Kurt Kranz
Early Form Sequences

Kurt Kranz
Frühe Form-Reihen

Kurt Kranz
Early Form Sequences
1927 - 1932

Kurt Kranz
Frühe Form-Reihen
1927 - 1932

Hans Richter
Werner Haftmann
Werner Hofmann

The MIT Press
Cambridge, Massachusetts

Copyright © by Hans Christians Verlag, Hamburg 1975
© Kurt Kranz for all works of art
Alle Rechte, auch die des auszugsweisen Nachdrucks und
der fotomechanischen Wiedergabe, sind vorbehalten
All rights reserved
Lithos Gries KG, Ahrensburg
Druck Christians Druckerei, Hamburg
Einband Verlagsbuchbinderei Ladstetter, Hamburg
ISBN: 3-7672-0236-0 (Christians Verlag)
ISBN: 0 262 11060 1 (MIT Press)
Library of Congress catalog card number: 75-27384
Printed in West Germany

Nichts
Im Nichts
Spur im Nichts
Spur im Nichts von Etwas
Etwas im Nichts wird Form
Form wird Wuchs
Wuchs will Ziel
Ziel will Lösung
Lösung wird Auflösung

Spur im Nichts von Etwas
Spur im Nichts
im Nichts
Nichts

K. K.

Index

Inhaltsverzeichnis

The arrow is Cupid's weapon,
Apollo's threat;
A sparsely feathered bird,
of love as well as death,
intent on its aim and unfailing,
attracted by the centre of his target,
wherever and whoever it may be.
A dogmatist,
holding his victim fast.
But who knows his secret self?
Where and how does it live?
As feathered kinetic?
As maelstrom in a saturated environment?
As a cutting of the air?
As generator of forces and counter-forces,
of with- and anti-arrows, craters, fissures and spirals
up to the subtle splitting of itself?
The arrow which meets the anti-arrow,
deciphers it,
and deflects it towards the lyrical,
to the bonds of intimacy and affection.
When split by chance, it becomes
conscious of its hitherto undiscovered powers,
part of our surging, atomic environment.
From shooting to hovering,
from striking to embracing.
Farewell and homecoming in one,
a reunion with itself.
In the poetry of graphics
a wreath *
in which the arrow flies, stands and reflects itself.
An anti-arrow of reconciliation.

Hans Richter

The private life of an arrow
To the drawings and film sequence by Kurt Kranz

* wreath = Kranz

Der Pfeil ist Cupidos Waffe,
Apollos Drohung.
Ein sparsam gefederter Vogel
der Liebe wie des Todes.
Richtungsbesessen-unbeirrbar,
angezogen vom Mittelpunkt,
wo immer und wer immer es sei.
Ein Rechthaber,
der sein Opfer festhält.
Aber wer kennt sein geheimes Sein?
Wo und wie lebt er sich selbst?
Als gefiederte Kinetik?
Als Wirbel in einer saturierten Umwelt?
Als ein Zerschneider der Luft?
Als Erzeuger von Kräften und Gegenkräften,
von Mit- und Gegen-Pfeilen, Trichtern, Spaltungen und Spiralen . . .
bis zum subtilen Sich-selbst-Zerteilen?
Der Pfeil, der den Gegenpfeil trifft,
entziffert ihn,
biegt ihn ins Lyrische ab,
zu Bändern der Verbundenheit.
Abgespalten im Zufall
seiner unentdeckten Möglichkeiten
wird er fühlend,
Teil unserer wogenden atomaren Umwelt.
Vom Schießen zum Schweben,
vom Zieltreffen zur Umarmung,
Abschied und Heimkehr vereint,
Wiedersehen mit sich selbst.
In der Poesie der Graphik
ein Kranz,
in dem der Pfeil fliegt, steht und sich selbst spiegelt.
Ein Anti-Pfeil der Versöhnung.

Hans Richter

Das Privatleben eines Pfeils
Zu den Zeichnungen und Filmfolgen von Kurt Kranz

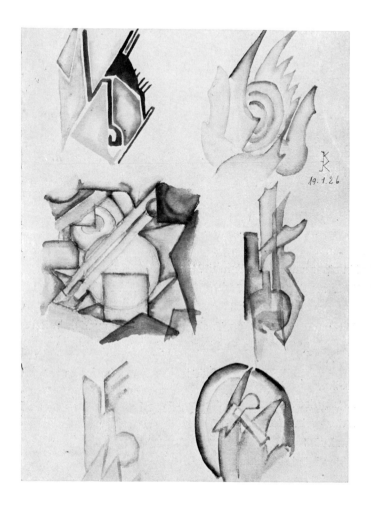

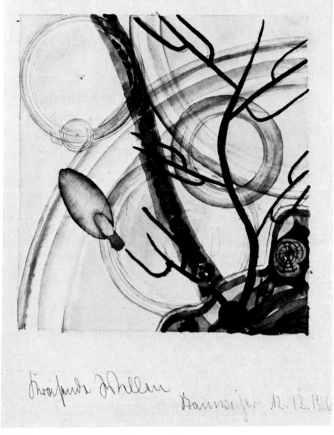

Page from a sketchbook 1925/26
Here already are form variations produced by watercolour brush
and a few pencil lines. The forms originate from the expressionism of the
decorative painters which has now developed into decor. The 16-year-old
finds inspiration and models in his workaday surroundings.

Seite aus einem Skizzenbuch von 1925/26
Hier schon sind Formvarianten aus dem Aquarellpinsel
und wenigen Bleistiftstrichen entstanden. Die Formen stammen aus dem
zum Dekor gewordenen Expressionismus der Dekorationsmaler.
Der 16jährige findet Anregung und Vorbild in seiner alltäglichen Umwelt.

Circling waves, watercolour 10 x 12 cm ???, 1926
This is not a nature study, but an abstraction from memory. The rings on the
surface of the water are accentuated by the elliptical form
of a duck. A stylized tree, containing a formsequence, is projected
onto the plane.
With their decorative style, something between art nouveau and
expressionism, the teachers at the school of arts and crafts influenced
at that time the form world of their young student.

Kreisende Wellen, Aquarell, 1926
Dies ist keine Naturstudie, sondern eine Abstraktion aus dem Gedächtnis.
Die Ringe auf der Wasseroberfläche sind durch die
elliptische Form einer Ente akzentuiert. Ein stilisierter Baum mit der
Andeutung einer Formreihe ist in die Fläche geklappt.
Die Lehrer an der Kunstgewerbeschule beeinflußten mit ihrem
dekorativen Stil, der zwischen Jugendstil und Expressionismus lag, die
damalige Formwelt des Kunstgewerbeschülers.

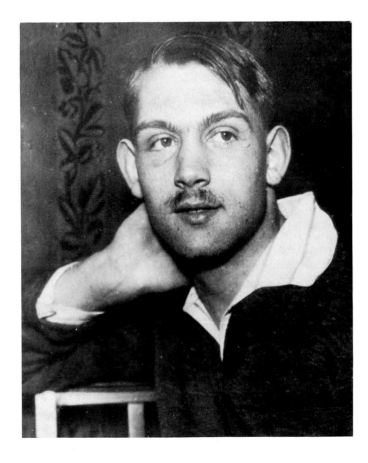

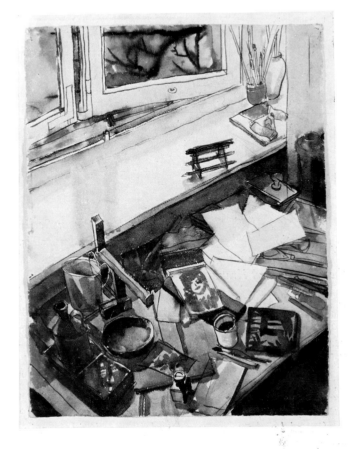

Kurt Kranz, at the age of 18, photographed by his friend.
The new miniature camera had such a low power lens that an exposure time of 15 seconds was required. Taken in the petit bourgeois atmosphere of a small provincial town, Kranz has here the air of a real revolutionary with his Schiller collar, typical badge of the youth movements of the day.

Kurt Kranz im Alter von 18 Jahren, von seinem Freund fotografiert.
Die neue Kleinbildkamera hatte ein so schwaches Objektiv, daß eine Belichtungszeit von 15 Sekunden notwendig war. Aufgenommen in dem begrenzten Verhältnissen seines Provinzmilieus, wirkte er damals mit dem Schillerkragen, dem typischen Requisit der Jugendbewegung, recht revolutionär.

"Work-table" 1928/29, watercolour on Whatman, 60 x 48 cm.
The table shown is the same size as a drawing-board. It is covered with tools and sketches. In the foreground lies a linocut, just begun. On this makeshift table in his bedroom in Bielefeld were composed the gouaches and watercolours of "20 pictures" and the suite "Black-White".

„Arbeitstisch" 1928/29, Aquarell auf Whatman, 60 x 48 cm.
Der dargestellte Tisch hat die Größe eines Reißbrettes. Er ist mit Werkzeugen und Skizzen überfüllt. Im Vordergrund liegt ein begonnener Linolschnitt. An diesem provisorischen Tisch in der Schlafkammer in Bielefeld sind die Gouachen und Aquarelle der „20 Bilder" und die „Suite Schwarz : Weiß" entstanden.

Discussion between Professor Dr. Werner Haftmann and the painter Kurt Kranz recorded on the 11th September, 1974 in Berlin.

This discussion took place mid-September 1974 in Berlin in the National Gallery when two friends, Professor Dr. Werner Haftmann, director of the National Gallery and the painter, Kurt Kranz, from Hamburg, met each other.
The first prints of the form-sequences were at hand and the discussion dealt with the many facets of these early works produced between 1928–1932 by Kurt Kranz. Werner Haftmann's penetrating questions attempted to establish the relation between these serial pictures and the role they play in the work of Kurt Kranz.
This discussion pinpoints the distinctly now contemporary nature of these from sequences which has been subsequently confirmed by the present usage of film and video equipment.

Haftmann = H, *Kranz* = K.

H
How did you hit upon the idea of making picture sequences such as these?
K
I produced these examples here during my youth in Bielefeld. In 1927 I was still naive enough to believe that I had discovered the process of abstract picture sequences. For example I painted "20 pictures in the life of a composition" in vertical format without giving any thought to the possibilities of film. And then, the second sequence, the Black/White storyboard consisted of many circles and other geometrical elements which involuntarily led one to think of Kandinsky. But the theme is really about geometrical forms which were familiar to me through my usage, as a lithographer, of the compass and drawing pen.
H
But from where did you derive the stimulus to develop this form of time sequence. When I look at these pictures here in front of me, they seem to develop out of one particular formal theme, they really have a certain film character. But don't misunderstand me when, as a historian, I point out that similar attempts already existed in 1919/20 when Viking Eggeling and Hans Richter drew the first abstract reels and then very quickly transferred them into films. At that time you were a schoolboy living in rather out-of-the-way Bielefeld, weren't you?

Gespräch zwischen Professor Dr. W. Haftmann und dem Maler Kurt Kranz, aufgezeichnet am 11. September 1974 in Berlin.

Dieses vorliegende Gespräch wurde Mitte September 1974 in Berlin aufgezeichnet. In der Nationalgalerie trafen sich zwei Freunde, Professor Dr. Werner Haftmann, Direktor der Nationalgalerie, und der Maler Kurt Kranz aus Hamburg.

Es lagen die ersten Andrucke der Formsequenzen vor, und das Gespräch durchleuchtet die vielen Facetten dieses Frühwerkes von Kurt Kranz, das in den Jahren 1928 bis 1932 entstanden ist. Werner Haftmann stellt durch beharrliches Fragen die Bezüge her zwischen den Bildreihen und ihrer Rolle im Œuvre des Malers Kurt Kranz.

Das Gespräch macht deutlich, daß die Formsequenzen ausgesprochen aktuellen Charakter haben, der durch die heutige Handhabung von Film- und Videogeräten bestätigt wird.

H

Wie kamst du auf die Idee, derartige Bildreihen zu machen?

K

Die vorliegenden Bildfolgen sind in meiner Jugendzeit in Bielefeld entstanden. 1927 war ich so naiv zu glauben, die abstrakte Bildfolge erfunden zu haben. Ich malte z. B. „20 Bilder aus dem Leben einer Komposition" im Hochformat und dachte zunächst gar nicht an Film, sondern an ein Bilderbuch. Dann folgte Nummer 2, die Formreihe Schwarz: Weiß, die nun schon viele Kreise und andere Geometrien hat, so daß man sich unwillkürlich an Kandinsky erinnert. Aber es handelt sich um geometrische Formen, die mir durch den Gebrauch von Zirkel und Ziehfeder als Lithograph geläufig waren.

H

Woher kam der Anstoß, solch zeitliche Sequenzen zu entwickeln? Wenn ich die Bilder hier vor mir sehe, so entwickeln sie sich doch aus einem bestimmten formalen Thema; es ist eigentlich eine filmische Unternehmung. Nimm es mir nicht übel, wenn ich dir als Historiker sage, daß es ja schon 1919/20 ähnliche Bestrebungen gegeben hat, als damals Viking Eggeling und Hans Richter die ersten abstrakten Rollen zeichneten und dann sehr schnell zu Zeichenfilmen übergingen. Du lebtest doch damals im etwas abgelegenen Bielefeld als Schüler oder ...?

K

I was a lithography apprentice and went in the evening to the Polytechnic to do live drawing.

H

At that time had you ever, in any form at all, come across or heard about the efforts of Hans Richter and Viking Eggeling?

K

Unfortunately not!

H

As a painter, you allow pictorial themes to develop in phases; actually a rather musical undertaking.

K

Already as a 16 year old I had painted four or five sequences of phases. I was always searching for new variations. It is quite natural for me to see form, not as static, but in a process for growth.

H

Let us go back to the time sequence of "20 Pictures". They show a development in sequence from a so to speak zero point, then circular forms begin to move out of the white area. These one could imagine as cosmic circles or something similar, to use Kandinsky's terminology (which is certainly not yours). We see a formal development which emerges out of the circle theme; then it takes on a sort of "eye-point theme" which reveals itself in the third area and is expressively accentuated until the end. I would now like to know what you as a young man of 18 or 19 actually conceived here as content over and above the formal content. When I, as a writer, look at your picture sequence and see how "cosmic" spiral forms and the like are sparked off by a bright light-point ...

Did you have in mind any conception of the nature of the content?

K

As an eighteem year old I naturally worked quite emotionally. The invention was nearly ruined by my over-enthusiasm. The idea came of its own accord and this yellow field which deepens into green and blue grew together with all the other accompanying forms into a "whole". I was completely convinced by my work.

H

Actually one is often cleverer at 19 than at 90 because one has more faith.

K

When one has sufficient spontaneity, there is no room for intellectual doubt.

H

But when I imagine you as a young man, an apprentice, in Bielefeld ... Had you seen anything of Kandinsky's work at that time? I find it quite astonishing that a young man living in Bielefeld at that time should have attempted such a theme at all with no outside stimulation.

K

I only knew very few reproductions of Kandinsky, one of which was a coloured Hanfstaengel print, but in the winter of 1929 I bought Klee's "Pedagogical Sketchbook". In the autumn Moholy-Nagy gave a lecture about the Bauhaus and at the same time presented an exhibition of original works of some Bauhaus masters in a gymnasium. I was so enthusiastic and overwhelmed that I decided to join the Bauhaus immediately after my apprenticeship. I then saw a corroboration for my drawing sequences, which were long since finished.

H

When did you start studying at Dessau?

K

In April 1930. I wanted to take my drawing sequence to Kandinsky. When I arrived in Dessau I discovered that he gave only one lecture a week, and that one had to attend the basic course of Josef Albers first. There was no painting or film class in the whole Bauhaus at this time, so I had only an attic studio for my work. In order to obtain entrance to the Bauhaus I was forced to register myself in

K

Ich war zu dieser Zeit Lithographenlehrling und ging abends in die Kunstgewerbeschule, um Akt zu zeichnen.

H

Hast du damals in irgendeiner Form von den Bemühungen von Richter und Eggeling gehört?

K

Leider nicht!

H

Du als Maler läßt ein Bild in Phasen wachsen – eigentlich eine musikantische Unternehmung.

K

Ich habe schon als 16jähriger in meinem Skizzenbuch, sagen wir vier oder fünf Phasen, gemalt. Ich suchte immer neue Varianten. Es ist mir ganz natürlich, eine Form nicht statisch zu sehen, sondern in ihrem Wuchs.

H

Wollen wir noch einmal über die zeitliche Abfolge der 20 Bilder sprechen. Sie zeigen eine serielle Entfaltung. Sozusagen vom Nullpunkt, von der weißen Fläche aus beginnen sich Kreisformen zu bewegen, die man im kandinskyschen Sprachgebrauch (der sicher nicht der deine ist) sich als ‚kosmische‘ Kreise oder ähnliches vorstellen könnte. Wir sehen eine formale Entfaltung, die aus dem Kreisthema sich entwickelt, dann eine Art von „Augenpunktthema“ hinzunimmt, das im dritten Feld aufklingt und sich bis zum Schluß expressiv steigert. Ich möchte von dir gern wissen, was du dir als junger Mann von 17 oder 18 Jahren als inhaltliche, über das Formale hinausgehende Konzeption vorgestellt hast. Wenn ich deine Bilderfolge als ein schreibender Mensch betrachte und sehe, wie sich von einem hellen Lichtpunkt aus „kosmische“ Wirbel formen und ähnliches entzünden ... lag da bei dir eine Vorstellung inhaltlicher Natur zugrunde?

K

Im Alter von 18 Jahren arbeitete ich natürlich ganz aus dem Gefühl heraus; die Erfindung wird fast von der Be-

geisterung erdrückt. Der Einfall kam wie von selbst, und das gelbe Licht, das sich ins Grüne und Blaue verdunkelt, wuchs – und mit ihm alle Begleitformen zu einem Ganzen. Ich war von meiner Arbeit völlig überzeugt.

H

In der Tat – man kann mit 19 Jahren sehr viel klüger sein als mit 90 Jahren, weil man gläubiger ist.

K

Wenn genügend Spontaneität in der Sache ist, ist kein Platz für intellektuelle Zweifel.

H

Ich stell' mir dich jetzt als Junge, als Lehrling in Bielefeld vor, hast du damals etwas vom Werk von Kandinsky gekannt? Denn ich finde es ungemein verblüffend, daß man in Bielefeld damals und als junger Mann – und ohne Anregung von außen – sich ein solches Thema überhaupt stellen konnte.

K

Ich habe nur wenige Reproduktionen von Kandinsky gekannt, darunter einen farbigen Hanfstängel-Druck, aber im Winter 1929 kaufte ich mir das „Pädagogische Skizzenbuch“ von Klee; im Herbst hatte Moholy-Nagy bei uns einen Vortrag über das Bauhaus gehalten und gleichzeitig in einer Turnhalle die originalen Werke einiger Bauhausmeister ausgestellt. Ich war so begeistert und überwältigt, daß ich den Entschluß faßte, gleich nach meiner Lehre zum Bauhaus zu gehen. In alldem sah ich für meine Bildreihen, die längst fertig waren, eine Bestätigung.

H

Wann hast du deine Studien in Dessau begonnen?

K

Das war im April 1930. Ich wollte mit meinen Bildreihen zu Kandinsky. Als ich in Dessau ankam, stellte ich fest, daß sein Seminar lediglich einmal in der Woche stattfand und daß man zuerst einmal in den Grundkurs zu Josef Albers mußte. Es gab zu dieser Zeit im ganzen Bauhaus weder eine Malklasse noch eine Filmklasse. Ich war mit meiner

the class of Joost Schmidt. Naturally I attended every seminar of Kandinsky and Klee as I admired them so much.

H

One could well presume that the Bauhaus had reached a certain crisis situation at this time due to the appointment of Hannes Meyer and also due to the accentuation of functionalism in architecture. The free painters Klee, Kandinsky, Schlemmer and Feininger who were there to provide the broad artistic background – within that architectural functionalism which the Bauhaus aimed at – ever increasingly lost their influence. It was a political crisis aggravated by the marxist ideas of Hannes Meyer, which were directed – as we are still today sick and tired of hearing – against the elite, the authoritarian in art. Also the work of art as an individual object of intrinsic worth was rejected as unsuitable; the only purpose of artistic activity was to provide support in one form or another for society.

K

Naturally my reaction as a 20 year old was to withdraw into my drawing sequences and photomontages.

H

Did this unexpected over-accentuation of politics in the Bauhaus help to drive Klee away?

K

Probably yes. I remember that right at the beginning in the introductory lectures of Albers, Hannes Meyer appeared and explained to us that art was quite dead now, it was nothing more than the esoteric luxury of the capitalists and that one should rather design chairs and housing for the workers. This was more sensible as then humanity would be able to develop. Suddenly we were caught between two fires, we were all to become architects and industrial designers although we had actually come to the Bauhaus to study with the great painters. And so a greater part of the students left the course.

H

What was your reaction as a creative artist?

K

As a 20 year old, I retreated into my attic studio and, as I have already said, worked on photomontages. Intuitively I composed them in a cryptic language, which I can easily decipher today; for instance "Play your game" referred to the Bauhaus Masters, in "Isolation" I was referring to myself, who at that time could establish no contact; "clear distinction" was a symbol for intellectual logic-chopping. After a speech by Hitler, in which he screamed that "Heads will roll", I produced a "Head Store".

H

So these were the metaphors which occurred to you during the production of these photomontages. Did the photomontages of Moholy-Nagy have a strong influence on you when you came to the Bauhaus?

K

Yes, but at this time Moholy was already in Berlin and I was dependent on reproductions.

H

But didn't Peterhans help you there?

K

I couldn't make any abstract films in his class, but I did learn photography. I made serial photos then, variations on eyes, noses, mouths and hands, about 30 of each, which seem to be an anticipation of conceptual.

H

But let us return to this Black/White series which you had already developed by then and which you brought to the Bauhaus. What was Kandinsky's opinion of it?

K

He attached a great deal of importance to it and insisted on having it printed. He knew of a patron in Nuremberg, a Mr. Wiesner, to whom he wrote immediately. A short while later Kandinsky informed me that our plans had been defeated by lack of funds.

Arbeit auf die Dachstube angewiesen. Um einen Studienplatz zu bekommen, blieb mir nichts anderes übrig, als mich bei Joost Schmidt einzuschreiben. Selbstverständlich habe ich jedes Seminar von Kandinsky und Klee im Bauhaus wahrgenommen, da ich diese Meister gläubig verehrte.

H

Nun muß man wohl voraussetzen, daß damals das Bauhaus bereits in eine Krise geraten war durch die Berufung von Hannes Meyer und durch die Betonung des Funktionalismus in der Architektur. Die ‚freien‘ Künstler, wie Klee, Kandinsky, Schlemmer, Feininger, die ja eigentlich da sein sollten, um den künstlerischen Hintergrund zu entwerfen – innerhalb der funktionalistischen Architektur, die das Bauhaus anstrebte –, verloren doch zunehmend an Wirksamkeit. Es war eine politische Krise, denn durch Hannes Meyer wurden die marxistischen Ideen gefördert, die sich – was wir ja heute zum Überdruß immer wieder hören – gegen das Elitäre, das Autoritäre der Kunst richteten. Auch das Kunstwerk als das einzelne erlesene Werk wurde als unbrauchbar beiseite getan. Es lief darauf hinaus, soziales Leben durch künstlerische Tätigkeit in irgendeiner Form zu unterstützen.

K

Die Reaktion eines 20jährigen war, sich auf seine Reihenbilder und Fotomontagen zurückzuziehen.

H

Hat dieses unerwartete Übergewicht des Politischen auch Klee vom Bauhaus weggetrieben?

K

Vermutlich ja. Ich entsinne mich, ganz zu Anfang, im Vorkurs von Albers erschien Hannes Meyer und erklärte uns, daß die Kunst nun völlig tot sei, sie sei nichts als esoterischer Luxus der Kapitalisten, und man sollte jetzt lieber Stühle und Häuser für Werktätige bauen. Das sei vernünftiger, dann würde die Menschheit sich bessern. Da saßen wir nun zwischen zwei Stühlen, wir sollten nun alle Architekten und Industrial Designer werden, obwohl wir ja wegen der großen Maler ans Bauhaus gekommen waren; und so reiste auch ein großer Teil der Studenten wieder ab.

H

Wie war deine Reaktion als bildnerischer Mensch?

K

Mit 20 Jahren habe ich mich in meine Dachstube zurückgezogen und, wie ich schon sagte, Fotomontagen gemacht. Intuitiv habe ich hier in einer verschlüsselten Sprache verfaßt, was ich heute sehr gut lesen kann, mit „Spielt euer Spiel“ z. B. waren die Bauhausmeister gemeint. In „Vereinsamung“ meinte ich mich selbst, der keinen Anschluß fand. Mit der „Klaren Trennung“ war das Verhackstücken durch den Intellekt symbolisiert. Nach Hitlers Rede, in der er lauthals schrie: Köpfe sollen rollen! legte ich einen „Kopfvorrat“ an.

H

Das waren Metaphern, die dir bei den Fotomontagen zufielen. Hatten Moholys Fotomontagen einen Einfluß auf dich, als du ans Bauhaus kamst?

K

Ja, aber zu dieser Zeit befand sich Moholy schon in Berlin, ich war wieder auf die Reproduktionen angewiesen.

H

Hat sich Peterhans da nicht eingeschaltet?

K

Bei ihm konnte ich keine abstrakten Filme machen, aber ich lernte zu fotografieren. Ich machte damals Fotoreihen: Variationen von Augen, Nasen, Mündern und Händen, je etwa 30, die heute wie eine Vorwegnahme des Conceptuals anmuten.

H

Wollen wir wieder zurückgehen zu der Schwarzweißserie, die du damals entwickelt hast! Mit ihr kamst du zum Bauhaus . . . und was sagte Kandinsky dazu?

K

Er fand die Arbeit so wichtig, daß er sie unbedingt gedruckt

H

Did you know anything about the efforts of Malevich and El Lissitzky or of the Styl-group?

K

I first became acquainted with their work in various Bauhaus books in the Bauhaus, although Lissitzky's "Abstract Cabinet" of 1925 was only an hour away by train from Bielefeld, in the Hanover museum.

H

It is quite amazing anyway that these things came so easily to you through the medium of commercial art.

K

Naturally I was familiar with "Elementary typography" before entering the Bauhaus.

H

What is astonishing is not only the chronological emergence of a form which develops from simple elements into complexity, but also the development of the luminosity of the Black/White and the spatial stages. Here we have not only an emergence of light, which grows to an extreme point and then loses itself again, in addition we have a dramatic spatiality which develops itself in the chronological fulfilment of the sequence. What interests me is how this time sequence idea came to you, the conception of a sort of pictorial fugue which develops in chronological phases as in music. Painting by its very nature recognizes no point of time; painting produces a static self-contained entity, in which the point of time plays no part.

But that about 1910 the time element became extremely important is shown by Boccioni and the Futurists. Certainly they show it in a still very simple form. They seek to translate the impression of a train rushing by, its speed and its background noise, into pictorial forms. What they achieved was a sort of realistic, descriptive illustration of speed. But all these movement processes are contained within the pictorial elements, for instance in a line. While our eye follows its movement, it itself develops into the passage of time. Movements can also be expressed through the medium of colour. In 1912 Delaunay stated that, for instance, when the eye wanted to observe the transition from red to orange, it required a certain amount of time. And Klee explained that in his pictures he constructed paths for the eye, along which the eye could wander. Thereby the picture, to use a musical expression, assumed a certain fugue-like structure. Then as the structure develops and the eye follows its paths, the time element is formulated. Much of this technique is apparent in the picture sequence which you made as a young man in Bielefeld. Did the film help you in any way here?

K

At that time I could not think of the production of a film because not only the financial but also the technical means did not exist, but I undertook the production of these film ideas afterwards in 1972. When we return for example to the Black/White series, I can say that here I was completely uninfluenced in my discovery of a rhythmical order. I developed a certain theme to a climax which, in this case, is continually wiped away by white forms to make place for a new theme.

H

I find the expression which you have just used, "the rhythmical order", an extremely enlightening phrase because it not only expresses something of musical rhythm but also something about poetry and lyricism. The rhythmical form is actually a lyrical mode of expression.

K

During my time in Bielefeld I was in contact with various enthusiastic young poets. What was important for me then was that the single elements of my picture sequences should be absorbed in the new totality of the whole concept, and this total concept which was born and died and was reborn and so on, meant a kind of symbol of existence to me.

sehen wollte. Er wußte auch einen Mäzen in Nürnberg, Herrn Wiesner, dem er sofort schrieb. Wenig später aber teilte mir Kandinsky mit, daß aus Geldgründen aus diesem Plan nichts würde.

H

Hast du damals von den Bestrebungen der Russen Malewitsch und El Lissitzky oder von der Styl-Gruppe gewußt?

K

Erst im Bauhaus erfuhr ich durch die Bauhaus-Bücher davon. Obgleich Lissitzkys „Abstraktes Kabinett" von 1925 im Museum von Hannover nur eine Zugstunde von Bielefeld entfernt war.

H

Das ist erstaunlich! So flog dir manches über die Gebrauchsgraphik zu?

K

Ich kannte natürlich die „Elementare Typographie" schon vor dem Bauhaus.

H

Das Erstaunliche an der Sache ist nicht nur die Idee der zeitlichen Entfaltung einer Form, die sich von einfachen Elementen zu reichen Formen steigert, sondern auch die Steigerung der Lichthaltigkeit des Schwarz-Weiß und der räumlichen Stufungen. Es handelt sich ja nicht nur um eine Entfaltung zeichnerischer Lineaturen, sondern auch um eine Entfaltung des Lichtes, die sich zum äußersten Punkt entwickelt und sich dann wieder verliert; dazu kommt auch eine dramatische Räumlichkeit, die sich im zeitlichen Nachvollzug der Folge entwickelt. Mich interessiert, wie die Idee des Zeitlichen in dir zustande kam, die Vorstellung von einer Art bildnerischer Fuge, die sich wie in der Musik in zeitlicher Abfolge abspielt. Malerei kennt aus ihrer Natur ursprünglich das Zeitmoment nicht. Malerei bringt ein statisches, abgeschlossenes Gebilde hervor, in dem das Zeitmoment zunächst keine Rolle spielt. Daß aber das Moment der Zeit ungefähr um 1910 auch für die Malerei außerordentlich dringlich wurde, zeigen Boccioni und die Futu-

risten. Sie zeigen es freilich noch in einfacher Weise. Sie suchen den Eindruck eines vorbeirauschenden Zuges, seine Geräuschkulisse und seine Geschwindigkeit in bildnerische Formen umzusetzen. Was sie erreichten war eine Art von realistischer beschreibender Illustration von Geschwindigkeit. Aber innerhalb der bildnerischen Mittel selber sind Bewegungsabläufe auch enthalten, z. B. in einer Linie. Indem unser Auge ihren Bewegungen folgt, entfaltet sie sich im zeitlichen Ablauf. Auch innerhalb der Farbe lassen sich Bewegungsvorgänge anschaulich machen. 1912 sagte Delaunay, daß z. B. die Abfolge von Rot zu Orange für das aufnehmende Auge Zeit erfordert. Und Klee erklärte, daß er in seinen Bildern dem Auge Wege einrichte, die das Auge abläuft. Dadurch nähme das Bild, musikantisch ausgedrückt, eine bestimmte fugenartige Struktur an. Indem sich diese Struktur entfaltet und das Auge ihren Wegen folgt, gestaltet sich das zeitliche Moment. In deinen Bildreihen, die du als Junge in Bielefeld gemacht hast, ist vieles Derartiges angeschlagen. Hat dir der Film dabei geholfen?

K

Damals habe ich nicht an die Herstellung eines Films denken können, weil mir sowohl die Technik als auch das Geld fehlte, aber die filmischen Aufnahmen habe ich 1972 nachgeholt. Doch sprechen wir noch einmal von dem Aufbau z. B. der Schwarz-Weiß-Reihe. Ich fand hier ganz von selbst eine strophische Ordnung, entwickelte ein Thema zu einem Höhepunkt, das im vorliegenden Fall durch weiße Punkte weggewischt wird, um immer einem neuen Thema Platz zu machen.

H

Ich finde diesen Ausdruck von der strophischen Ordnung ein ungewöhnlich erhellendes Wort. Es sagt nicht nur etwas über die musikantische Strophenform, sondern auch noch etwas über die Poesie und den Lyrismus aus. Die strophische Weise ist eine lyrische Art, sich auszudrücken.

H

Here we find ourselves within the structure of our modern culture, confronted with a completely new conception of reality, a reality which has long since dissolved into the abstract and has long since been operating with movement and the processes of growth and decay.

K

I designed two further form sequences in the Bauhaus, "The Arrow" from 1930 till 1931 and "Leporello" from 1931–32.

H

If I remember correctly, it was in about 1928 to 1929 that Klee, in his lectures, used continually to refer to the arrow. This was a very much discussed theme in the Bauhaus. How then did you arrive at the irea of developing such a theme in your long picture sequence where the arrow is born out of nothingness, assumes a specific direction becoming increasingly sharper, more precise and pointed in order to penetrate various obstacles so that it may finally enter a circle.

K

Arrow and Bauhaus! One could practically call the arrow the sign of the Bauhaus because it was so frequently employed in pictures or publications there. I was, however, more interested in the idea of really setting this arrow in motion.

H

Even in the "Pedagogical Sketchbook" by Klee there is a section about the arrow. He had given a great deal of thought to the concept of the arrow, at least during his pedagogical development, and had attached various metaphysical meanings to it.

K

His text about the arrow reads like a modern lyric.

H

That is what is so wonderful about Klee. He starts out from a rational logical thought, but then in an extraordinary inversion, blends this logical thought into pure poetry. Klee can proceed from simple geometrical conceptions, and suddenly the square on its own or the arrangement of triangles are transformed into a single entity in a lyrical concept.

K

In your book on Klee you give a very good example ... "because the finished form is the result of its development, that is 'forming', one cannot start at the end". In the beginning, it was very difficult to understand Klee in his seminars, but one didn't dare to question him even when one could not follow his line of thought. Up front he virtually delivered a monologue. Unfortunately my time with Klee was far too short. As I said, he went to Düsseldorf, and shortly afterwards the Bauhaus had to leave Dessau.

H

Did you go with the Bauhaus to Berlin?

K

Yes, I accompanied the Bauhaus to Berlin-Steglitz and on Goebbels' order, was interrogated by the police. It was all extremely unpleasant and I was very happy when Josef Albers and Herbert Bayer gave me good references because otherwise I would never have received an artist's licence from the "Reichskulturamt". There all the Bauhaus artists were classified as culture bolshevists. In order to survive I had to undertake commercial art work until the 2nd world war.

H

We were together in the Hamburg Academy of Art and it was then that I saw your suite "Bandolina", another picture sequence in which you were preoccupied with surrealism. This sequence seems to touch upon the essence of your pictorial work. I was amazed to see how you identified yourself with your students and let them develop certain sequences and processes. I also admired you for your monk-like devotion in abstaining from your own artistic work

K

In meiner Bielefelder Zeit hatte ich Kontakte zu schwärmerischen jungen Dichtern. Wichtig war für mich damals aber, daß die einzelnen Teile meiner Bildreihen in einem Gesamtbild aller Strophen aufgehen und daß die große Form, die geboren wird und stirbt . . . wieder aufersteht usw., für mich ein Sinnbild der Welt bedeutet.

H

Ja, wir sehen uns innerhalb der Struktur unserer modernen Kultur einer ganz neuen Vorstellung von Wirklichkeit gegenüber, einer Wirklichkeit, die sich längst ins Abstrakte aufgelöst hat, längst mit Bewegungsformen, mit Zerfall- und Aufbauformen arbeitet.

K

Im Bauhaus habe ich zwei weitere Formsequenzen entworfen. 1930–31 den „Pfeil" und 1931–32 das „Leporello".

H

Wenn ich mich recht erinnere, so war es ungefähr 1928–29, als Klee ständig in seinen Vorlesungen auf den Pfeil zu sprechen kam. Dies war ein groß angelegtes Thema im Bauhaus. Wie kamst du dazu, ein solches Thema in deiner langen Serie zu entfalten, – wo sich der Pfeil aus dem Nichts entwickelt, eine Richtung annimmt, immer schärfer, präziser, spitzer wird, durch Widerstände hindurchgeht, um dann zum Schluß in einen Kreis einzugehen?

K

Der Pfeil, man könnte fast von einem Signet des Bauhauses sprechen, so häufig wurde der Pfeil auf Bildern oder in Publikationen des Bauhauses verwandt. Mich aber reizte es, diesen Pfeil nun wirklich in Bewegung zu setzen.

H

Auch im „Pädagogischen Skizzenbuch" von Klee gibt es eine Abhandlung über den Pfeil. Er hat, zumindest innerhalb seiner pädagogischen Entwicklung, über den Pfeil gründlich nachgedacht und ihn mit allerlei, auch metaphysischer Bedeutung beladen.

K

Der Text über den Pfeil von Klee liest sich wie moderne Lyrik.

H

Das ist ja das Wunderbare bei Klee, daß er von einem rationalen logischen Gedanken ausgeht, diesen logischen Gedanken aber in sonderbarer Umkehrung in reinste Poesie hinüberspielt. Klee kann von einfachen geometrischen Vorstellungen ausgehen, und plötzlich verwandelt sich das bloße Quadrat oder die Zusammenordnung von Dreiecken zu einer Einheit in einem lyrischen Konzept. In einem zauberischen Moment seiner Einbildungskraft gelingt es ihm, die Logik umzudrehen und in Poesie zu verwandeln.

K

In deinem Buch über Klee führst du ein schönes Beispiel auf, „. . . weil die fertige Form Ergebnis eines Weges ist – also Formende, kann man nicht mit dem Ende beginnen . . ." Zu Beginn war das Verständnis bei Klee in den Seminaren sehr schwer, man wagte ihn nicht zu fragen, selbst wenn man seinem Gedankengang nicht folgen konnte; es lief da vorne ein Monolog ab.

K

Leider war die Zeit bei Klee viel zu kurz. Wir sagten schon, er ging nach Düsseldorf. Bald darauf mußte das Bauhaus Dessau verlassen.

H

Bist du damals mit nach Berlin gegangen?

K

Ja, ich habe den Umzug des Bauhauses nach Berlin-Steglitz mitgemacht, wurde auch auf Goebbels Befehl von der Polizei verhört. Es war sehr unerfreulich, und ich war froh, als mich Josef Albers an Herbert Bayer empfahl, denn ich hätte ja nie von der Reichskulturkammer eine Lizenznummer als Maler bekommen. Dort hießen alle Bauhäusler „Kulturbolschewisten". Bis zum zweiten Weltkrieg habe ich Gebrauchsgraphik gemacht und mich damit über Wasser gehalten.

in order to be a teacher pure and simple, a teacher of basic principles like Albers, who for a long time carried on Bauhaus tradition, albeit modified, at the expense of his own productivity.

K

This teaching activity was very important for me as it formed a basis for my own work.

H

Your reputation as a teacher has spread far beyond the USA.

K

I have taught in Japan as well as in the USA and finally at Harvard.

H

So you have used "The training of the means" as Klee put it, and then the completely different approach of Josef Albers' "creative form theory" as basis.

K

Yes, I based my work on that. I added, however, a few new processes and attempted new themes, for example new methods of combination, transformation and new sequences and variation techniques and virtual volumes.

H

And how did you go on from there?

K

In 1955 I began to occupy myself with structure. I employed a form of "fugue-technique" or if you like "12 tone technique". The picture area was divided into a grid. A pre-selected sequence in mirroring, inversion and stretto was fitted into this grid.

My colleague, Max Bense the computer theorist, has pointed out to me that the grid corresponds to the "Bits". The sequences make up the sign repertoire and this results in the programme.

H

What are you doing now, back in your house in Suzette?

What are you up to there? Are you working on pictures or are you producing further sequences?

K

I am working hard for my next exhibition.

H

So you are painting for your next exhibition, but all the same you are still working on a specific sequence basis as you were at the age of 20, where one picture provokes the next and the next picture again summons up the one after and so on . . .

K

You've said it exactly.

H

Wir waren doch beide zusammen an der Hochschule in Hamburg, und was ich damals von deiner Malerei sah, war die Suite „Bandolina". Wieder eine Bildreihe, in der du dich mit dem Surrealismus auseinandergesetzt hast, diese Reihe berührte auch den Kern deiner bildnerischen Arbeit.

Damals sah ich mit Erstaunen, wie du dich mit deinen Schülern identifiziertest und auch sie bestimmte Reihen und Verfahren entwickeln ließest. Ich bestaunte die Mönchshaftigkeit, mit der du dich von deiner eigenen malerischen Tätigkeit zurückhieltest, indem du einfach nur Lehrer warst, ein Grundklassenlehrer, wie Albers, der die modifizierte Bauhauslehre weitergab und eigentlich seine eigene Produktivität lange Zeit beiseite ließ.

K

Diese Lehrtätigkeit war mir sehr wichtig, sie war meine eigene Grundlagenforschung.

H

Dein Ruf als Pädagoge ist ja weit über die USA hinausgegangen.

K

Ich habe sowohl in Japan als auch in den USA und zuletzt in Havard gelehrt.

H

Du hast dabei die „Aufzucht der Mittel", wie Klee es nannte, und den so ganz anderen Ansatz des „Werklichen Formunterrichts" von Josef Albers als Grundlage benutzt.

K

Ja, darauf fuße ich. Ich habe aber einige neue Verfahren hinzugefügt, neue Themen aufgegriffen, z. B. Kombinatorik, Transformation, Variationstechnik, Reihentechnik und virtuelle Volumen.

H

Und wie ging es weiter?

K

1955 beginnt meine Auseinandersetzung mit der Struktur. Ich wandte eine Art Fugentechnik, wenn du willst „Zwölfton-Technik" an. Die Bildfläche war in Raster eingeteilt. Eine vorgegebene Reihe wurde in Spiegelung, Umkehrung und Engführung in dieses Raster eingetragen. Mein Kollege Max Bense, der Informationstheoretiker, hat mich darauf aufmerksam gemacht, daß das Raster den „Bits" entspricht. Die Formreihen bilden das Zeichenrepertoire. Aus diesem Programm resultiert das Ergebnis. Das ist eine Vorwegnahme der späteren Computer-Technik.

H

Was machst du jetzt, wenn du in deinem Haus in Suzette sitzt? Was treibst du da? Malst du Bilder, oder machst du weiter Serielles?

K

Ich male fleißig für die nächste Ausstellung.

H

Du malst für die nächste Ausstellung, aber immerhin, genau wie mit 20 Jahren auf einer gewissen seriellen Basis, indem ein Bild das andere provoziert und das nächste wieder das andere herbeiruft, so, so . . .

K

Ja, du sagst es.

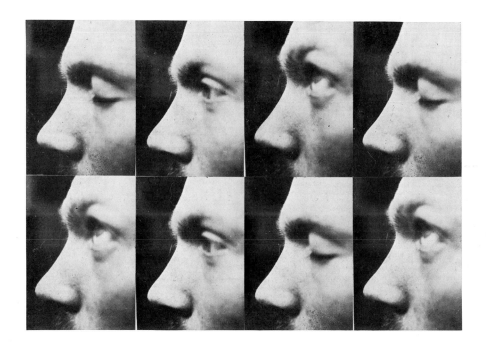

Eye and nose profiles, 1930/31
Self-portrait sequences with variations of gesture taken by a fixed camera.

Augen- und Nasenprofile, 1930/31
Reihen-Selbstporträts mit gestischer Variante bei feststehender Kamera.

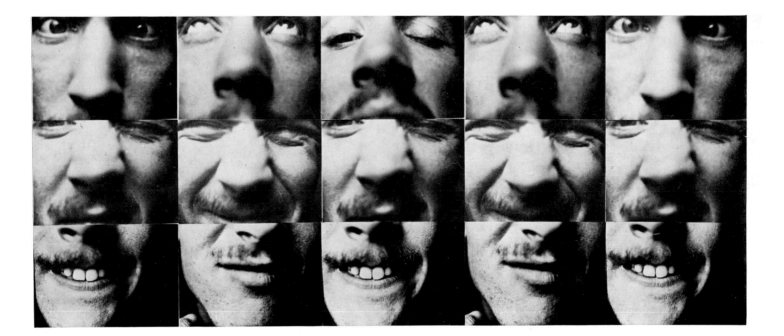

Kranz, during the winter semester 1930/31 in the Bauhaus, Dessau, enrolled in the class of Joos Schmidt, practising photography in Walter Peterhans' course.

Self-portrait in defensive postures, 1930/31
Photo-sequences of eye and mouth gestures were made in cooperation with Kurt Schmidt (page 200). Is Kurt Kranz here grimacing in the face of an imaginary enemy? This sujet was as topical at that time as it is today. Conceptual and video very frequently make use of the distorted or deformed face in sequences.

Kranz während des Wintersemesters 1930/31 im Bauhaus Dessau, eingeschrieben in der Klasse Joost Schmidt und im Kurs bei Walter Peterhans Fotografie praktizierend.

Selbstporträt in Abwehrgesten, 1930/31
In Zusammenarbeit mit Kurt Schmidt entstanden Fotoreihen von Augen- und Mundgesten (Seite 200). Grimassiert Kurt Kranz hier gegen einen imaginären Gegner? Dieses Sujet war damals so aktuell wie heute. Conceptual und Video verwenden sehr häufig das verzerrte und deformierte Gesicht in Reihen.

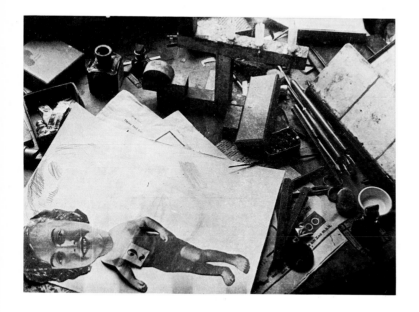

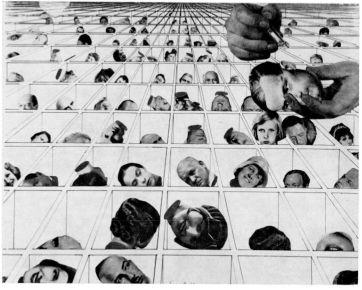

Head store; 1932, 50 x 64 cm, photomontage newsprint with pencil, watercoloured.
The Hitler slogan "Heads will roll" is countered in ironic fashion with a "Head store". This reminds one of slaves' cant. It is a way registering in code their fear and distress in the face of the power of their masters, in this case the Nazis. The young Bauhaus student—standing between broadsheet and agit-prop, the battle slogans of the political movements from right and left demonstrating on the streets—asked himself—Quo vadis?

Kopfvorrat, 1932, 50 x 64 cm, Fotomontage, Zeitung und Bleistift, koloriert mit Aquarell.
Die Hitler-Parole „Köpfe werden rollen" wird mit einem Kopfvorrat ironisch beantwortet. Dies erinnert an Sklavensprache und verschlüsselt die Not und Furcht vor der Macht der anderen, den Nazis.
Der junge Bauhäusler fragte sich – zwischen Flugblatt und Agit-Prop, den Kampfparolen der politischen Strömungen von links und rechts und ihren Demonstrationen stehend – wohin?

Kurt Kranz's work-table in Dessau, 1930/31
In the foreground on a drawing with a grimacing self-portrait lies part of a photomontage. The finished work has unfortunately been lost. The inks, pens and watercolour utensils spread over the table are the materials with which the picture-sequences, "Leporello" and "Heroic arrow", were made.

Der Arbeitstisch von Kurt Kranz in Dessau, 1930/31
Im Vordergrund auf einer Zeichnung mit grimassierendem Selbstporträt liegt ein Teil einer Fotomontage. Die fertige Arbeit ist leider verlorengegangen. Die auf dem Tisch ausgebreiteten Tuschen, Federn und Aquarellutensilien sind die Materialien, mit denen hier die Bildreihen „Leporello" und „Heroischer Pfeil" entstanden sind.

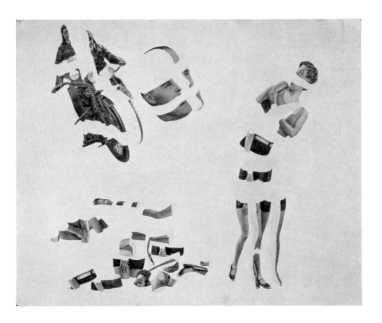

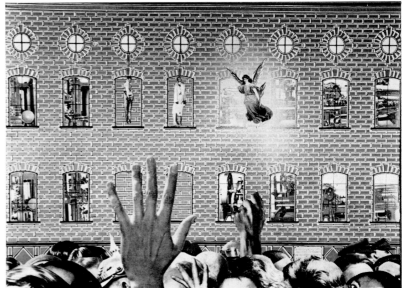

Clear cut distinction, 1930, 51 x 65 cm, photomontage, photo and watercolour.
Through the constructivist occupation with the human body, geometrical
simplification and cuts were much used in the Bauhaus, Oscar Schlemmer as
well as Joost Schmidt employed both in their classes. Here "cutting"
becomes bloody pink reality in a "photoreality". Surrealist, intellectual cutting
serves both as experiment and sarcasm.

Klare Trennung, 1930, 51 x 65 cm, Fotomontage, Foto und Aquarell.
Durch die konstruktive Beschäftigung mit dem menschlichen Körper
waren geometrische Vereinfachung und Schnitte im Bauhaus
häufig. Sowohl Oscar Schlemmer als auch Joost Schmidt verwandten
beides in ihrem Unterricht. Hier wird das „Zerschneiden"
rosa-blutige Wirklichkeit in einer „Foto-Realität". Das surrealistische,
intellektuelle Zerteilen ist Experiment und Sarkasmus zugleich.

No solution, 1930, 50 x 60 cm, collage, wallpaper und newsprint.
Kranz illustrates topical events. Here is shown the anonymous mass
which lynches its enemies and cannot be soothed by a lacquered angel
of peace.

Keine Lösung, 1930, 50 x 65 cm, Collage, Tapete und Zeitungsdruck.
Kranz illustriert Zeitgeschehen. Dargestellt ist die anonyme Masse, die ihre
Gegner lyncht und nicht von einem Lackbild-Friedensengelchen
besänftigt werden kann.

Werner Hofmann

Early Form Sequences by Kurt Kranz

I.

More than 80 years ago, Wölfflin wrote about Marées: "He is sparing with his media, but what he uses produces the maximum effect, not through ostentation but because it is placed in exactly the right spot. In a good composition the miracle is brought to perfection in that everything suddenly falls into the right relationship, everything adds up, the scattered parts are integrated into a whole in which pulsates a life which is homogeneous and balanced. Without this summing up, without this invisible interplay of relationship which connects one part with the other, the combination of parts, be they ever so colourful individually, produces an effect of poverty and emptiness. Here the impression, which one so often has in modern pictures, that everything could have been equally well achieved by other means, does not hold good. The composition breathes necessity." This bears the trademark of permanence, of finality.

These and similar superlatives have been the stock-in-trade of form analysis since time immemorial. We have all, at one time or another, succumbed to the fascination of a pronouncement "ex cathedra" that "this and no other holds good" in the case of a Cézanne or a Raffael. Forms which are beyond compare also brook no argument. They stand, above all discussion, on the farthest limit of the horizon of our experience and are invested with the authority of the absolute. "The great works of art have been created by man in accordance with true and natural laws exactly like the greatest works of Nature. Everything arbitrary, everything imagined collapses; there is Necessity, there is God", pronounces Goethe, himself a demigod, if not more, to his contemporaries. A work of art can be accorded no higher recognition.

The judgement of such an emotional pronouncement is as a general rule not made in a vacuum. It is based on a handful of formal rules which it lays down as natural laws. These are measurable factors, definite proportions, the rules of symmetry, the golden mean and other basic patterns of solid and plane geometry. To conclude from the above that only normative form and composition resting on a theory of art, based on and supported by mathematics, can reveal the pleasant certainty of the "necessary" and the "unshakeable" would, however, be erroneous. All these positive criteria only rationalize and aestheticize expectations whose roots lie deeper. What we call art today, the production of pictures and shapes, bears from the very beginning the stamp of the fixed, the immutable. One has only to think of the very first imprint of a hand. Something is preserved, its use reserved for magical or other purposes; what has been preserved turns out to be materially recorded. Vis à vis the fluc-

26

Werner Hofmann

Frühe Formreihen von Kurt Kranz

Vor mehr als achtzig Jahren schrieb Wölfflin über Marées: „Er ist sparsam in den Mitteln, aber alles wirkt bei ihm mit höchster Kraft; nicht weil es sich vordrängt, sondern weil es am richtigen Platz sitzt. In der guten Komposition vollzieht sich das Wunder, daß plötzlich alles Beziehung zueinander gewinnt, alles zusammenschießt, die zerstreuten Teile zu einem Ganzen sich fügen, in dem einheitliches, gleichmäßiges Leben pulsiert. Ohne dieses Zusammenschießen, ohne das unsichtbare Ziel der Beziehungen, die von Teil zu Teil gehen, wirkt die bunteste Versammlung im Bilde leer und arm ... Der Eindruck, den man vor modernen Gemälden so oft hat, daß alles ebenso gut auch anders sein könne, fehlt hier. Die Komposition atmet Notwendigkeit." Diese Notwendigkeit trägt den Gütestempel des Unverrückbaren, Endgültigen.

Mit solchen und ähnlichen Superlativen arbeitet die Formanalyse seit eh und je. Wir alle sind irgendwann einmal der Faszination eines Kanzelwortes erlegen, das angesichts eines Cézanne oder Raffael sein „So und nicht anders" verkündet. Formen, die keinen Widerruf kennen, dulden auch keinen Widerspruch: sie stehen, der Diskussion enthoben, an der äußersten Grenze unseres Erfahrungshorizontes und treten mit der Autorität des Absoluten auf. „Die hohen Kunstwerke sind zugleich als die höchsten Naturwerke vom Menschen nach wahren und natürlichen Gesetzen hervorgebracht worden. Alles Willkürliche, Eingebildete fällt zusammen, da ist Notwendigkeit, da ist Gott", verkündet Goethe, seinen Zeitgenossen ein Halbgott, wenn nicht mehr. Man kann dem Kunstwerk kein höheres Prädikat zusprechen.

Das Verkündungspathos urteilt in der Regel nicht freischwebend. Es stützt seine Aussagen auf eine Handvoll formaler Regeln, die es als Gesetzmäßigkeiten ausgibt. Das sind meßbare Faktoren: bestimmte Proportionen, die Spielarten der Symmetrie, der Goldene Schnitt und andere Grundmuster der geometrischen Körper- und Flächenteilung. Daraus zu schließen, daß erst die mathematisch abgesicherte kunsttheoretische Kanonbildung die schöne Gewißheit des Notwendigen und Unverrückbaren zu offenbaren vermochte, wäre jedoch ein Irrtum. Alle diese positiven Maßstäbe rationalisieren und ästhetisieren bloß Erwartungen, deren Wurzeln tiefer liegen. Was wir heute Kunst nennen, das Herstellen von „Bildern" und „Gebilden", trägt von allem Anfang an das Merkmal des Fixierten. Man denke bloß an den allerersten Handabklatsch. Etwas wird festgehalten, für magische oder andere Zwecke gebannt. Das Festgehaltene erweist sich als materiell festgelegt. Gegenüber der Fluktuation der Erscheinungen und Ereignisse ist es dadurch abgehoben, daß es sich nicht verändert. Es soll dauern. Das macht seine Überlegenheit

tuations of phenomena and historical events, it is thus secured against change. It is intended to endure. This gives it its superiority. And on this rests still today the aesthetic of "This and no other" when it plays off the certainty of the work of art against the uncertainties and fortuities of the world outside art. When, for instance, Kandinsky describes as sacred all art media which are intrinsically "necessary", he is thus secularizing – guided perhaps by his Russian ancestry – a concept value which was originally attached to an art object designed for religious use, namely the icon. (In like manner, of course, Kandinsky is sanctifying the language he uses for the practice of his art). The diversified motivation for the reverence they inspire has made of certain icons paramount examples to be copied as exactly as possible. This slavish adherence to a form shaped once and for all in a definite pattern was an assurance that the miraculous qualities of the original would be transferred to the copy. Constancy of form guarantees the believer the fulfilment of his expectations. In this manner the chosen icon assumes formal authority and becomes an obligatory pattern for "This and no other".

From this we can see that wishful thinking directed towards "Necessity" has a history rooted in religious or ritual behaviourism, i. e. that the need for finality and certainty derives from the very beginnings of human environmental orientation. This correct conduct, produced with the help of ruler and compass, is only a later secularized product of these ideals.

2.

This detailed foreword was unavoidable because here the argument is concerned with two different concepts of art. The still predominant one derives its cultural prestige from the characteristics described above. To these are added others. The worship of the masterpiece, long since recognized as an inner substitute for religion, is nothing other than the sociological equivalent in art of a set of hierarchical values, authoritatively laid down. Combined with these are the demands which furnish an alibi for the creative process of art, the more it becomes a theme in itself: the demand for innovation, for originality, for uniqueness of the great achievement (Originality and original are coupled; this has, as we know, far reaching consequences for the marketing of art). There is no way back from this one-way street; with each work the artist has to be better, i. e., (if these comparatives existed), more unique and more inimitable. Incidentally it is not disputed that there are, or rather must be, masterpieces, for logically they belong to an art concept based on formal and material finality. We now contrast this closed concept, closed because it is limited by its confining form, with another art concept which we call open because, in its sphere of application, the definite, the permanent is not recognized. Reduced to a single formula, included in this open art concept are all productions in which the possibilities of processed change of the accepted vocabulary of form are tried out. Thus form is regarded as a series, not as a final exclusive end, as a dynamic process, not as a static monument. The view is gradually becoming more widespread that the shift of emphasis from the single work to the work-chain represents the process, most fraught with consequences, in the art of our century. This chapter of history began more than five centuries ago. Its pre-history has not yet been written. Material for it can be found in the "second rate" or, from the perspective of the "high arts", in the peripheral art forms: in ornamentation, in so far as the alteration or transformation of a motif (= basic theme) can be attributed to it; in grotesque, caricature and so called fantastic art, in so far as they rely for their effects on the merging of heteromorphic characters (an example: the two "dreams" of Grandville); further material can be found in the calligraphic script pattern books and also in the figure alphabets, in fact everywhere where one or several char-

aus. Darauf beruht heute noch die Ästhetik des „So und nicht anders", wenn sie die formale und materielle Gewißheit des Kunstgebildes gegen die Ungewißheiten und Zufälligkeiten der außerkünstlerischen Erfahrungswelt ausspielt.

Wenn etwa Kandinsky alle Kunstmittel „heilig" nennt, die innerlich notwendig sind, so säkularisiert er – von seiner russischen Herkunft gelenkt? – eine Wertvorstellung, mit der ursprünglich ein Kunstgegenstand des religiösen Gebrauchs behaftet war: die Ikone. (Zugleich freilich sakralisiert Kandinsky die Sprachmittel seiner Kunstpraxis.) Ihre verschieden motivierte Verehrungswürdigkeit machte bestimmte Ikonen zu Vorbildern und empfahl sie der möglichst genauen Nachahmung. Das sklavische Festhalten an der ein für alle Male gefundenen Formgestalt verbürgte, daß die Wunderwirkung vom Original auf die Kopie überging. Formale Konstanz garantiert dem Gläubigen die Erfüllung seiner Erwartungen. Solcherart gewinnt die ausgezeichnete Ikone formale Autorität, sie wird zum verbindlichen So-und-nicht-anders-Muster.

Daraus ersehen wir, daß die auf „Notwendigkeit" abzielenden Wunschvorstellungen eine in magischen und religiösen Verhaltensweisen wurzelnde Vorgeschichte haben, daß also das Bedürfnis nach Endgültigkeit und Gewißheit in den Anfängen der menschlichen Umweltorientierung gründet. Das mit Hilfe von Lineal und Zirkel ermittelte Wohlverhalten, genannt „Notwendigkeit", ist erst ein spätes, verweltlichtes Produkt dieser Wunschbilder.

2.

Die ausführliche Vorbemerkung war unerläßlich, denn es geht hier um die Auseinandersetzung zweier Kunstbegriffe. Der immer noch herrschende bezieht sein kulturelles Prestige aus den eben beschriebenen Merkmalen. Dazu kommen andere. Die Anbetung des Meisterwerks, schon längst als verinnerlichter Religionsersatz erkannt, ist ja nichts anderes als die kunstsoziologische Entsprechung autoritär entschiedener Werthierarchien. Damit verknüpft sind die Forderungen, die dem Kunstgeschehen, je mehr es sich selbst zum Thema wird, das Alibi liefern: die Forderung nach permanenter Innovation, nach Erst- und Einmaligkeit des großen Wurfes. (Originalität und Original sind miteinander gekoppelt: das hat bekanntlich für die Vermarktung von Kunst weitreichende Folgen.) Auf dieser Einbahnstraße gibt es kein Zurück, der Künstler muß mit jedem Werk besser, d. h. (wenn es diesen Komparativ gäbe) einmaliger und unwiederholbarer werden. Es sei übrigens nicht bestritten, daß es Meisterwerke gibt, richtiger: geben muß, denn sie gehören folgerichtig zu einem auf formale und materielle Endgültigkeit angelegten Kunstbegriff.

Wir stellen nun diesem von der abschließenden Form getragenen, *geschlossenen* Kunstbegriff einen anderen gegenüber, den wir *offen* nennen, weil in seinem Geltungsbereich kein Definitives, kein Dauerzustand anerkannt wird. Auf eine Formel gebracht: zu diesem offenen Kunstbegriff rechnen alle Hervorbringungen, in denen die Möglichkeiten der prozeßhaften Veränderung des formalen Vokabulars erprobt werden. Also Form als Reihe, nicht als exklusiver Endpunkt; als dynamischer Ablauf, nicht als statisches Monument.

Allmählich setzt sich die Einsicht durch, daß das Umdenken vom Einzelwerk auf eine Werkkette den folgenreichsten Prozeß in der Kunst unseres Jahrhunderts darstellt. Dieses Geschichtskapitel begann vor mehr als fünf Jahrzehnten. Seine Vorgeschichte ist noch nicht geschrieben. Material dazu findet man bei den „zweitrangigen" oder – aus der Sicht der „Hochkünste" – peripheren Kunstpraktiken: im Ornament, sofern ihm die Verwandlung oder Abwandlung eines Motivs (= Grundthemas) zugestanden wird; in Groteske, Karikatur und sogenannter phantastischer Kunst, sofern sie ihre Wirkung aus dem Ineinanderblenden heteromorpher Zeichen beziehen (ein Beispiel: die beiden „Träume" von Grandville); weiteres Material wartet in den kalligraphischen Schriftmusterbüchern, aber auch in den Figurenalphabeten – überall dort also, wo ein oder mehrere

acters are tried out for their mutability or are arranged at different levels of meaning. A systematic investigation of these sectors of art world arrive at the conclusion that a processed trial of the various possibilities of form is one of the characteristics of the marginal and applied arts. In these sectors the licence of ambiguity is permitted. The right to invent mixed forms, to project the human figure on the outline of a letter, a crescent in an umbrella, and to change the latter into a bellows – this freedom of expression makes the marginal arts more mobile and pliable in form than the "high arts" (painting, sculpture, architecture) as long as the latter are fettered to the defined finality and thus to the unequivocalness of their vocabulary. In our time these practices of mutation are leaving their sub-cultural ghetto and are finding a place of honour among the "high arts". They will be ennobled exactly to that extent to which these high arts are prepared to emerge from their category of seclusion and turn towards the open concept of art.

The pioneer role of the marginal arts, research on which is still inadequate, should not distract our gaze from an important episode which took place in painting towards the end of the 19th century. I mean the three cycles which Monet painted in the nineties: the poplars, the haystacks and the cathedral at Rouen. Here we are given a demonstration of how light never ceases to change the objects which we perceive. The empirical analysis of a moment ("impression") expands into a time sequence of light conditions. Thus occurs, reduced to a simple formula, a sort of phase record, the sum of which, compared with the single picture, offers an increase of information, but again this increase is relative as there is no order of sequence among the light conditions, and none of them can be awarded the predicate of finality. Amongst themselves all the pictures are equal, their sequence has as little end or beginning as the continuous process of Nature, which we divide into day and night. We come to the conclusion

that the picture theme dissolves into variations or vice versa, the variation becomes the theme.

In the classic theory of art, the religious or mythological historical picture took pride of place. For this it was doubly predestined, firstly through the dignity and gravity of its content, and secondly through the dominant role of the human figure elevated to an ideal formula. Below this category were ranged landscapes, portraits and still-life, all excluded from the ideality of the historical picture because they were forced to compromise with empirical reality. It is not mere chance that the cycle of motif variation, which pioneered the way to the open concept of art, actually began in landscape painting, i. e. in one of the non-strict categories whose latent content – and not only since the Impressionists – is change: The interplay and sequence of the times of the day and the seasons of the year permit no final word, no "this and no other". Thus it is wrong when one describes a figure composition which has been "lumped together" as breathing and pulsating. Then, hereby, a processing quality would be foisted onto the figure pictures of von Marées which are in direct contrast to their permanence. On the other hand, the metaphor of breathing and pulsating can be used to describe the qualities which both unite and differentiate various pictures of Monet's.

It is not necessary to stress that the Impressionists were not painter naturalists, not passive recorders of light and colour phenomena, although their analytical integrity and their search for an objective conformity with natural laws did coincide with the new systematic approach of the natural sciences. This applies in still greater measure to Seurat and his circle. And even an art theoretician who did not take cognizance of these happenings in the latest trend of painting sensed at the same time the need for an objective basis, a thorough-bass, to use Goethe's words. "One can first start to work with accuracy", wrote Wölfflin in 1886 (at that time Seurat was

Zeichenrepertoires auf ihre Wandelbarkeit erprobt oder verschiedenen Bedeutungsebenen zugeordnet werden. Eine systematische Untersuchung dieser Bereiche käme zu dem Ergebnis, daß das prozeßhafte Durchspielen formaler Möglichkeiten eines der Merkmale der Rand- und Gebrauchskünste ist. In diesen Bereichen gilt die Lizenz der formalen Mehrdeutigkeit. Das Recht, Mischbildungen zu erfinden, die menschliche Gestalt auf den Umriß eines Buchstabens zu projizieren, eine Mondsichel in einen Regenschirm, diesen in einen Blasbalg zu verwandeln – diese Freizügigkeit macht die Randkünste formal beweglicher als die „Hochkünste" (Malerei, Plastik und Architektur), solange diese unter dem Zwang zur definitorischen Endgültigkeit und somit Eindeutigkeit ihres Vokabulars stehen. In unserer Tagen haben diese Verwandlungspraktiken ihr subkulturelles Getto verlassen und kommen in den „Hochkünsten" zu Ehren. Sie werden in eben dem Maße nobilitiert, in dem diese Hochkünste aus ihrer kategorialen Abgeschlossenheit heraustreten und sich dem *offenen* Kunstbegriff zuwenden.

Die noch ungenügend erforschte Vorläuferrolle der „Randkünste" sollte nicht den Blick auf eine wichtige Episode verstellen, die sich gegen Ende des 19. Jahrhunderts in der Malerei ereignete. Ich meine die drei Zyklen, die Monet in den 90er Jahren malte: die Pappeln, die Heuschober und die Kathedrale von Rouen. Darin wird uns demonstriert, daß das Licht ununterbrochen die Gegenstände unserer Wahrnehmung verändert. Die empirische Analyse eines Augenblicks („Impression") dehnt sich auf eine zeitliche Folge von Lichtzuständen aus. So entsteht, auf eine nüchterne Formel gebracht, eine Art Phasenprotokoll, dessen Summe zwar – gemessen am Einzelbild – ein Mehr an Information bietet, zugleich aber dieses Mehr wieder relativiert, da es keine Rangordnung zwischen den Lichtzuständen gibt und keiner das Prädikat der Endgültigkeit zuerkannt bekommt. Alle Bilder sind untereinander gleich, ihre Reihung hat ebensowenig Anfang und Ende wie der kontinuierliche Naturprozeß, den wir in Tag und Nacht zer-

legen. Fazit: das Bildthema löst sich in Variationen auf, oder umgekehrt: die Variation wird thematisiert.

In der klassischen Kunsttheorie nahm das religiöse oder mythologische Historienbild den höchsten Rang ein. Es war dazu doppelt prädestiniert: einmal durch die Würde seiner Inhalte, zum andern durch die beherrschende Rolle der auf einen idealen Kanon gebrachten menschlichen Gestalt. Unter dieser strengen Bildgattung rangierten Landschaft, Bildnis und Stilleben, allesamt von der Idealität des Historienbildes ausgeschlossen, weil zum Kompromiß mit der empirischen Wirklichkeit verurteilt. Es ist kein Zufall, daß die den offenen Kunstbegriff vorbereitende zyklische Motivvariation gerade in der Landschaftsmalerei beginnt, in einer der „unstrengen" Bildgattungen also, deren latenter Inhalt – nicht erst seit den Impressionisten – der *Wechsel* ist: das Ineinander und Nacheinander von Tages- und Jahreszeiten, das kein letztes Wort, kein „So und nicht anders" zuläßt. Deshalb ist es falsch, wenn man eine „zusammengeschossene" Figurenkomposition als atmend und pulsierend beschreibt. Den Figurenbildern von Marées wird damit ein Prozeßcharakter untergeschoben, dem ihre Unverrückbarkeit widerspricht. Hingegen läßt sich mit den Metaphern des Atmens und Pulsierens das umschreiben, was die verschiedenen Bilder Monets sowohl verbindet wie trennt.

Die Impressionisten, das muß man nicht betonen, waren keine malenden Naturforscher, keine passiven Protokollanten von Licht- und Farbphänomenen, obschon ihre analytische Redlichkeit und das Suchen nach objektiven Gesetzmäßigkeiten sich im Ansatz mit dem systematischen Vorgehen der Naturwissenschaften berühren. Das gilt in noch stärkerem Maße für Seurat und seinen Kreis. Auch ein Kunsttheoretiker, der diese Ereignisse der neuesten Malerei nicht zur Kenntnis nahm, verspürte zur gleichen Zeit das Bedürfnis nach einer objektiven Basis, einem Generalbaß, mit Goethe zu reden. „Man kann erst da exakt arbeiten", schrieb Wölfflin 1886 (damals vollendete Seurat „La Grande

finishing "La grande Jatte"), "where it is possible to record the flow of phenomena in solid forms. Mechanics, for instance, provides physics with these solid forms. The humanities are still lacking this fundamental; it can be looked for in psychology alone. This would allow art history also to reduce the particular to a general, to definite laws." It was on such considerations that the gestalt psychologists built up their theories: however what they discovered regarding conformity with natural laws was concerned less with "solid" forms than with morphogenetic processes.

One can suppose that the demand for objective, measurable systems of law has been provoked by doubt as to the validity of subjective judgements on taste. The more one realizes that the formal exemplariness of the historical picture was exhausting itself in the sterile repetition of the beauty ideal, the more pointedly will doubt be cast on this "law of beauty", until now firmly identified with the human shape, and it will be finally supplanted by Nature's "laws of life". This process has many chapters, and nowhere is it clearer than in the chapter which takes us from the Impressionists to Cézanne.

As fraught with consequences as this loss of prestige of the anthropo-centric scale of values may be, the search for refuge in the objective laws of Nature does not necessarily mean the abandonment of the principle of hierarchic thought, then the scientific world of the 19th century, geared to the concept of evolution, appealed, and there were many who did so, to the authority of the Aristotelian doctrine of the ascending scale, whose inner logic permits no mutations or caprices. (Then Aristotle states: "Not any creature can emerge from any seed; but only a particular creature from a particular seed.") Thus, on the one hand, the artist is directed by the methods of systematic science towards the processing character of form creation, and, on the other hand, he is regimented by an idea, strictly orientated towards a definite aim, which develops with inexorable necessity in "this way and no other". Basically it is a case of whether a painter who allows himself to be induced to try variations, for instance by Haeckel's glimpses into the processes of micro-organism (the 10 volumes of Art forms of Nature appeared between 1899 and 1904), strives to achieve a series of metamorphoses on an ascending scale, i. e. aims at complete finality, or whether he dares to make creations that are not "necessary" and "consequent", but arbitrary, and thereby not aim at finality. And here we are again with Goethe; but this time not with the stern judge of art, but with the bold discoverer of the Urpflanze, the prototypical form of the plant, who assumes for himself a right which he denies to the artist: "The Urpflanze is the most wonderful creation in the world, and one which Nature itself should envy my possessing. With this model and the key to it, one can invent plants ad infinitum, but they must be consequent, that is if they do not actually exist, they could exist." Limits are drawn to the breadth of this vision; the most wonderful creation is permitted, but it must be consequent. This fine balancing act between freedom and "necessity" is perfected by Klee and Kandinsky in the Bauhaus in the 1920s. In Klee's famous Jena lecture (1924), he speaks of the "secret key" which unlocks the "Urgrund" the fundamental form of cause, the Urgesetz, the fundamental form of law, but at the same time the artist, if he wants to give genesis permanence, rejects the regimenting "form-ends", for it is the "Formative forces that interest him more than the form-ends".

3.
At the age of 17, Kurt Kranz, born in 1910, began to take part in this process. In April 1926, the, for him, painful period of school had come to an end. With his school leaving certificate in his pocket, he goes to a Bielefeld printer to learn the techniques of lithography. At the same time he attends evening classes at the school of

Jatte"), „wo es möglich ist, den Strom der Erscheinungen in festen Formen aufzufangen. Diese festen Formen liefert der Physik z. B. die Mechanik. Die Geisteswissenschaften entbehren noch dieser Grundlage; sie kann allein in der Psychologie gesucht werden. Diese würde auch der Kunstgeschichte erlauben, das einzelne auf ein allgemeines, auf Gesetze zurückzuführen." Auf solchen Überlegungen bauten wenig später die Gestaltpsychologen auf: was sie an Gesetzmäßigkeiten entdeckten, betraf freilich weniger die „festen Formen" als die morphogenetischen Prozesse.

Man kann vermuten, daß das Verlangen nach objektiven, meßbaren Gesetzmäßigkeiten vom Zweifel an der Gültigkeit subjektiver Geschmacksurteile ausgelöst wurde. Je mehr man einsah, daß die formale Vorbildlichkeit des Historienbildes sich im sterilen Nachbeten des Idealschönen erschöpft, desto nachdrücklicher wird das bislang in der menschlichen Gestalt verankerte *Schönheits*gesetz in Zweifel gezogen und schließlich von den *Lebens*gesetzen der „Natur" verdrängt. Dieser Vorgang hat viele Kapitel – das von den Impressionisten zu Cézanne führende macht ihn am deutlichsten spürbar.

So folgenschwer der Prestigeverlust des anthropozentrischen Wertgefüges ist, so bedeutet das Zufluchtsuchen bei den objektiven Gesetzen der Natur keineswegs die unbedingte Preisgabe des hierarchischen Denkens, denn das am Leitbegriff der Evolution orientierte naturwissenschaftliche Weltbild des 19. Jahrhunderts beruft sich, durchaus vielstimmig, auf den aristotelischen Gedanken des nach oben führenden Stufenbaues, dessen innere Logik keine Mutationen und Willkürlichkeiten zuläßt. („Denn keineswegs wird aus jedem Samen ein beliebiges Wesen, sondern aus einem bestimmten nur ein bestimmtes", heißt es bei Aristoteles.)

So wird der Künstler von der naturwissenschaftlichen Systematik einerseits auf den Prozeßcharakter des Formgeschehens verwiesen, andererseits aber von einer zielorientierten Entwicklungsidee bevormundet, die eben mit unaus-

weichlicher Notwendigkeit „so und nicht anders" abläuft. Er muß sich also entscheiden. Es geht im Grunde darum, ob ein Maler, der sich etwa von Haeckels Einblicken in die Prozesse der Mikrolebewesen (die zehn Bände der „Kunstformen der Natur" erschienen zwischen 1899 und 1904) zu Variationen anstiften läßt, eine aufsteigende Metamorphosenreihe anstrebt, also auf geschlossene Endgültigkeit hinarbeitet, oder ob er sich dazu ermächtigt, nicht „notwendig" und „konsequent", sondern willkürlich zu erfinden und keine Endgültigkeit anzustreben. Damit sind wir wieder bei Goethe, diesmal nicht beim strengen Kunstrichter, sondern beim kühnen Erfinder der Urpflanze, der sich ein Recht herausnimmt, das er dem Künstler nicht zugesteht: „Die Urpflanze wird das wunderlichste Geschöpf der Welt, um welches mich die Natur selbst beneiden soll. Mit diesem Modell und dem Schlüssel dazu kann man als dann noch Pflanzen ins Unendliche erfinden, die konsequent sein müssen, das heißt, die, wenn sie auch nicht existieren, doch existieren könnten . . ." Der Offenheit dieser Vision bleiben Grenzen gezogen: das wunderlichste Geschöpf ist erlaubt, aber es muß konsequent sein. Diese Gratwanderung zwischen Freiheit und Notwendigkeit vollbringen Klee und Kandinsky in den 20er Jahren am Bauhaus. In Klees berühmtem Jenaer Vortrag (1924) fällt das Wort vom „geheimen Schlüssel", der den Urgrund, das Urgesetz aufschließt, zugleich aber schiebt der Künstler die bevormundenden „Form-Enden" von sich, möchte er *der Genesis Dauer verleihen,* denn es liegt ihm „mehr an den formenden Kräften als an den Form-Enden".

3.

Mit siebzehn Jahren beginnt Kurt Kranz, Jahrgang 1910, an diesem Prozeß teilzunehmen. Im April 1926 war die für ihn „qualvolle Schulzeit" zu Ende gegangen. Mit dem Reifezeugnis in der Tasche geht er zu einem Bielefelder Drucker, um die Lithographiertechniken zu lernen. Gleichzeitig besucht er die Abendkurse der Kunstgewerbeschule, übt sich in Naturstudien und im Aktzeichnen. Bei der Anmeldung

arts and crafts, and practises Nature studies and nude drawings. When applying he shows some of his attempts at art and hears the comment, "something in the style of Kandinsky". The name at the moment means nothing to him. Then in the school library he sees, for the first time, copies of Kandinsky's works, probably also his Bauhaus book entitled "Point and line to the plane", which appeared in 1926. Does the example of the great master have a retarding or an inciting effect on his impulses? The 16 year old takes refuge in Nature, he joins a youth group, and, paying homage to Hermann Löns, wanders through the Lüneburg Heath. In the second year of his evening classes, as he later calls to mind, he tortures himself trying to find a decorative "exploitation" for his Nature studies. In literature he busies himself with Rilke, Nietzsche and Hölderlin. An "Expressionist" exhibition (Heckel, Schmidt-Rottluff, Felixmüller) impresses him very much, but does not serve as a model for him.

In the autumn of 1927 Kranz begins his cycle "20 pictures from the life of a composition". In the title the intention is made clear that "composition" does not mean something final, something permanent, and "life" not a process aimed at unfolding and rounding off. Nevertheless the cycle has become a sort of commentary on the story of the creation, and the formula "from chaos to cosmos" would not have been inappropriate to its biomorphic energies.

From dark to light, from the sluggish mass ascending into transparent light – this is more or less how the series can be interpreted. But is this the only way of reading it? It seems to me that the signs could be changed round and the process thus reversed. In this case then, the way leads from the ethereal zone back into the "earthbound" (as Carus understood it) and the inscrutable. What was previously observed as the emergence of germ forms now becomes a withdrawal, where coagulation was expected, dissolution must now be assumed, extrusion becomes suction or vice versa. One could compare this ambivalence with the equation systole and diastole.

1928. As printer's apprentice Kranz considers that he is "disgracefully exploited". The evening courses, which he suffers for the sake of learning formal discipline, help to sharpen his inner conflict: "I'm completely confused and learn without knowing it." What emerges from this can be seen in the 40 sheets of the series Black:White 1928/29. The vocabulary is made up of only a few elements, which are sparingly used. A cool precision determines the sequence of the geometrical figures. The central motif is the circle. White circles thrust themselves vertically into a black field. Their tracks leave "staves" of various breadth. The third sheet poses the question: where are the positive energies at work, where is figure, where ground – in the white or black sector? Soon after a well balanced starting point is established; what has happened up to now was apparently only a prelude; now the confrontation of the two partners can begin. Then emerge, completely unexpectedly, black and white wedges and throw the whole vertical arrangement into confusion. In their train come white constellations of circles and occupy the surface. Suddenly in sheet 14 the white Dominant becomes the germ-cell of black "turning-points". Between this and the following print is applied what film people call Zoom. This shortening of the distance by jerks pushes the white Dominant out of our consciousness, and the black disks assume power. About the middle of the cycle a fleeting balance is restored (sheet 21). Immediately afterwards a new motif is introduced: the disks assume space energy, they resemble cones which meet at one point or radiate from there. White again sets the tone, but is then displaced by black. The wedges thicken into a black surface. Again the process is reversed. What was up to now the outline of a wedge establishes itself into linear white energy. The Zoom overrides this process (sheets 29 and 30). From the last set (32–36) emerge a confusion and discord, but unexpectedly

legt er einige seiner Versuche vor und hört die Bemerkung: „In der Art von Kandinsky". Noch kann er mit diesem Namen nichts anfangen. In der Bibliothek der Schule sieht er dann zum ersten Mal Abbildungen von Kandinskys Werken, wahrscheinlich auch dessen 1926 erschienenes Bauhaus-Buch „Punkt und Linie zu Fläche". Tritt das große Vorbild hemmend oder bestärkend zum eigenen Impuls? Der Sechzehnjährige flieht in die Natur, findet Anschluß an die Jugendbewegung, wandert mit seiner Lönsverehrung durch die Lüneburger Heide. Im zweiten Jahr des Abendkurses quält er sich – so sieht es später die Erinnerung – damit herum, seinen Naturstudien eine dekorative „Auswertung" zu finden. Literarisch beschäftigen ihn Rilke, Nietzsche und Hölderlin. Eine Expressionistenausstellung (Heckel, Schmidt-Rottluff, Felixmüller) beeindruckt ihn sehr, wirkt aber nicht als Vorbild.

Im Herbst 1927 beginnt Kranz den Zyklus „Zwanzig Bilder aus dem Leben einer Komposition". Im Titel wird die Absicht ausgesprochen: „Komposition" meint nichts Endgültiges, Unverrückbares, „Leben" keinen auf Entfaltung und Abgrund abzielenden Prozeß. Dennoch ist der Zyklus so etwas wie ein Kommentar zur Schöpfungsgeschichte geworden, und die Formel „Vom Chaos zum Kosmos" wäre seinen biomorphen Energien nicht unangemessen. Vom Dunklen ins Helle, aus der trägen Masse ins durchsichtige Licht aufsteigend – so etwa kann man die Folge ablesen. Ist das die einzige Lesart? Mir scheint, daß man die Vorzeichen auch umkehren und den Prozeß „rückläufig" machen darf. Dann führt der Weg von der ätherischen Zone zurück ins „Erdlebenhafte" (wie Carus es verstand) und Undurchschaubare. Was vordem als das Auftauchen von Formkeimen wahrgenommen wurde, wird jetzt ein Zurückweichen, wo sich Gerinnen ankündigte, muß nun Zerrinnen vermutet werden, aus dem Ausstülpen wird ein Einsaugen . . . oder umgekehrt. Man könnte diese Ambivalenz auf die Gleichung von Systole und Diastole bringen.

1928. Die Lehre beim Drucker wird als „ganz besonders schikanös" empfunden. Der Abendkurs, als Zwang zur formalen Disziplin erlitten, vertieft den Zwiespalt: „Bin völlig verzweifelt und lerne, ohne es zu wissen." Was daraus entsteht, zeigen die 40 Blätter der Folge *Schwarz : Weiß* (1928/29). Das Vokabular setzt sich aus wenigen Elementen zusammen, es wird sparsam eingesetzt. Kühle Präzision bestimmt den Ablauf der geometrischen Figuren. Das zentrale Motiv ist der Kreis. Weiße Kreise schieben sich senkrecht in ein schwarzes Feld: ihre Bahnen rufen verschieden breite „Stäbe" hervor. Das dritte Blatt stellt die Frage: Wo wirken die positiven Energien, wo ist Figur, wo Grund – im weißen oder im schwarzen Bereich? Bald danach richtet sich eine ausgewogene Ausgangsposition ein, was bis jetzt geschah, war offenbar nur Vorspiel, nunmehr kann die Auseinandersetzung der beiden Partner beginnen. Da tauchen, völlig überraschend, schwarze und weiße Keile auf und verwirren die Vertikalordnung. In ihrem Gefolge bemächtigen sich weiße Kreiskonstellationen der Fläche. Plötzlich, im 14. Blatt, wird die weiße Dominante zur Keimzelle von schwarzen „Wendepunkten". Zwischen diesem und dem folgenden Blatt wird das angewandt, was die Filmleute Zoom nennen. Die sprunghafte Distanzverkürzung verdrängt die weiße Dominante aus unserem Bewußtsein, die schwarzen Scheiben werden immer mächtiger. Etwa in der Mitte des Zyklus kommt wieder ein flüchtiges Gleichgewicht zustande (Blatt 21). Unmittelbar danach stellt sich ein neues Motiv ein: die Scheiben nehmen räumliche Energien an, sie gleichen Kegeln, die an einem Punkt zusammenlaufen oder von dort ausstrahlen. Wieder gibt Weiß den Ton an, wird aber dann von Schwarz verdrängt. Die Keile verdichten sich zur schwarzen Fläche. Wieder schlägt der Prozeß um: Was eben noch Kontur eines Keiles war, verselbständigt sich zu linearer weißer Energie. Der „Zoom" übersteigert diesen Vorgang (Blatt 29 und 30). Der letzte „Satz" (32–36) entfaltet laute, verwirrende Vielstimmigkeit, doch unvermutet tritt wieder Einstimmigkeit in ihr Recht, zieht sich die Energie

concord comes into its right again, and energy retires into a handful of circles. In this end there await new beginnings, i. e. one can read this series backwards as well. But a completely new series, beginning with sheet 40, would also be conceivable.

Every attempt to decode this sequence in formal dialogue should bear in mind that the vocabulary of the 40 ink drawings has, for reasons of form economy, been consciously strictly limited, but not based on predictable ("necessary") metamorphoses. We continually come up against shock-like irritations and disturbing interferences which distract the form process. We see that it is receptive for sudden changes, i. e. that it is not programmed. Perhaps the series drawn by hand makes these leapings and mutations clearer than the film can for which the prints were meant as a design, for the film optic does not show the phases side by side but connects them up into a flowing, uninterrupted continuity. Kandinsky, to whom Kranz showed the Leporello when he came to the Bauhaus in 1930, was interested in this film project and actually contacted a publisher. But the political confusion of the time and the economic crisis prevented its realization. Only later was the series given the title which designates it as a reversible form equation: white : black

$$\text{black : white}$$

1929. The printer's apprentice busies himself with designs for commercial art. The Bauhaus masters hold an exhibition in a Bielefeld gymnasium, Moholy-Nagy delivers a lecture which draws Kranz's attention to Klee's "Pedagogic sketch book" 1925. The latter means nothing to him but on the other hands he is fascinated by a very figurative story in picture form, namely Masereel's "Book of hours". He begins a new variation series. The theme is the distortions which perspective, when exercised from different viewpoints, can inflict on the actual object. The insistence of perspective on objectivation, its alleged exactness are thereby called into question. This means to catalogue and formally exploit the doubt which Cézanne has already cast on the arrangement of space and body dating from the renaissance. This arrangement was for hundreds of years one of the bastions of the aesthetic of finality, the abolition of which we spoke of in the introduction. All these designs have been lost. In 1930 the printer's apprentice receives his journeyman's certificate. A brochure by Hannes Meyer entitled "Young people, come to the Bauhaus" prompts him to go to Dessau. On the 15th of April Kranz is accepted by the Bauhaus. This new world confuses him; the artistic and ideological conflicts within the teaching body do not help to clarify the situation. A "simpleton from the province" (as he views the scene in retrospect) is thrust into an arrogantly sophisticated intellectual life. Kranz goes to Albers for instruction in the use of materials, to Kandinsky for analytical drawing and attends Klee's seminar ("even today he seems to be unapproachable"). In a new idea for a film, he makes use of the arrow, one of the emblems with which Klee used to instrument his changes of form. The 60 drawings are to be converted into a three minute film.

In music, ostinato denotes "a bass melody which persistently recurs, it can thereby be rhythmically changed and its notes varied with the same structure; it can also occasionally appear in another register and be transposed into another key ..." (Eberhard Thiel). The arrow also proves to be obstinate and stubborn; hence its epithet "heroic". Distracted from its course, multiplied, split, knotted or wound into loops, its basic form always recurs. Thereby, in some inexplicable fashion, its momentum proves to be artful and ingenious: even from a point in the innermost centre of a spiral, it suddenly finds an unexpected way out. Apart from the adventurous progress of this story, the series is presented as a new paraphrase of the theme "Figure and ground", whereby black and white once more take it in turns to play the main role. In

in eine Handvoll Kreise zurück. In diesem Ende warten neue Anfänge. Das heißt, daß man auch diese Reihe rückläufig lesen kann. Aber auch eine völlig neue Folge, mit dem 40. Blatt beginnend, wäre vorstellbar.

Jeder Versuch, diesen Ablauf formdialogisch zu entschlüsseln, sollte im Auge behalten, daß das Vokabular der 40 Tuschzeichnungen zwar aus Gründen der formalen Ökonomie bewußt eng gewählt, aber nicht auf voraussehbare („notwendige") Metamorphosen festgelegt ist. Immer wieder kommt es zu schockartigen Irritationen und störenden Eingriffen, die den Formprozeß umlenken. Wir sehen, daß er für überraschende Wendungen offen, also nicht programmiert ist. Vielleicht macht der gezeichnete Ablauf diese Sprünge und Mutationen deutlicher, als es der Film vermag, für den die Blätter als Vorlage bestimmt waren, denn die Filmoptik stellt ja nicht Phasen nebeneinander, sondern verbindet sie zu einem fließenden, bruchlosen Kontinuum. Kandinsky, dem Kranz den Leporello zeigte, als er im Frühjahr 1930 ins Bauhaus kam, war an diesem Filmprojekt interessiert und stellte den Kontakt zu einem Verleger her, doch verhinderten die politischen Wirren und die Wirtschaftskrise die Verwirklichung. Erst später kam die Reihe zu dem Titel, der sie als umkehrbare Formgleichung ausweist: weiß : schwarz

———————————

schwarz : weiß

1929. Der Druckerlehrling wird mit gebrauchsgraphischen Entwürfen beschäftigt. Die Bauhaus-Meister stellen in einer Bielefelder Turnhalle aus, Moholy-Nagy hält einen Vortrag, der Kranz auf Klees „Pädagogisches Skizzenbuch" (1925) hinweist. Aber er kann damit nichts anfangen, hingegen fesselt ihn eine sehr gegensätzliche Bilderzählung, Masereels „Stundenbuch". Eine neue Variationsreihe wird begonnen. Das Thema sind die Verzerrungen, welche die Perspektive, wenn man sie aus verschiedenen Standpunkten praktiziert, dem tatsächlichen Dingbestand zufügt. Der auf Objektivation pochende Anspruch der Perspektive, ihre

vorgebliche Richtigkeit wird damit in Frage gestellt. Das heißt den Zweifel thematisieren und formal auszubeuten, den schon Cézanne auf die von der Renaissance begründete Übereinkunft der Raum- und Körperwiedergabe richtete. Diese Übereinkunft war jahrhundertelang eine der Bastionen der Ästhetik der Endgültigkeit, von deren Abbau wir einleitend sprachen. Alle diese Entwürfe sind verlorengegangen.

1930 bekommt der Druckerlehrling seinen Gesellenbrief. Eine Broschüre von Hannes Meyer – „Junge Menschen kommt ans Bauhaus" – gibt den Anstoß, nach Dessau zu gehen. Am 15. April wird Kranz in das Bauhaus aufgenommen. Die neue Welt verwirrt ihn, die künstlerischen und kunstideologischen Konflikte innerhalb des Lehrkörpers tragen nicht zur Klärung bei. Ein „Simplicissimus aus der Provinz" (so sieht er die Situation im Rückblick) stößt auf „hochgestochenes, intellektuelles Leben". Kranz geht zu Albers in die Material- und Werklehre, er lernt analytisches Zeichnen bei Kandinsky und besucht das Seminar von Klee („noch heute erscheint er mir unnahbar"). In einer neuen Filmidee greift er nach dem Pfeil, einem der Embleme, mit denen Klee häufig seine Formwanderungen instrumentierte. Die sechzig Blätter sollten in einen Drei-Minuten-Film umgesetzt werden.

Ostinato nennt man in der Musik „eine Baßmelodie, die ständig wiederkehrt, wobei sie rhythmisch verändert und bei gleichem Aufbau auch tonlich variiert werden, gelegentlich auch in einer anderen Stimme und transponiert erscheinen kann . . ." (Eberhard Thiel). Obstinat, hartnäckig zeigt sich auch der Pfeil, was ihm den Beinamen „heroisch" eingetragen hat. Abgelenkt, vervielfacht, gespalten, verknotet oder verschlungen, setzt sich seine Grundgestalt doch immer wieder durch. Dabei erweist sich ihre Stoßkraft auf unerklärliche Weise pfiffig und einfallsreich: selbst aus dem innersten Punkt einer Spirale gibt es plötzlich einen unvermuteten Ausweg. Sieht man vom abenteuerlichen Verlauf dieser Story ab, stellt sich die Reihe als neue Paraphrase

the first sheet countless mini-arrows, from above and below, aim to reach the white ground, so that the latter itself is outlined into a superarrow, i. e. becomes a figure which soon rejuvenates itself in linear form but can at any moment release new showers of arrows. Towards the end the process is again reversed; the pointed linear energy thickens into the black surface, but at the same time a delicate white line is permitted to strike the final circling chord. Here classical dialectic is made clear in visible form: the self-establishment of a principle means its dissolution. Of necessity, then, a completely different form thesis appears on the scene: the circle. In contrast to the two earlier variation series, this one is irreversible, which, of course, does not exclude the possibility of continuing it. Only once, when arrow stands against arrow (26–30), do contra-rotating impulses come into play. More than the other two series, the "arrow" does give some consideration to its conversion into a film. The layout of each individual print is transitory i. e. geared to the function allotted to it between the earlier and the later phases.

When Kranz came to Dessau, the Bauhaus was already undergoing its ascetic phase. A strongly marxist coloured functionalism set the tone and stigmatized the artists at the Bauhaus as relics of bourgeois aestheticism. Hannes Meyer, who took over the direction of the school after Gropius' departure, used to make fun of "the Kleefeld (clover field) of young Bauhaus artists planted by the most wonderful of all individualistic painters". Kranz did not let this bother him. In 1930 his occupation with typography and photomontage results in a film project which, after the sober black and white phase, allows the painter to come into his own once more. Something was to be created which still did not exist in Europe at that time: a colour film; such was the original title of this project, which, of course, at first again only remained at the paper stage. Today this series is named "Leporello", in accordance with the form in which Kranz pasted the 32 gouaches

together. Colour brings spatial dimensions into action. The flowing space which it evokes cannot be pinned down to axes of perspective nor can it pervade the picture as an ultimate spread. It changes quickly from being a cell, body, micro- or macrostructure, open on all sides or rounded in spiral form. In the final phase it becomes a veiled colour space from which all sorts of possibilities can be expected. If one takes at random individual phases, every fifth print for example, out of the sequence and places them side by side, they give the impression of being completely unconnected and self-contained. We miss the "leitmotiv" thread, the "thorough-bass". The formal breadth of variation is much wider, the possibility of reversal is consequently even more freely observable than in the earlier cycles. The seams joining the individual prints, the shrewd observer notes, are welded with the help of the film optic What is distant is potentially near, what is minute can turn out to be a "world in a nutshell". All this is effected by the volatile shortening and lengthening of distance. As soon as a tumescent large form has reached its saturation point, i. e. the edge of the print, our eye is directed near to the centre. It discovers that the large form (super sign) releases micro-forms from itself, which in their turn strive to achieve saturation. This process will also taper off at a periphery and the centre will again release new impulses. Kranz builds on the self-producing power of his vocabulary, which gives genesis its permanence.

4.

Only today, more than 40 years later, are these variation series available as films. They run in direct contrast to Malraux's theory when he once tried to ease painting of some of the burden of its content by making the film take over the epic role: "Since we have had film, painting need no longer exercise the function of telling stories." But historical facts have disregarded such lines for the demarcation of competency. When the traditional two-dimensional arts (painting and graphics) started reflecting on

auf das Thema „Figur und Grund" dar, wobei Schwarz und Weiß wieder abwechselnd die Hauptrollen spielen. Im ersten Blatt streben unzählige Minipfeile von oben und unten auf den weißen „Grund" zu, so daß dieser selbst zum Superpfeil eingegrenzt, also zur „Figur" wird, die sich alsbald linear verjüngt, aber jederzeit neue Pfeilscharen freisetzen kann. Gegen Ende schlägt der Prozeß wieder um: die zugespitzte lineare Energie verdickt sich zur schwarzen Fläche, zugleich aber darf eine zarte weiße Linie den kreisenden Schlußakkord anschlagen. Hier wird klassische Dialektik anschaulich gemacht: die Selbstverwirklichung eines Prinzips bedeutet dessen Selbstauflösung. Notwendig tritt sodann eine ganz andere Formthese auf: der Kreis. Anders als die beiden früheren Variationsreihen ist diese irreversibel, was freilich die Möglichkeit, sie fortzusetzen, nicht ausschließt. Nur einmal, als Pfeil gegen Pfeil steht (26–30), kommen gegenläufige Impulse ins Spiel. Mehr als die beiden anderen Reihen nimmt der „Pfeil" auf die filmische Umsetzung Rücksicht. Jedes Einzelblatt ist transitorisch angelegt, d. h. von der Funktion geprägt, die ihm zwischen den früheren und den späteren Phasen zukommt.

Als Kranz nach Dessau kam, stand das Bauhaus bereits in seiner asketischen Phase. Eine stark marxistisch gefärbter Funktionalismus gab den Ton an und stempelte die Künstler am Bauhaus zu Relikten der bürgerlichen Ästhetik. Hannes Meyer, der nach Gropius' Weggang die Leitung der Schule übernahm, spottete über „das Kleefeld junger Bauhauskünstler, gezüchtet vom wundersamsten Maler-Individualisten". Kranz ließ es sich nicht verdrießen. In die Beschäftigung mit Typographie und Photomontage schiebt sich 1930 ein Filmprojekt, das nach der nüchternen Schwarz-Weiß-Phase wieder den Maler zu Wort kommen läßt. Etwas sollte entstehen, das es damals in Europa noch gar nicht gab: ein „Farbfilm" – so lautete der ursprüngliche Titel des Projekts, das freilich vorerst wieder auf dem Papier blieb. Heute heißt die Reihe „Leporello" gemäß der Form, in der

Kranz die 32 Gouachen aneinandergeklebt hat. Die Farbe bringt räumliche Dimensionen in das Geschehen. Der fließende Raum, den sie evoziert, läßt sich weder auf Perspektivachsen festlegen noch als endliche Erstreckung durchwandern. Es ist bald Zelle, bald Leib, Mikro- oder Makrostruktur, nach allen Seiten offen oder spiraloid gerundet. In der Schlußphase wird er zum verschleierten Farbraum, der viele wartende Möglichkeiten in sich trägt. Greift man willkürlich einzelne Phasen – etwa jedes fünfte Blatt – aus der Sequenz heraus und stellt sie nebeneinander, wirken sie völlig unverbunden und eigenmächtig. Wir vermissen den leitmotivischen Faden, den „Generalbaß". Die formale Variationsbreite ist viel breiter, die Möglichkeit des Umschlagens wird folglich noch freier wahrgenommen als in früheren Zyklen. Die überbrückenden Nahtstellen – das erkennt der aufmerksame Blick – kommen mit Hilfe der Filmoptik zustande. Das Ferne ist potentiell ein Nahes, das Winzige kann sich als eine „world in a nutshell" entpuppen. Das alles bewirkt die sprunghafte Distanzverkürzung oder -vergrößerung. Sobald eine anschwellende Großform ihre saturation (d. h. den Blattrand) erreicht hat, wird unser Auge nahe an das Zentrum herangeführt. Es entdeckt, daß die Großform (Superzeichen) neue Mikroformen aus sich entläßt, die ihrerseits der Sättigung zustreben. Auch dieser Prozeß wird an einer Peripherie auslaufen, und wieder wird das Zentrum neue Impulse freisetzen. Kranz baut auf die selbstzeugende Kraft seines Vokabulars, der Genesis Dauer verleihend.

4.

Erst heute, mehr als vierzig Jahre später, liegen diese Variationsreihen als Filme vor. Sie widersprechen dem Wort, mit dem Malraux einmal versuchte, die Malerei inhaltlich zu entlasten und den Film auf seine epische Rolle zu verpflichten: „Seit wir Film haben, braucht die Malerei keine Geschichten mehr zu erzählen." Die historischen Tatsachen kümmerten sich nicht um solche Kompetenzabgrenzungen. Als die traditionellen Flächenkünste (Malerei und Graphik)

the autonomous possibilities of their vocabulary – the formula for this is known as Abstraction – together with the question of the syntactic arrangement of this element material, there arose at once the problem of kinetic concatenation, serial progress and its systematization. This transition from the closed art concept of finality to an open system of variability was, in the first instance, tried out in painting. Its first phase extends roughly from Monet's cycles to Mondrian. The second generation of pioneers unhesitatingly seized the opportunity of instrumenting serialization with the help of film media. Viking Eggeling and Hans Richter did this immediately after the first world war. In their painted "picture rolls" they reproduced successive form phases in a juxtaposed picture strip. At the same time were made the first abstract films, Eggeling's "Diagonal symphony" (1919) and Richter's "Rhythm 21" (1921). Kranz first saw these films in 1931/32 when Richter showed them in Dessau. He was no less affected when he learned that Werner Graeff, a friend of Richter's, was concerning himself with ideas on abstract films at the Bauhaus. Already in Weimar, in the first year of the Bauhaus, Kurt Schwerdtfeger and Ludwig Hirschfeld-Mack had shown "reflecting moving pictures" (1923/24), in which they investigated the variable behavioural possibilities of geometrical form motifs. "Stencils in different colours, showed hither and thither and on top of one another, were projected onto the back of a transparent screen so that, on the side facing the public, appeared a kinetic coloured abstraction." (Wingler). A sort of score programmed the running of these pictures without, however, in any way restricting the free rein for hazardous flights of fancy. At each performance there were fresh variations for the programme. Mechanical media, hidden from the public, created the appearance of pictures from immaterial form and colour constellations. In his "Lichtrequisit" (1922–30), Moholy-Nagy attempted to integrate these two levels by making the apparatus (the motivating force of the moving pictures) visible during the performance in such a way that the basic material figure, i. e. the apparatus, and its transformation into light and shadow could be observed simultaneously. In the film this experiment was also carried to its logical end.

The Bauhaus was no exclusive laboratory for the ideas of geometrical purists. While, for instance, Albers extended systematic constructivism to cover the familiar alphabetic symbols, Walter Peterhans, head of the photographic department since 1929, devoted his attention to photographing material montages out of which he made variation series. Here it is not a question of element distillates, geometrically purified, but of still-life type combinations of items of the most varying provenance. The influence of surrealist alienation is unmistakable. These works were for Kranz an important incentive. He also recalls the impression which, in 1930, the surrealist manifest made on him. Apparently he did not regard Breton's much vaunted imagination "which knows no limits" (before it becomes the slave of utility) as the antipole of his morphogenetic investigations – just as we today recognize that the possibilities of variability and combinatorial analysis are spread over a number of executions and contact can be established between them. Geometrical combinatorial analysis is, in comparison, the strictest and the purest, the biomorphic tends more to the vaguely non-committal, and finally the surrealist, with its startling transformations, provokes the impression of anarchy and waywardness, whose object is to cause total confusion. Ernst's collage novel, "La Femme 100 têtes" (1929), made a great impression on Kranz. In 1930 he made his first photomontages. One print is called "No solution". Behind a many-headed crowd, over which hovers a trivial angel, there arises a wall with two rows of windows. Some of the 16 windows are bricked-in. 16 "glimpses", 16 phases of a surrealist variation sequence, which can be thought of as being continued indefinitely. The pessimistic "No solution" also

in die Reflexion über die autonomen Möglichkeiten ihres Vokabulars eintraten – die Formel dafür heißt Abstraktion –, stellte sich mit der Frage der syntaktischen Gliederung dieses Elementarmaterials sofort das Problem der kinetischen Verkettung, des Reihenablaufes und seiner Systematisierbarkeit. Dieser Übergang vom geschlossenen Kunstbegriff der Endgültigkeit zum offenen System der Variabilität wurde zunächst im Gestaltungsbereich der Malerei erprobt. Seine erste Phase reichte etwa von den Zyklen Monets bis zu Mondrian. Unverzüglich nahm die zweite Generation der Pioniere die Chance wahr, die Serialisierung mit filmischen Mitteln zu instrumentieren. Das taten Viking Eggeling und Hans Richter unmittelbar nach dem Ersten Weltkrieg. In ihren gemalten „Rollenbildern" gaben sie das Nacheinander von Formphasen im Nebeneinander eines Bildstreifens wieder. Gleichzeitig entstanden die ersten abstrakten Filme, Eggelings „Diagonal-Symphonie" (1919) und Richters „Rhythmus 21" (1921). Kranz sah diese Filme erst 1931/32, als Richter sie in Dessau vorführte. Nicht minder betroffen war er, als er davon erfuhr, daß Werner Graeff, ein Freund Richters, sich am Bauhaus mit abstrakten Filmideen beschäftigte. Schon in Weimar, in den ersten Bauhausjahren, hatten Kurt Schwertfeger und Ludwig Hirschfeld-Mack „Reflektorische Lichtspiele" 1923/24) vorgeführt, in denen sie die variablen Verhaltensmöglichkeiten geometrischer Formmotive untersuchten. „Schablonen in verschiedenen Farben wurden, vor Scheinwerfern hin- und her- und übereinandergeschoben, auf die Rückseite eines transparenten Bildschirms projiziert, so daß auf der dem Publikum zugewandten Vorderseite eine kinetisch farbige Abstraktion erschien" (Wingler). Eine Art Partitur programmierte diese Abläufe, ohne jedoch aleatorischen Einfällen den Spielraum zu versagen. Bei jeder Vorführung konnten dem Programm neue Variationen erschlossen werden. Apparative Mittel erzeugten, dem Publikum verborgen, Scheinbilder aus immateriellen Form- und Farbkonstellationen. In seinem „Lichtrequisit" (1922–30) versuchte Moholy-Nagy diese beiden Ebenen zu interpretieren, indem er den Apparat, Anlaß der Lichtspiele, sichtbar in den Ablauf einbezog, solcherart die materielle Grundfigur und deren Verwandlung in Licht und Schatten der simultanen Wahrnehmung zugänglich machte. Auch dieses Experiment erreichte in der Filmaufzeichnung seine letzte Konsequenz.

Das Bauhaus war kein exklusives Ideenlabor geometrischer Puristen. Während z. B. Albers die konstruktivistische Systematik sogar auf das vertraute Zeichenrepertoire des Alphabets ausdehnte, beschäftigte sich Walter Peterhans, seit 1929 Leiter der Photoabteilung, mit Photographien von Materialmontagen, aus denen er Variationsreihen bildete. Hier geht es nicht um geometrisch gereinigte Elementdestillate, sondern um stillebenhafte Kombinationen aus Gegenständen verschiedenster Herkunft. Der Einfluß der surrealistischen Dingverfremdung ist unverkennbar. Diese Arbeiten waren für Kranz ein wichtiger Anstoß. Er erinnert sich auch des Eindrucks, den er um 1930 vom Surrealistischen Manifest empfing. Offenbar hat er die von Breton gepriesene Phantasie, „die keine Grenzen kennt" (ehe sie unter das Diktat der Nützlichkeit gerät), nicht als Gegenpol seiner morphogenetischen Untersuchungen gesehen – gleichwie wir heute erkennen, daß die Möglichkeiten von Variabilität und Kombinatorik sich auf mehrere Spielarten verteilen, zwischen denen es Konflikte geben kann. Die geometrische Kombinatorik ist vergleichsweise die strengste und „reinste", die biomorphe neigt zur schweifenden Unverbindlichkeit, die surrealistische schließlich provoziert mit ihren Verwandlungsschocks den Eindruck anarchischer Willkür, die totale Verwirrung stiften möchte.

Ernsts Collagen-Roman „La Femme 100 têtes" (1929) hat Kranz sehr beeindruckt. 1930 machte er seine ersten Photomontagen. Ein Blatt heißt „Keine Lösung". Hinter einer vielköpfigen Menge, über der ein verheißender Trivialengel schwebt, erhebt sich eine Mauer mit zwei Fensterreihen. Einige der 16 Fenster sind vermauert. Sechzehn „Einblicke" – sechzehn Phasen einer surrealistischen Variationsreihe,

means "No end". The montage, "Stock of heads" (1932), is an ironic answer to the untranslatable play on words "Femme 100 têtes". About 100 heads without bodies are, like props, kept in a box. They form the macabre working material of adventurous association sequences.These and other ingenious ideas one must place alongside the 4 film sequences in order to recognize that Kurt Kranz, from the very beginning, was quite at home with the various aspects of combinatorial analysis. What he took with him from his three Bauhaus years was to influence decisively his conscious experimentation, which, right up to the present day, never considers attaching itself permanently to the finality of any particular synthesis. New inventions provide ever fresh proof of this mobility, the folding and graduated pictures, and now the sequences with plastic objects: "From outside to inside", "From one into the other". The repertoire of the material montages includes geometrical figures, items of rubbish and junk, bits of jewellery and toys etc. If we were to see these collections of items all mixed up higgledy piggeldy in a drawer, they would only give the impression of the disparate. The montage arranges the conglomeration into series of associations out of unexpected juxtapositions. Geometrical patterns, organic "informel" and surrealist objets trouvés form poetic combinations over which the fairy's magic wand seems to wave. That childish credulity of the fables, which imagines that out of anything everything can be made, here comes back into its own. From "outside to inside" could equally well be called from "inside to outside", then each sequence can be read in at least two directions; his picture field is a multi-dimensional playing field. One is reminded once more of Goethe's oft quoted saying:

Nothing is within, nothing is without

Then what is within is without.

This poem refers to the "Contemplation of Nature" but it seems to suit better a "Contemplation of art" which the doctrine, "always regard one as all", applies to the open systems of variation sequences of artistic provenance, and thereby discovers that these non-predetermined processes are reversible, that they are made up of associations as well as dissociations. And therein the question concerning the consequences of the open concept of art, mentioned at the beginning, has its binding and valid answer; for the first time since art has existed, the construction and dissolution of form constellations stand side by side as processes of equal rank and status. By appropriating this terrain of new experiences with form and new behavioural attitudes, Kurt Kranz has, as artist and teacher, introduced a whole series of important and significant discoveries.

Werner Hofmann

die man endlos fortgesetzt denken kann. Das pessimistische „Keine Löung" bedeutet auch „Kein Ende". Die Montage „Kopf-Vorrat" (1932) antwortet ironisch auf das unübersetzbare Wortspiel der „Femme 100 têtes". Rund 100 Köpfe ohne Körper sind gleich Requisiten in einem Schachtelraster untergebracht. Sie bilden das makabre Spielmaterial von abenteuerlichen Assoziationsreihen.

Diese und andere Einfälle muß man den vier Filmsequenzen zur Seite stellen, um zu erkennen, daß Kurt Kranz von Anfang an in den verschiedenen Spielarten der Kombinatorik zu Hause war. Die Ausbeute der drei Bauhausjahre wurde bestimmend für sein etperimentelles Bewußtsein, das bis zum heutigen Tag nicht daran denkt, bei der Endgültigkeit irgendeiner Synthese vor Anker zu gehen. Diese Beweglichkeit belegen immer neue Erfindungen: die Falt- und Stufenbilder, neuerdings die Reihen mit plastischen Objekten: „Von Außen nach Innen", „Vom Einen ins Andere". Das Repertoire dieser Materialmontagen erstreckt sich auf geometrische Figuren, Gegenstandsabfall und Kleinkram, Schmuck- und Spielzeugfragmente u. a. m. Sähen wir diese Dingversammlungen in einer Schublade durcheinander geworfen, böten sie bloß den Eindruck des Disparaten. Die Montage ordnet das Konglomerat zu Assoziationsreihen aus unerwarteten Nachbarschaften. Geometrische Muster, vegetabiles „Informel" und surreale Fundstücke gehen poetische Verbindungen ein, über denen der Zauberstab des Märchens zu walten scheint. Der fabulierende Kinderglaube, der aus allem alles zu machen vermeint, kommt hier wieder zu seinem Recht. „Von Außen nach Innen" könnte auch „Von Innen nach Außen" heißen, denn jede Reihe läßt sich mindestens nach zwei Richtungen lesen, das Bildfeld ist ein mehrdimensionales Spielfeld. Da fällt einem wieder einmal das vielzitierte Goethe-Wort ein:

> Nichts ist drinne, nichts ist draußen:
> Denn was innen das ist außen.

Dieses Gedicht bezieht sich auf das „Naturbetrachten", doch scheint es besser auf ein „Kunstbetrachten" zu passen, das die Lehre

> Immer eins wie alles achten

auf die offenen Systeme von Variationsreihen *künstlicher* Herkunft anwendet und dabei entdeckt, daß diese nicht prädeterminierten Prozesse umkehrbar sind, daß sie sich sowohl aus Assoziationen wie aus Dissoziationen zuammensetzen. Darin hat die Frage nach dem Ertrag des eingangs erörterten *offenen Kunstbegriffs* ihre bündige Antwort: zum ersten Mal, seit es Kunst gibt, stehen der Aufbau und der Abbau von Formkonstellationen als gleichberechtigte und gleichrangige Prozesse nebeneinander. Bei der Aneignung dieses Terrains neuer Formerfahrungen und -verhaltensweisen hat Kurt Kranz als Künstler und als Pädagoge eine Reihe wichtiger Entdeckungen eingebracht.

Werner Hofmann

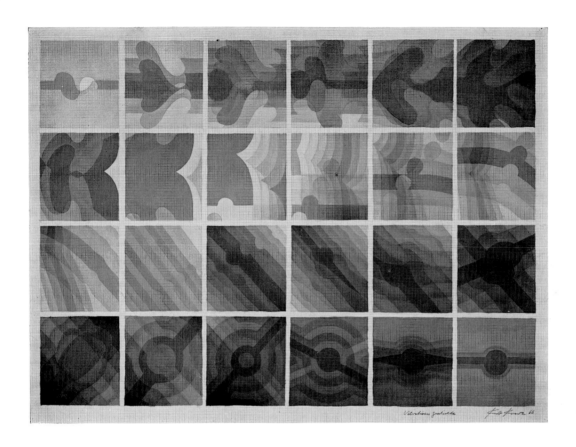

Kranz: Vibration story, 1966, 56 x 76 cm, watercolour
24 variations make up a form sequence which can be read like a story.
The abstract form action can be seen growing or shrinking by comparing
the individual variations with one another. Thereby is released a poetic
message, not definable in words. Nevertheless it is a picture story, a cartoon.

Kranz: Vibrationsgeschichte 1966, 56 x 76 cm, Aquarell.
25 Variationen bilden eine Formreihe, die man wie eine Geschichte lesen
kann. Das abstrakte Formgeschehen wird durch den Vergleich der
einzelnen Variationen untereinander wachsend und abbauend gesehen. Dabei
wird eine durch Worte nicht definierbare poetische Botschaft frei. Trotzdem
ist es eine Bildergeschichte, ein Cartoon.

P. 45

From outwards to inwards, 1970, 98 x 118 cm, Mixed media, canvas and wood.
The sequence theme shows the change from great to small. Forms and
objects leap star-shaped in 16 rows on cold and warm grey graduations, trans-
forming themselves into the smallest symbol, into the centre of the picture.
The colours of these objects and signs follow this cold/warm jump-turn
into the blind centre. The readability of the sequence can be interpreted
in several ways. The riddle of the bifurcations, of the doors leading
to nowhere, of the symmetrical ornamentation etc. contribute as a whole
to the wealth and meaning of this composition.

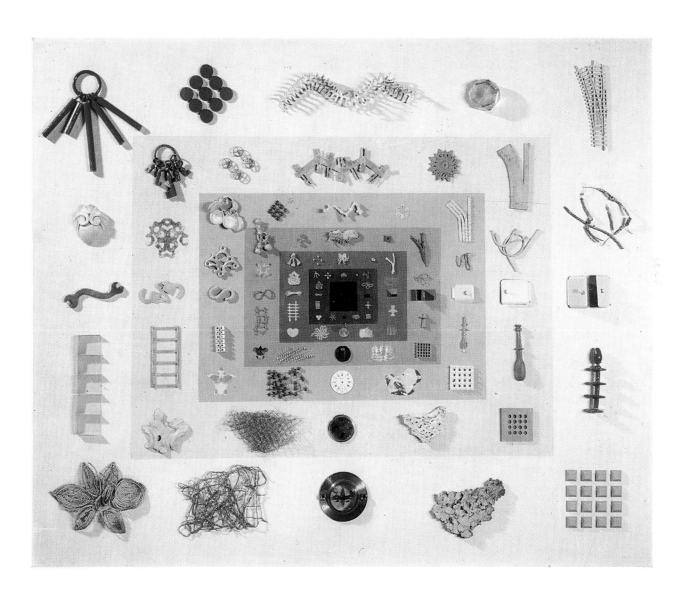

Von Außen nach Innen, 1970, 98 x 118 cm, Mixed media, Leinwand und Holz.
Das Reihen-Thema zeigt die Veränderung vom Großen zum Kleinen.
Formen und Objekte springen sternförmig, in 16 Reihen auf
kalten und warmen Graustufen sich zum kleinsten Symbol verwandelnd,
in die Bildmitte hinein. Die Farben der Objekte und Zeichen folgen

diesem Kalt-Warm-Umsprung bis zur blinden Mitte. Die Ablesbarkeit der
Reihe ist mehrdeutig angelegt. Das Rätsel des Verzweigten,
der Türen ins Nichts, der Ornamentsymmetrien usw. sind in ihrem Ganzen
der Reichtum und Sinn dieser Komposition.

Bernhard Kerber

Comments on the readability of picture sequences.

As a theme, intelligibility presupposes a transformation of shape. It aims its elements not at identity but at form genesis, at metamorphosis, and thus encourages inventiveness. Combinatorial analysis, change, evolution and transformation require plurality. Sequences sacrifice simultaneity and the autonomy of the field of view. The single picture is only one brick in the building.

The lack of finality relieves the individual picture of the pressure of composition, encourages the fortuitous cut-out character of the frame and directs the attention to a larger whole. The picture, just because it is pars pro toto (not a fragment), can keep unspoilt the painting process, the dynamics of its creation. It preserves its intrinsic action.

Picture sequences, Leporelli, display themselves in the course of time. This stimulates the observer to personal structural initiative. He shares the responsibility, in combination and in participation he constructs strophic form families. The permanence of picture roll and frieze is the precondition for the film. "The tempi are the real ingredients of the film vis à vis the timeless and impersonal time of the observer of the picture sequence" (Kranz).

Morphogenesis knows mutation. Spontaneous deviation in the parameter is a hindrance to construction and serialization, manifests the relevance of determination, opens the system. Creative imagination is equivalent to life.

From the life of a composition.

"From the life of a composition" transposes the single picture into the whole of a Leporello sequence. A biomorphic surrealism completes the form osmosis of mostly transparent shapes until their dissolution in multi-dimensional light spaces through which the observer appears to hurry with changing degrees of proximity.

Bernhard Kerber

Anmerkungen zur Lesbarkeit der Bildreihen.

Ablesbarkeit als Thema setzt Gestaltwandel voraus. Sie legt ihre Elemente nicht auf Identität, sondern auf Formgenese, auf Metamorphose an und macht also erfinderisch. Kombinatorik, Verwandlung, Evolution und Transformation bedürfen der Pluralität. Sequenzen opfern Simultaneität und Autonomie des Bildfeldes. Das einzelne ist nur Baustein.
Der Mangel an Endgültigkeit entlastet vom Kompositionszwang, fördert den zufälligen Ausschnittcharakter des Bildrahmens, verweist auf ein größeres Ganzes. Das Bild kann, gerade weil pars pro toto (nicht Fragment), den Malvorgang, die Dynamik seiner Entstehung ungefährdet enthalten. Es bewahrt Eigentätigkeit.

Bilderreihen, Leporellos entfalten sich in der Zeit. Diese stimuliert den Betrachter zu strukturierender Eigentätigkeit. Er ist mitverantwortlich. Kombinierend und teilend bildet er strophische Formfamilien.

Zeithaltigkeit von Bilderrolle und Fries ist die Bedingung des Films. „Die Tempi sind die wirkliche Zutat des Films gegenüber der zeitlosen und unpersönlichen Zeit des Betrachters der Bilderreihe." (Kranz.)

Morphogenese kennt die Mutation. Spontane Abweichung im Parameter verhindert Konstruktion und Serialität, relativiert die Determination, öffnet das System. Kreative Phantasie ist Äquivalent fürs Leben.

Aus dem Leben einer Komposition.
„Aus dem Leben einer Komposition" transponiert das einzelne Bild in das gesamte einer Leporellofolge. Ein biomorpher Surrealismus vollzieht die Formosmose meist transparenter Gestalten bis zu ihrer Aufhebung in multidimensionalen Lichträumen, welche der Betrachter mit wechselnder Gegenstandsnähe scheinbar durcheilt.

White against Black.
White circular forms drive vertical tracks into the black. With varying speeds, self-contained semicircular black tracks follow after. Picture 7 introduces the diagonal. Interior forms wander out of the circles and overlay one another. In a positive-negative exchange, the process is repeated. White and black staves wander over the circles and obliterate them. Cylindrical constellations appear out of the depths of the picture, grow, give birth to black forms out of their interiors, which expand until they split. The fissures release black and white circles. They drive tracks into chaos. The process is reversed. At the end stands, almost cyclically, the negative of the beginning.

The heroic arrow.
The heroic arrow, whose dimensions at first the surface of the picture could scarcely contain, shrinks on a horizontal track under the attacks of its foes to a line, escapes, pierces the darkness and shakes off its pursuers. It tears apart new resistances, flies through a network of man-traps, is split by the counter-movement of an opponent, joins itself together again and finds its way into a spiral labyrinth, hostile to movement, from the centre of which it surprisingly emerges into the open. It gains in size, expands over the whole screen, its "soul" becomes visible and goes into the "circle of timelessness".

Movement and counter-movement, offensive and defensive, active and passive, gain in size and loss in size, penetration, flowing back into itself, progressive change and relativity of the time scale, all this demonstrated on the arrow (and spiral as well) was Paul Klee's favourite theme when Kranz, as a student at the Bauhaus, used to attend his afternoon courses.

Design of a colour film.
The "heroic arrow" lived on the plane. The "design of a colour film" introduces the spatial element and through the medium of the zoom takes the eye from the distant view to the close up view. The macrocosm, geometrically ordered, sets free a microcosm of biological forms. Colour illusionism and light/dark give support to the suggestion of space. Microscopic magnification reveals non-static pictures. The repertoire of forms is to an extent familiar: circles, often arranged concentrically, bundles of staves, spirals. The end is arbitrary and triggers off a dynamic process of life.

Weiß gegen Schwarz.
Weiße Kreisformen treiben Vertikalbahnen in das Schwarz. Mit unterschiedlicher Geschwindigkeit rücken halbrund geschlossene Schwarzbahnen nach. Bild 7 führt die Diagonale ein. Binnenformen wandern aus den Kreisen und überlagern einander. Im Positiv-Negativ-Tausch wiederholt sich der Prozeß. Weiße und schwarze Stäbe überwandern die Kreise und löschen sie aus. Zylindrische Konstellationen tauchen aus der Bildtiefe auf, wachsen, gebären schwarze Formen aus ihrem Inneren, welche sich dehnen bis zum Zerspalten. Die Risse entlassen schwarze und weiße Kreise. Sie treiben Bahnen ins Chaos. Der Prozeß kehrt sich um. Am Schluß steht fast zyklisch das Negativ des Anfangs.

Der heroische Pfeil.
Der heroische Pfeil, dessen Dimensionen die Bildfläche anfangs kaum einzufangen vermag, schrumpft auf horizontaler Bahn unter den Attacken der Widersacher zur Linie, entkommt, durchstößt das Dunkel und schüttelt die Verfolger ab. Er zerreißt neue Widerstände, durchfliegt ein Netz von Fußangeln, wird von der Gegenbewegung eines Kontrahenten gespalten, schließt sich wieder und gerät in ein bewegungsfeindliches spiraliges Labyrinth, aus dessen Zentrum er überraschend ins Freie stößt. Er gewinnt an Größe, dehnt sich über die Leinwand, seine „Seele" wird sichtbar und geht ein „in den Kreis der Zeitlosigkeit".
Bewegung und Gegenbewegung, Offensive und Defensive, Aktiv und Passiv, Zu- und Abnahme, Durchdringung, Ineinanderströmen, progressive Veränderung und Relativierung des Zeitmaßes, dies alles am Pfeil (und auch der Spirale) demonstriert, war Lieblingsthema Paul Klees, dessen Nachmittagskurse der Bauhausschüler Kranz besuchte.

Entwurf eines Farbfilms.
Der „Heroische Pfeil" lebte in der Fläche. Der „Entwurf eines Farbfilms" bringt die Raumgestaltung ein und führt mittels des Zoom von der Fern- zur Nahsicht. Der geometrisch geordnete Makrokosmos gibt einen Mikrokosmos biologischer Formen frei. Farbillusionismus und Helldunkel unterstützen die Raumsuggestion. Mikroskopische Vergrößerung enthüllt unstatische Bilder. Das Formenrepertoire ist z. T. bekannt: Kreise, oft konzentrisch geordnet, Stabbündel, Spiralen. Das Ende ist willkürlich, Setzung eines dynamischen Lebensprozesses.

Kurt Kranz
20 Bilder
aus dem Leben einer Komposition
1927–28

Original in Aquarell und Tempera
im Papierband gebunden, Privatbesitz
auf der Titelseite signiert
Größe des Papierbandes: 28 x 24 cm
Größe der Tafeln: 15,7 x 22,5 cm
Gesamtlänge des Leporellos: 220 cm
beidseitig bedruckt

verfilmt 1972
Filmtechnik: Robert Darroll

Der siebzehnjährige Lithographenlehrling Kurt Kranz wurde zwischen Druckereiwerkstatt und Kunstgewerbeschule hin- und hergezerrt. Aussterbendes, von der Photo-Lithographie abgelöstes Handwerk einerseits – und Naturstudium, Dekor und Neue Sachlichkeit an der Kunstgewerbeschule andererseits waren die Möglichkeiten. Die freie Aussage, eine Privatangelegenheit, wurde weder da noch dort angenommen.
Die Arbeit am Fensterbrett der Schlafstube war seine Zuflucht. Hier entstanden Formreihen, Kompositionen im Vokabular der zwanziger Jahre, wie Kranz es von Bielefeld aus sah. Die damaligen Kunstberichte waren unvergleichlich dürftig gegenüber der Flut von Informationen von heute.

Die nach innen gerichtete Neugier und das Erfinden eigener Bilder wie „Aus dem Leben einer Komposition" waren Zuflucht und Quelle. Die vorliegende Bildreihe, im Hochformat entworfen und gemalt, jedoch nicht als Film geplant, entstand vermutlich im Herbst 1927. Die Materialien sind Aquarell und Tempera, die ebenfalls wie Wasserfarbe vermalt wurden. Dadurch ist der Leimanteil sehr verdünnt worden und die pastellartige Wirkung entstanden, aber auch die Haftfähigkeit der Farbpartikel stark gemindert.
Die Blätter sind damals von einem Schulkameraden eingebunden worden, der Titel in der „neuen" Schablonenschrift gezeichnet.
(„Die lebende Komposition" war eine Idee, die sich Kranz aus seiner früheren Arbeit anbot. Ein Bändchen „Abstrakte Formen", begonnen 1925, zeigt bereits in einer Sequenz gesammelte „Kompositionen".)
1972 ist diese Bildergeschichte zum Farbfilm geworden. Ein Bild durchdringt das andere, eins löst das andere ab. Die Durchdringungen zeigen neue Wirkung. Der zeitliche Ablauf läßt das Leben der Komposition deutlich nachempfinden. Um das winzige Filmformat auszunutzen, war es notwendig, das Bild seitlich zu kippen. Dieser Film ist mit den Filmen „Schwarz : Weiß", „Der heroische Pfeil" und „Leporello" zusammengesetzt worden und hat eine Spieldauer von 22 Minuten. Eine aus der Malweise heraus entwickelte, aufbrechende Farbfläche zeigt Formen halb biologischer, halb abstrakter Art. Die Formgruppen kontrastieren zu einem kristallinen Schub. Ein Farbablauf steigert diese Schritte, der in einer dunklen, pastellartigen, trockenen Farbigkeit zu erstarren scheint. Eindringende Bläue, von Gelb abgelöst, endet in äußerster Helligkeit. Die expressive Farbigkeit und die Formkontraste beruhigen sich. Transparente Eiformen, die an Laich und Seifenblasen denken lassen, beenden diese Reihe. Ein Storyboard, bei dem sich die Phantasie des Betrachters von Bild zu Bild die Schritte der Veränderung hinzudenkt, vor- und zurückschreitend, wie es das Leporello erlaubt.

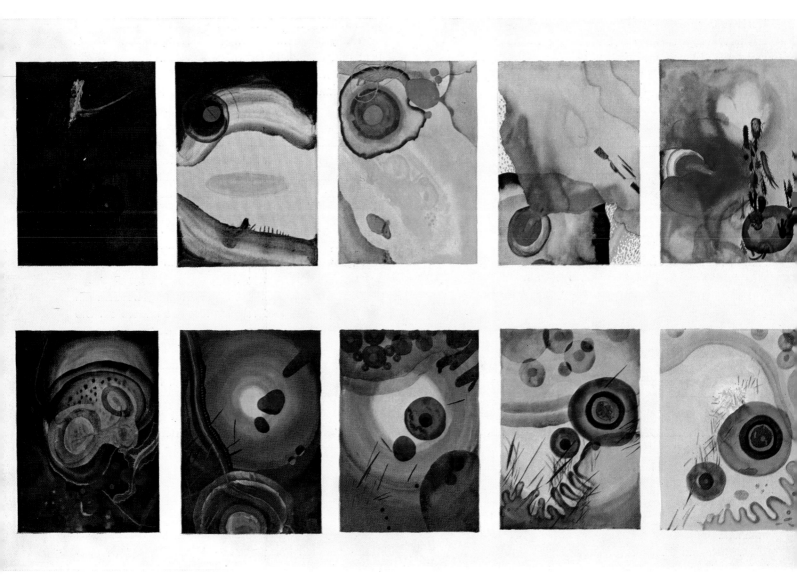

Panel showing complete picture-sequence "20 pictures from the life of a composition".

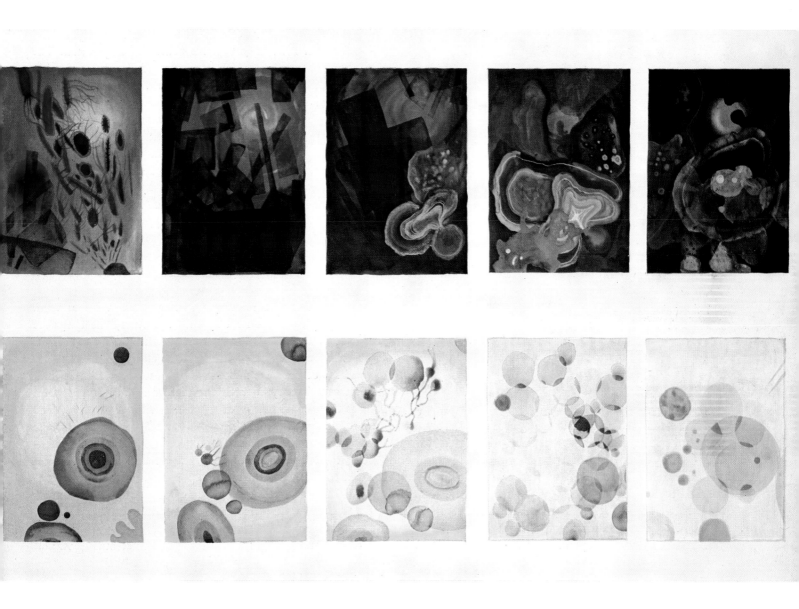

Übersichtstafel der Bildreihe „20 Bilder aus dem Leben einer Komposition"

Kurt Kranz
20 Phases
in the life of a composition
1927–28

Original in watercolour and tempera,
paper bound, in private ownership,
signed on the title page
Size of the paper cover 28 x 24 cm
Size of the panels: 15,7 x 22,5 cm
Total length of the Leporello: 220 cm
printed on both sides

Filmed 1972
Film technology: Robert Darroll

The seventeen-year-old lithograph apprentice, Kurt Kranz, was torn hither and thither between printing workshop and school of arts and crafts. He was faced with two alternatives, on the one hand, a handicraft that was dying out and being supplanted by photo-lithography, and on the other hand, the study of nature, decor and the New Functionalism at the school of arts and crafts. Free expression, his own private work, was accepted at neither.
His only refuge was the window-sill in his bedroom. Here were produced form sequences, compositions in the vocabulary of the twenties, as Kranz saw them from his Bielefeld perspective. Reports on art generally were at that time few and far between in comparison with the flood of information nowadays.

His own works such as "From the life of a composition" were both his refuge and his source of inspiration. The picture sequence shown here, designed and painted in upright format, but not planned as a film, was probably made in 1927. The media are watercolour and tempera, which was also applied like watercolour. Thereby the proportion of glue was very much thinned down so that a pastel-like effect emerged; but the adhesiveness of the paint particles was also considerably reduced.
At that time the sheets were bound by a schoolmate. The title is drawn in what was then the "new" stencil lettering.
(The living composition was an idea which occurred to Kranz as a result of his earlier work. A little book of "Abstract Forms", begun in 1925, already shows a sequence of collected "compositions".)
In 1972 this picture story was made into a colour film. One picture forces its way into the other, one takes the place of the other. The penetrations reveal a new effect. The life of the composition can be clearly read from the passage of time. To make full use of the tiny film format, it was necessary to turn the picture sideways. This film has been combined with the films "Black : White", "The Heroic Arrow" and "Leporello" and has a running time of 22 minutes. A colour surface, developed from the painting technique, emerges and shows forms, half biological and half abstract in type. The form groups form a contrast to a crystalline thrust. A colour sequence accelerates these steps and appears to coagulate in a dark, pastel-like, dry colouring. Penetrating blue, displaced by yellow, ends up in extreme brightness. The expressive colourfulness and the form contrasts settle down quietly. Transparent egg forms, reminding one of soap bubbles and spawn, complete this sequence. A storyboard in which the observer has to imagine in his mind the changing steps between picture and picture, pacing back and forth, as he can do when looking at the Leporello.

20 Phases in the life of a composition 1927-28
All plates in original size
after water colors and gouaches

20 Bilder aus dem Leben einer Komposition 1927-28
Alle Tafeln in Original-Größe
nach den Aquarellen und Gouachen

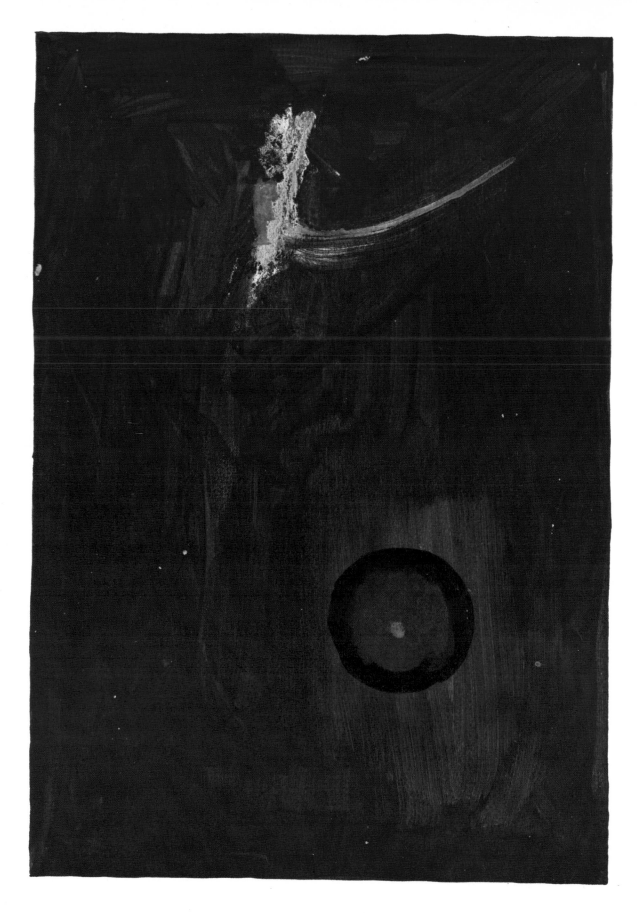

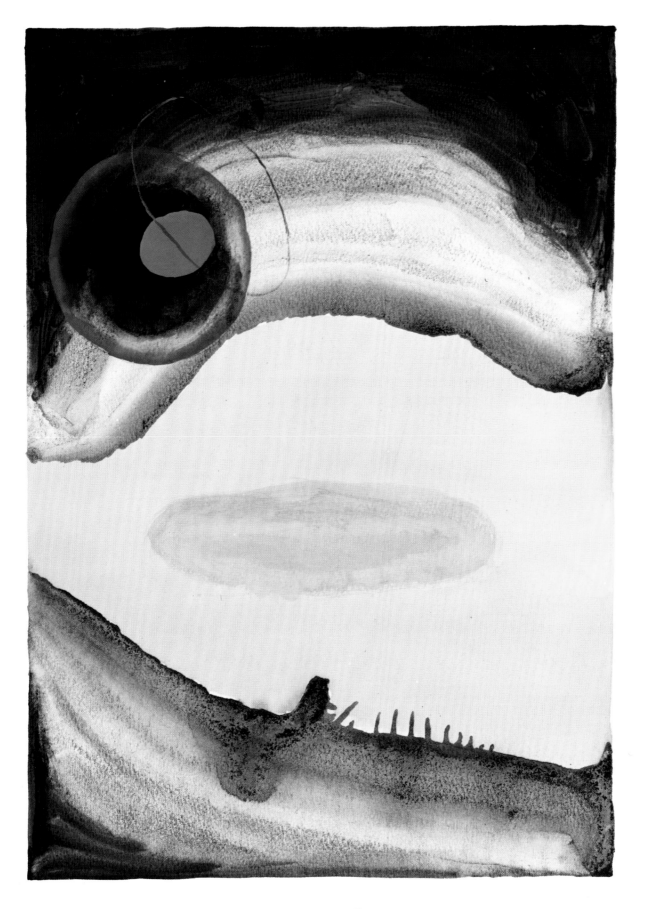

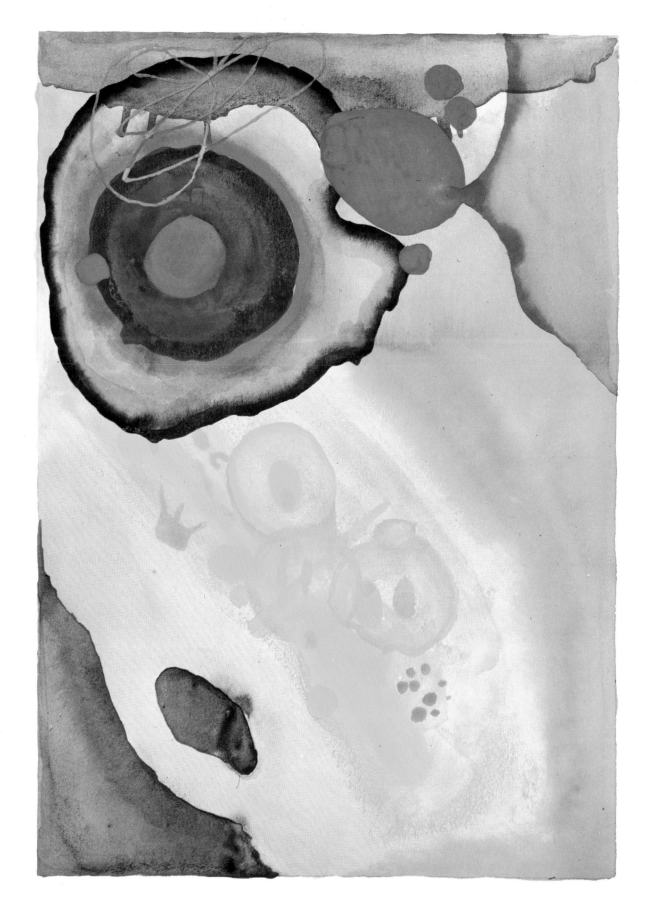

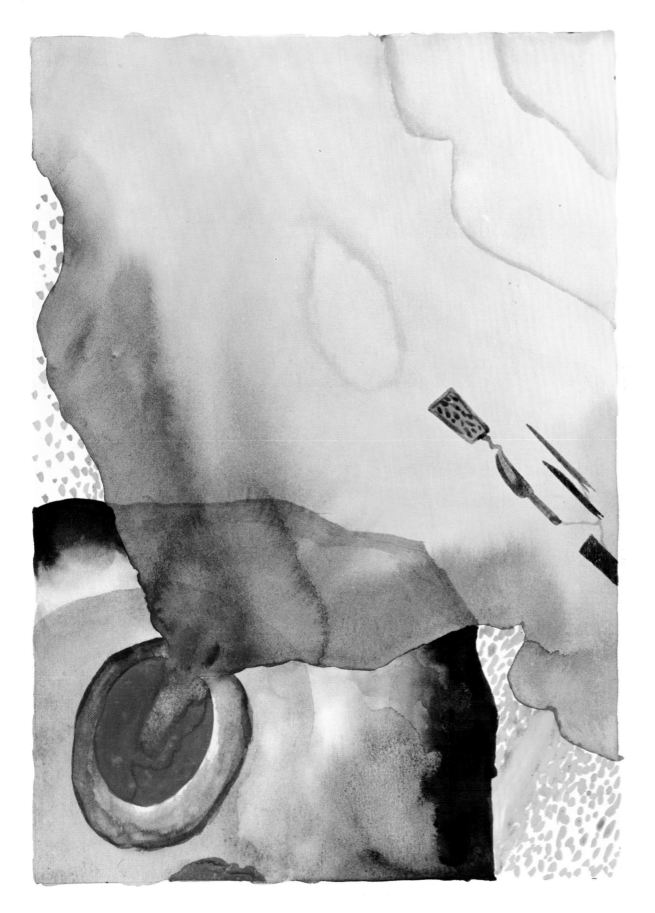

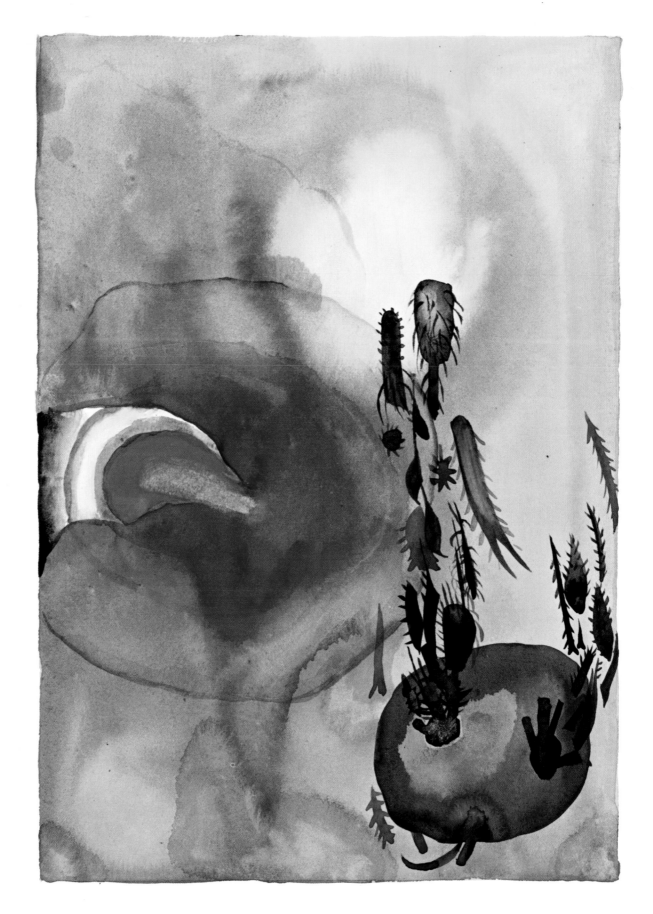

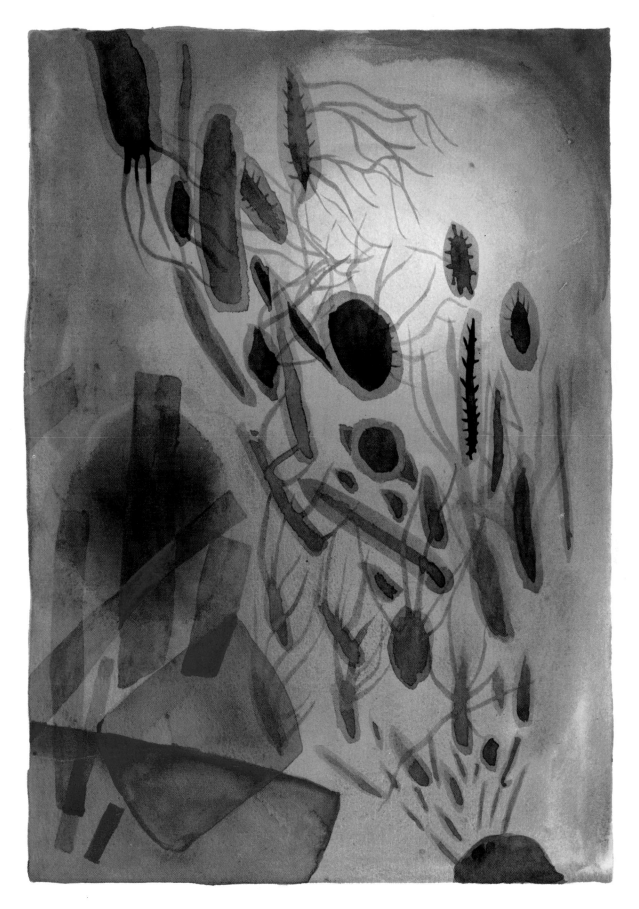

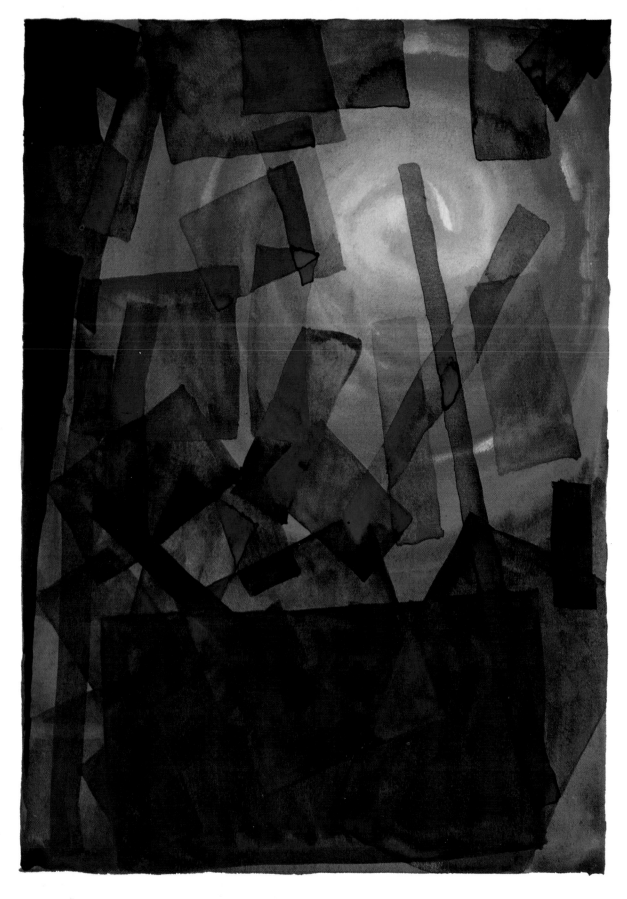

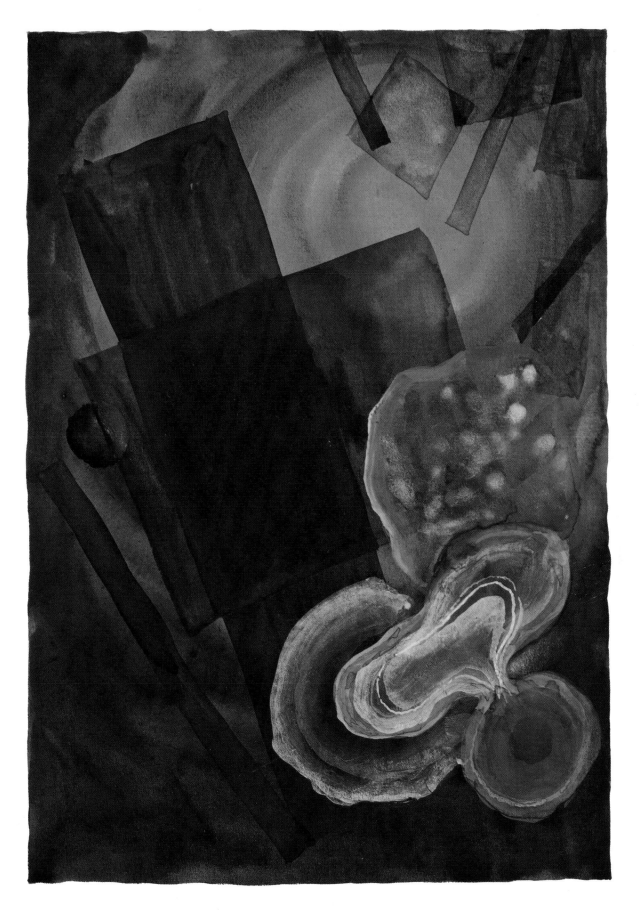

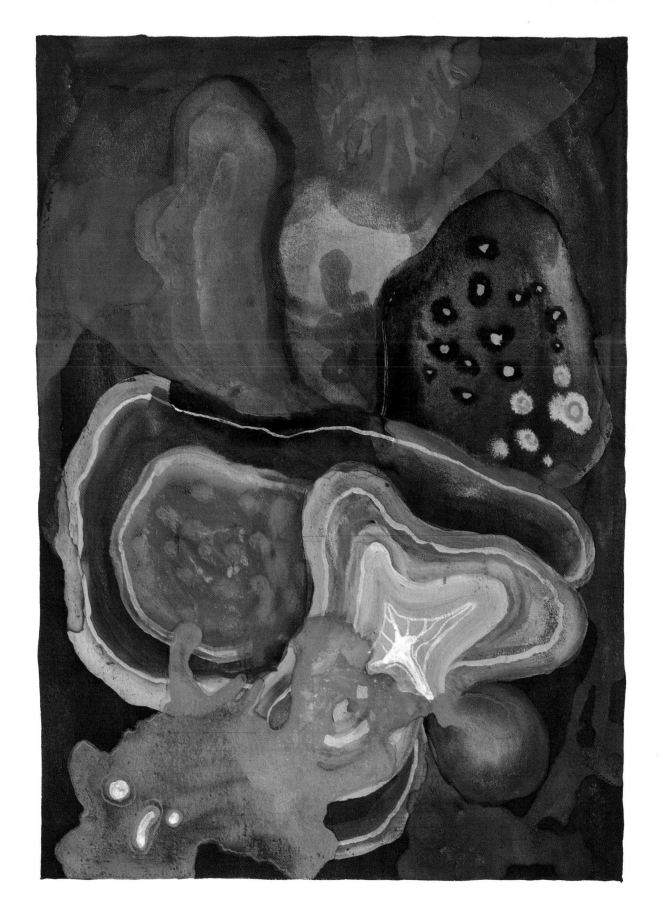

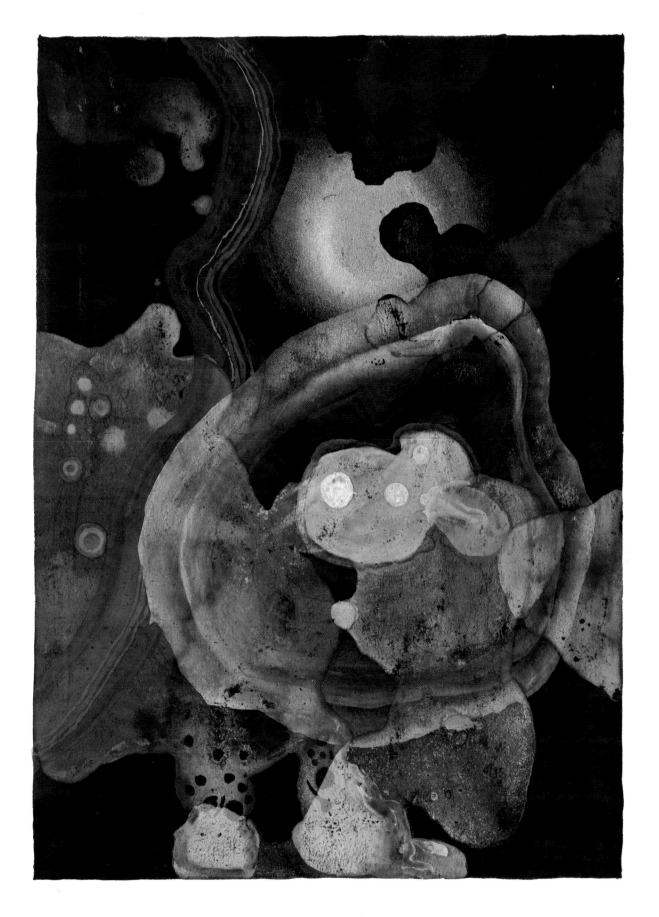

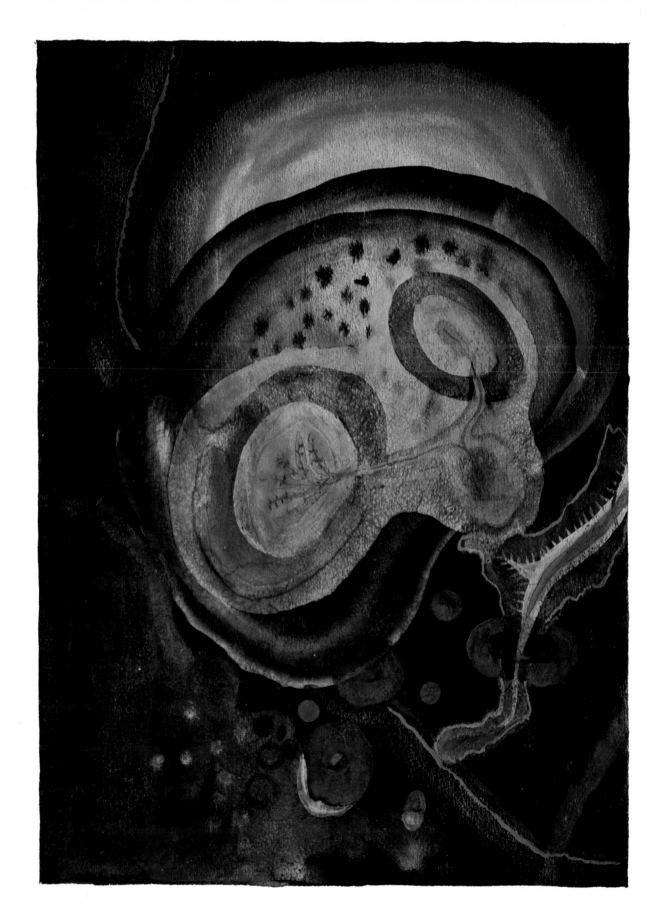

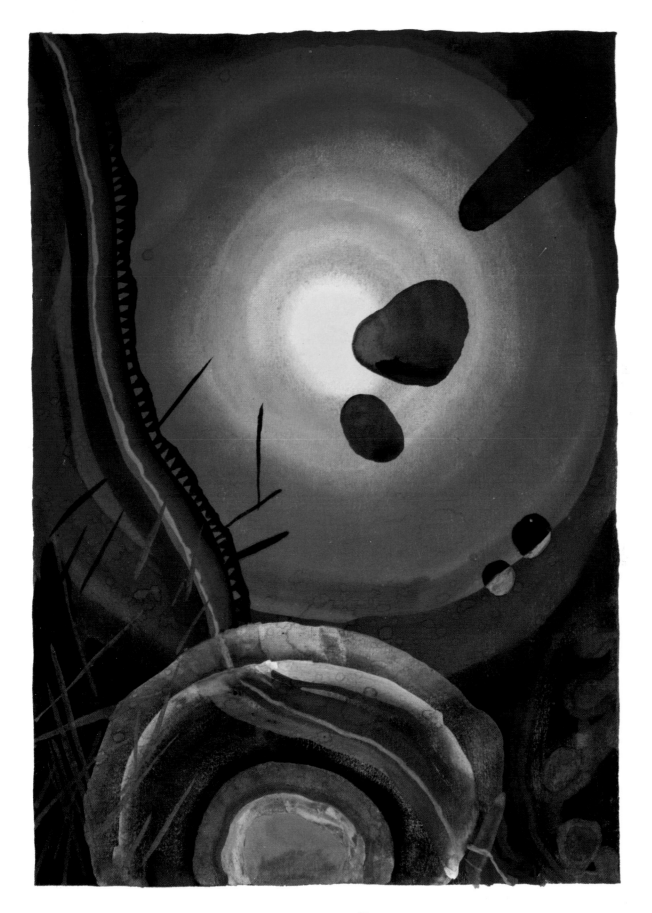

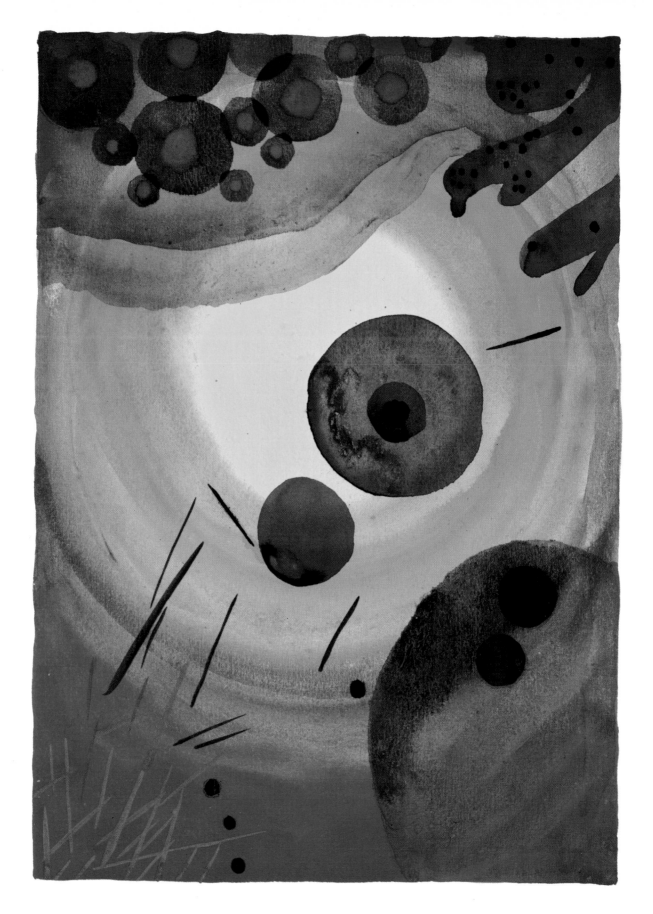

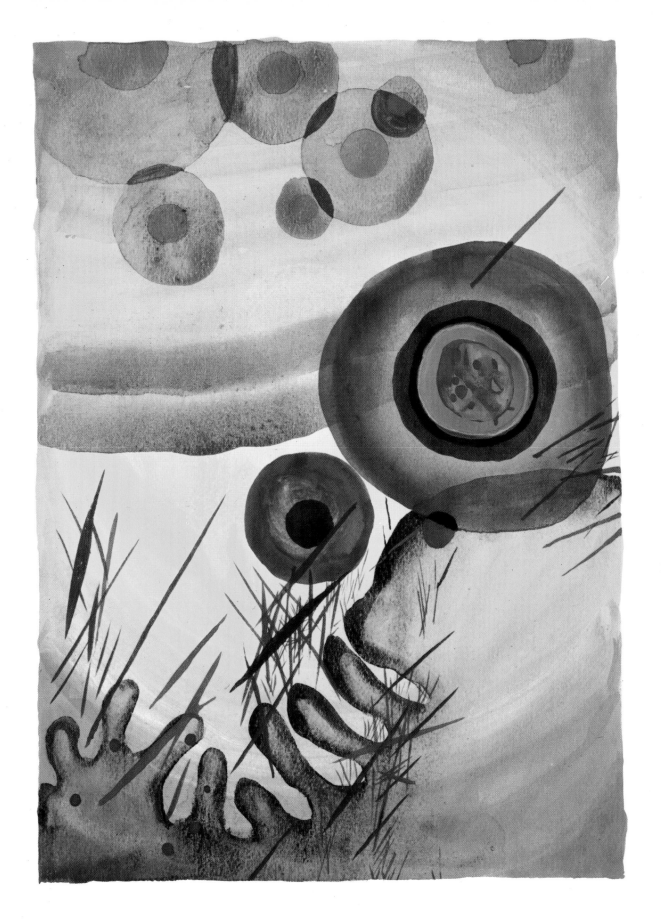

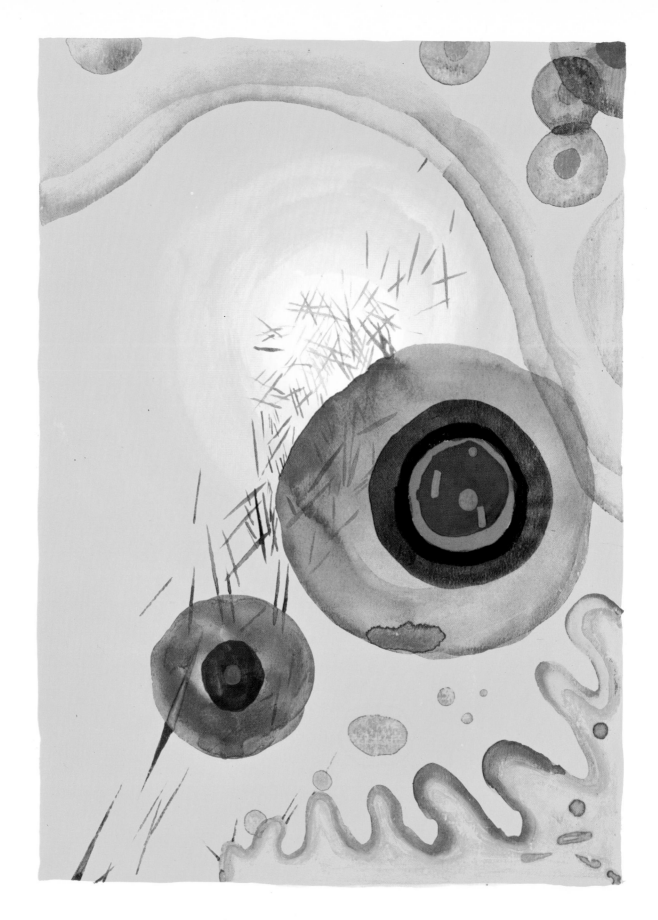

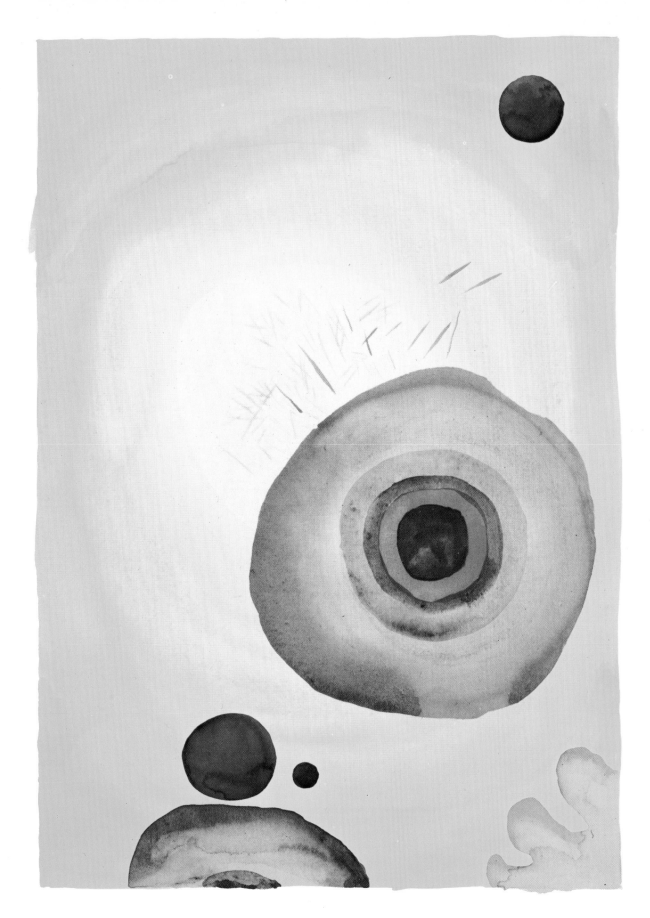

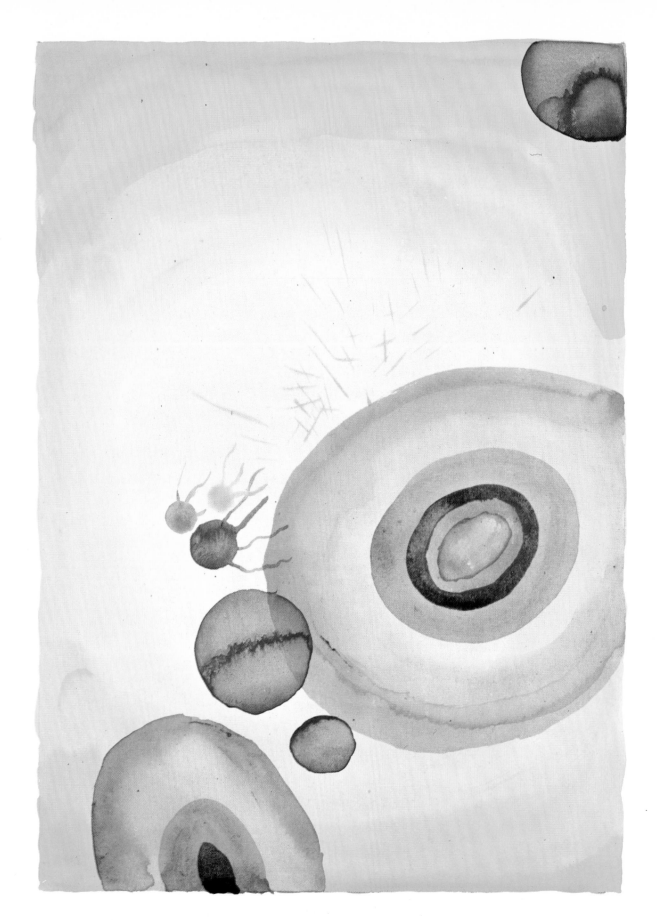

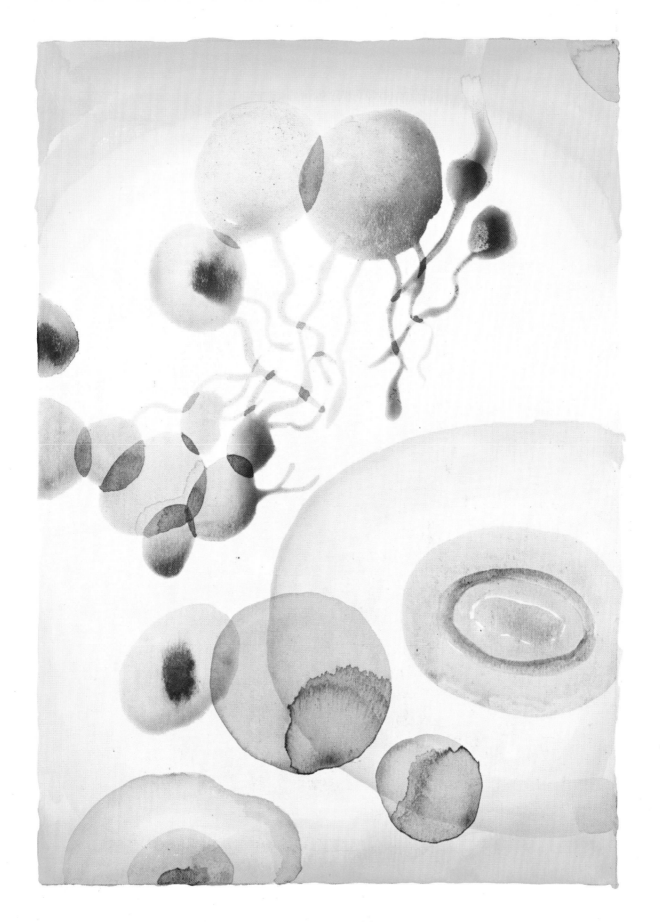

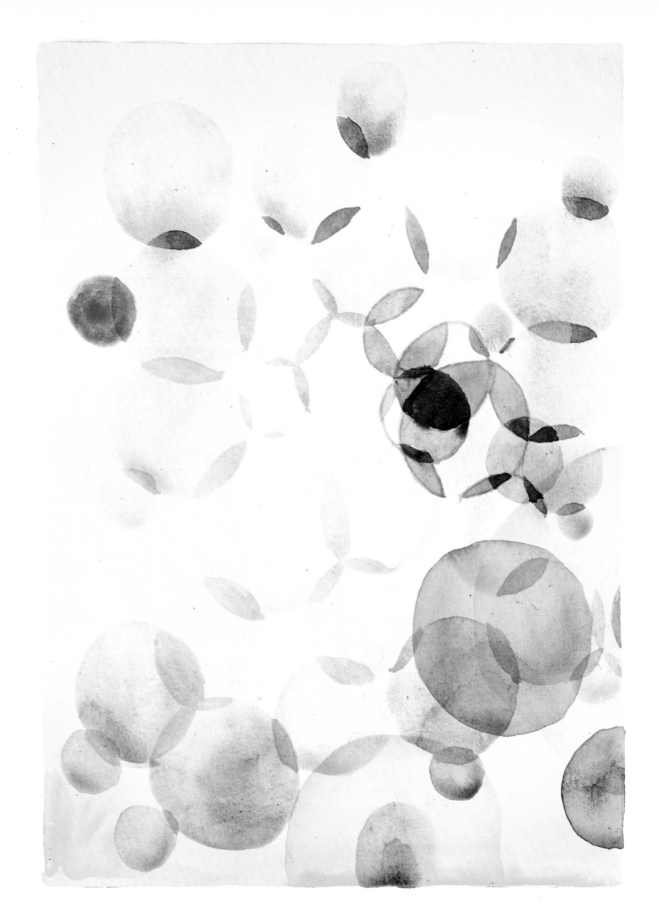

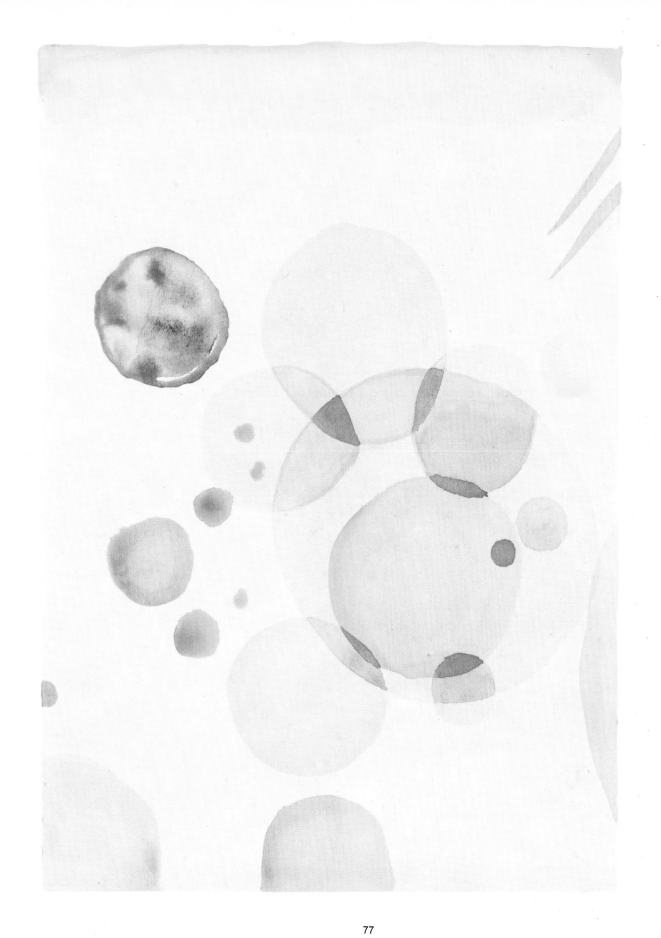

Kurt Kranz
Schwarz : Weiß

Weiß   : Schwarz
1928–29

40 Tuschzeichnungen mit Weiß gehöht
im Papierband gebunden, Privatbesitz
auf der Titelseite signiert
Größe des Papierbandes: 19 x 15 cm
Größe der Zeichnungen: 14 x 10,5 cm
Länge des Leporellos: 220 cm
beidseitig bedruckt

Schwarz : Weiß

Weiß   : Schwarz
Mit dieser Formel hat Kurt Kranz diese Bildreihe oft be-
zeichnet. 1928 ist gleich nach der Fertigstellung der „20
Bilder" mit den Zeichnungen begonnen worden. Mitte des
Jahres wurden die Lagen von dem Schulkameraden W.
Bergmann gebunden. Kranz arbeitete in dem Band bis
Januar 1929.
Die Materialien sind schwarze Tusche und Deckweiß. Die
Bilder stehen ebenfalls im Hochformat. An einen Film war
damals nicht gedacht. Aus der damaligen Perspektive erschien die Filmtechnik als etwas Unerreichbares.
1919 haben Hans Richter und Viking Eggeling auf Papierrol-
len Formthemen gemalt. Das Finanzproblem zu ihrer Verfilmung schien ihnen gigantisch. Da Viking Eggeling am 19. 5.
1925 starb, ist die Diagonalsymphonie vermutlich vor 1924
bei der UFA gedreht worden. 1931 hat Kranz die Diagonalsymphonie bei dem Besuch eines Filmvortrages von Hans
Richter mit Begeisterung und Entsetzen gesehen.
1929 entstand die Bildreihe Schwarz : Weiß von Kurt Kranz
als Bilderbuch.
Das Format der Graphiken entspricht dem Filmeinzelbild,
wenn man es seitlich kippt. So konnte man den Band wie
ein Blockbuch quer durchblättern. Darum ist hier die Reproduktion in horizontaler Lage angeordnet. Die 40 Tuschzeichnungen sind strophisch aufgebaut. Die zu Anfang auftauchenden großen weißen Punkte dringen in das Bildfeld
und wischen hinweg. Daraus entwickeln sich Gleichge-
wichte und deren Störungen. Sich bildende Formfamilien
wachsen allmählich und werden von Schwarzweiß-Umkeh-
rungen verdrängt, von neuen weißen Punkten schließlich
ausgelöscht. Sie machen einem anderen Thema mit seinen
Varianten und Umkehrungen Platz. Der Reichtum dieser
Veränderungen wird in einem Tutti, bei dem die ersten
Themenkreise hinzukommen, gesteigert. Der Höhepunkt ist
das Eindringen der auslöschenden Kreise, die den Schau-
platz für die Umkehrung befreien, die dann schwarze Punkte
vor weißer Fläche als die Umkehrung zeigt.
Dank Moholy, der im Frühjahr 1929 mit einem Vortrag über
das Bauhaus nach Bielefeld kam, lernte Kranz die Bilder
z. B. von Lissitzky, Mondrian und Malewich mit ihrem kon-
struktivistischen Formarsenal kennen.
Moholy zeigte etwa 40 Stücke der Bauhaus-Meister in der
Turnhalle eines Lyceums und sprach im naturwissenschaftlichen Verein. Der damalige Kunstverein hielt diese Arbeiten für zu avantgardistisch.
Kranz fand in dieser Zeit leider keine Möglichkeit, die
Sammlung eines Bielefelder Bürgers mit Werken von Kandinsky zu sehen.
Nur im Buchhandel und in der Bibliothek konnte er sich
lückenhaft über ihn informieren. Der kurze Weg nach Hannover, um Lissitzkys „abstraktes Kabinett" im Landesmuseum zu sehen, entfiel für Kranz, weil ihn in der Provinz
niemand darauf aufmerksam machte.
Auch diese Bildreihe wurde 1972 von Robert Darroll verfilmt. Durch das Überschneiden der verschiedenen Motive
ergeben sich im starken Maße Graustufen.
Im Zusammenspiel mit den „20 Bildern" und den anderen
Bildreihen entsteht ein malerisches Schauspiel.

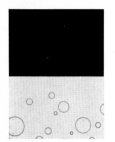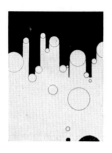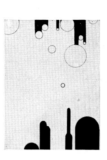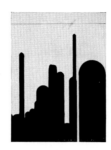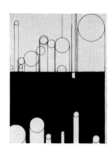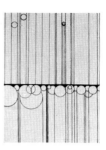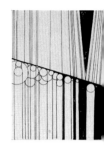

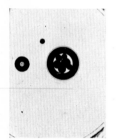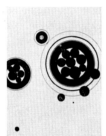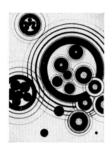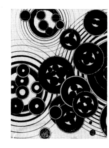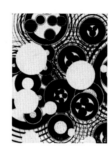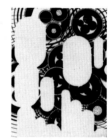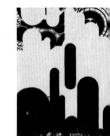

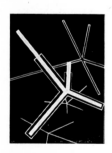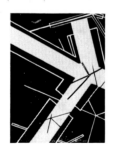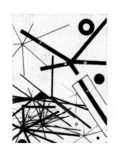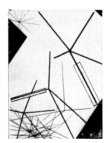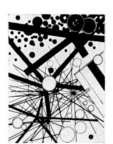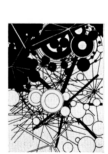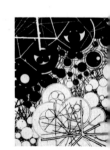

Panel showing complete picture-sequence black : white
                                         white : black

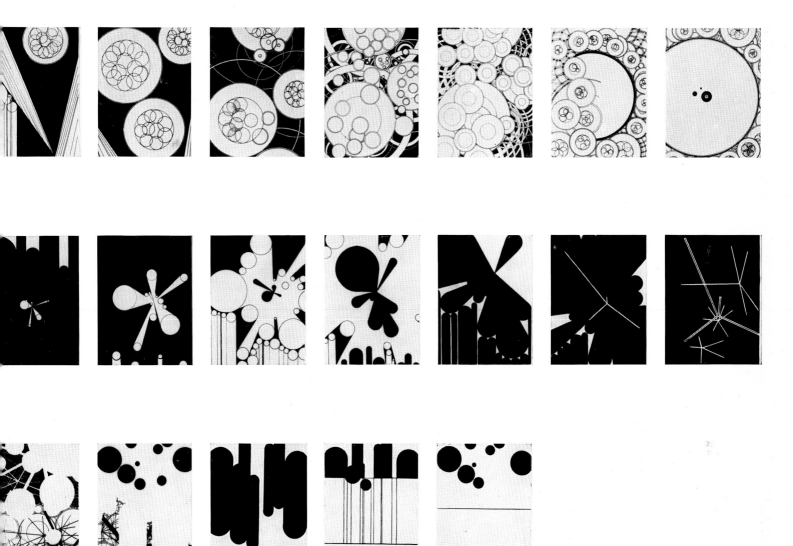

Übersichtstafel der Bildreihe schwarz : weiß
weiß   : schwarz

Kurt Kranz
Black : White

White : Black

1928–29

40 pen and ink drawings heightened with
white, bound in paper, in private ownership,
signed on the title page.
Size of the paper cover 19 x 15 cm
Size of the drawings 14 x 10,5 cm
Length of the Leporellos: 220 cm
printed on both sides.

Black : White

White : Black

Kranz has often used this formula to describe this picture
sequence. In 1928, immediately after the completion of the
"20 pictures", he started work on the drawings. In the
middle of the year the sheets were bound by his schoolmate, W. Bergmann, and Kranz worked on the book until
January 1929.
The media are black ink and tempera white. The pictures
are likewise in upright format. At that time a film was
not considered. From the perspective of the period, film
technique was regarded as something unattainable. In 1919
Hans Richter and Viking Eggeling had painted form
themes on rolls of paper. But the financial problem of
having them filmed seemed enormous. As Viking Eggeling
died on 19. 5. 25, the diagonal symphony had presumably
been filmed by UFA before 1924. In 1931 Kranz, while
attending a film showing by Hans Richter, saw the diagonal symphony and was both enthusiastic and horrified.
The format of the graphic works corresponds to that of
the individual film frame, when held sideways. Thus it
was possible to leaf through the book like a block-book.
This is the reason that here the reproduction is arranged
in horizontal order. The 40 pen and ink drawings are

built up in verses. The large white points which first
emerge penetrate into the image field and wipe it away.
From this develop balances and their disturbances. Self-
creating form families gradually begin to grow and are
displaced by black and white reversals and finally oblit-
erated by new white points. These then make room for
another theme with its variations. The profusion of these
changes expand in a tutti to which are added the first
theme circles. The climax is the penetration of the oblit-
erating circles which make the space free for the reversal,
which then show black points before a white surface as the
reversal.
In 1928 constructivist pictures were new. Lissitzky, Moholy, Malewich had reached Bielefeld, nevertheless the
constructivist arsenal of forms is unmistakable. In this
case it is applied directly and in a very naive manner by
an eighteen-year-old. In the spring of 1929 Moholy came
to Bielefeld and delivered a lecture on the Bauhaus. He
showed about 40 works in the gymnasium of a lyceum and
spoke to the local association of natural sciences. The art
club regarded the works of the Bauhaus master as in-
artistic. At that time Kranz also had no opportunity of
looking at the private collection of a Bielefeld citizen,
which contained works by Kandinsky. One could only
see reproductions in bookshops and in the library. At this
time Kandinsky was busy with his constructivist period,
and individual characteristic works of his had been reproduced, for instance "single circles". Kranz failed to
make the short journey to Hanover to see Lissitz's
"abstract cabinet" in the Landesmuseum there, because
no one in the provinces had seen fit to draw his attention
to it.
This picture sequence was also filmed by Robert Darroll in
1972. The overlapping of the different motives result in
an impressive effect of grey graduations. From the interplay of the "20 pictures" with the picture sequence there
emerges a pictorial drama.

Picture sequence
black : white

Bildreihe
schwarz : weiß

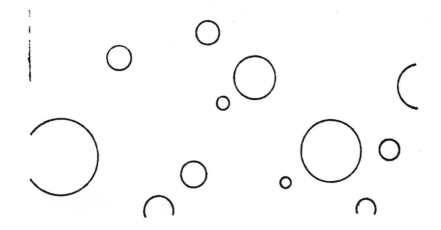

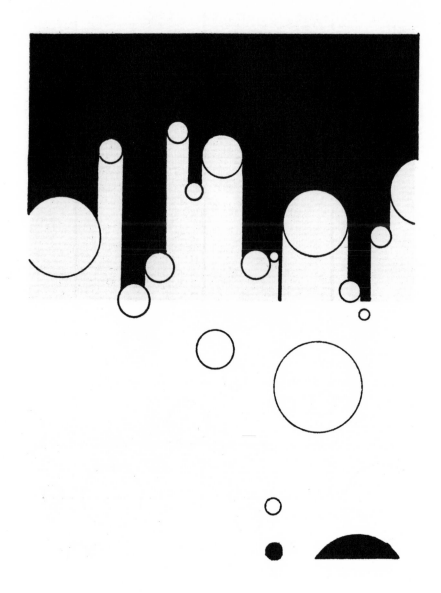

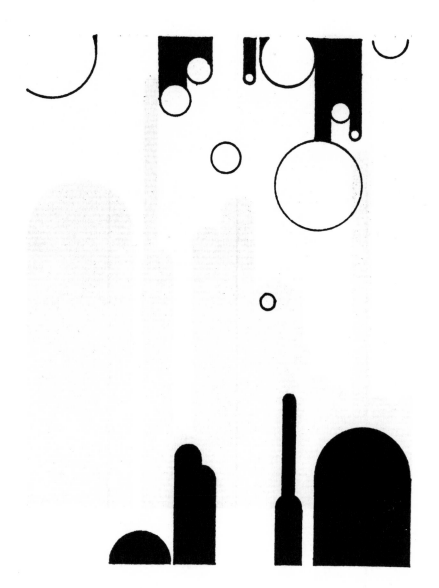

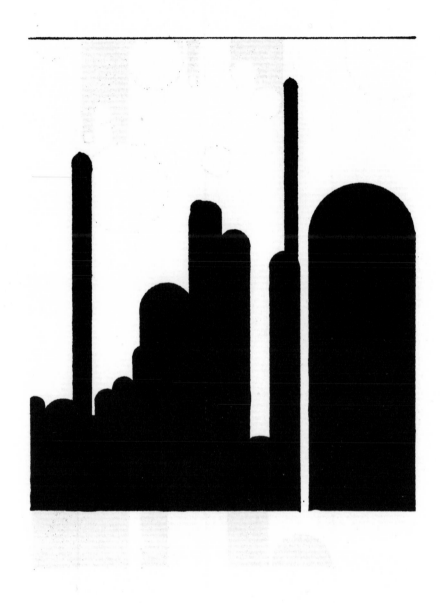

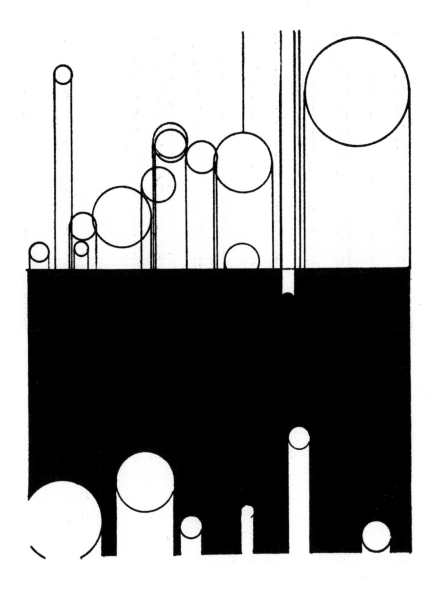

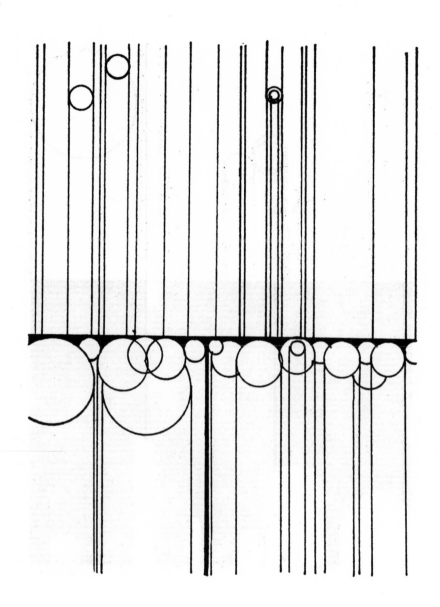

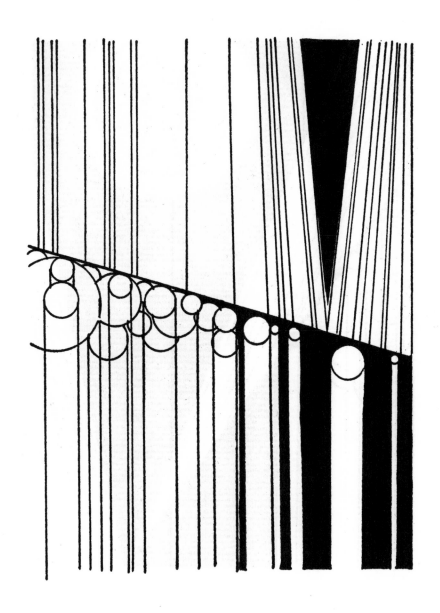

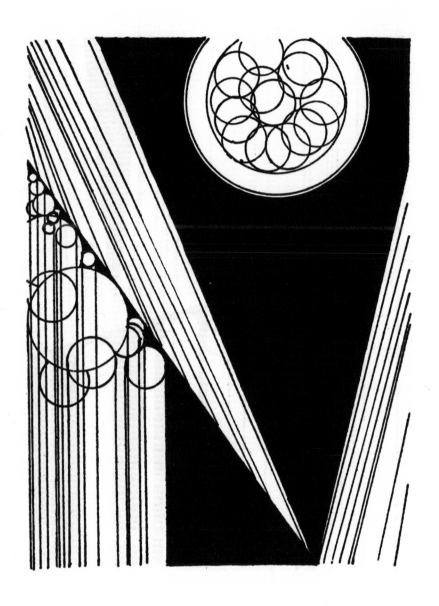

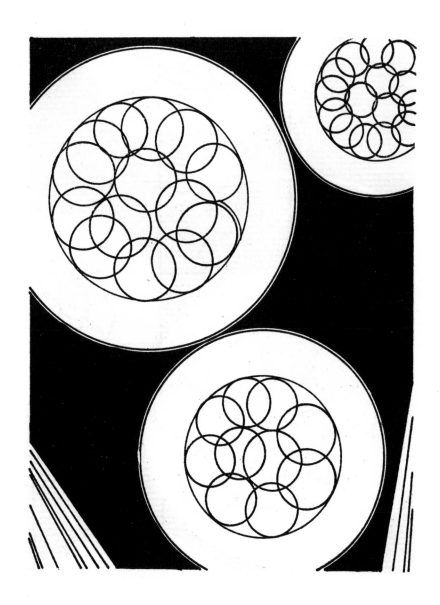

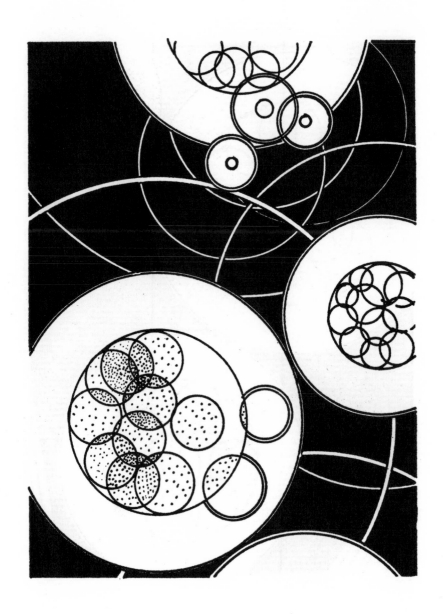

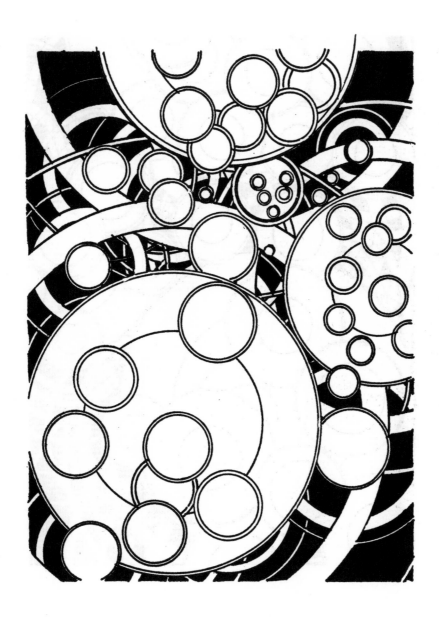

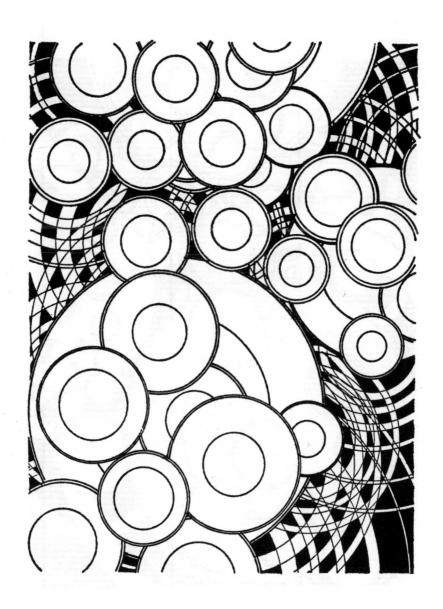

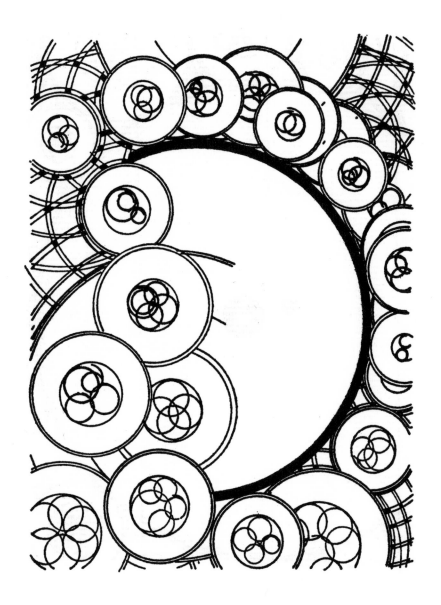

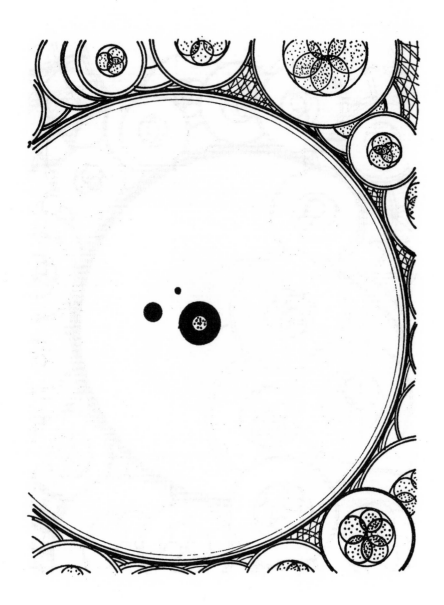

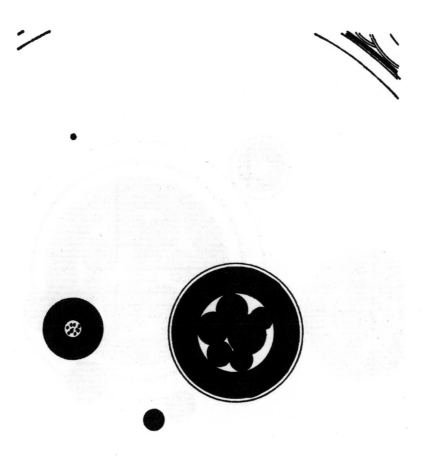

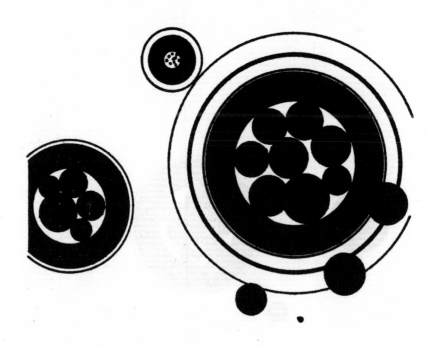

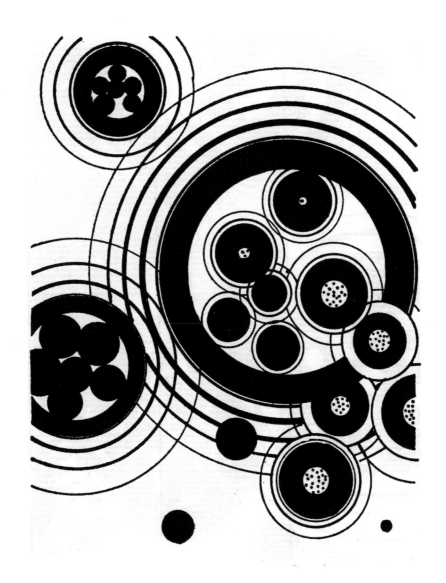

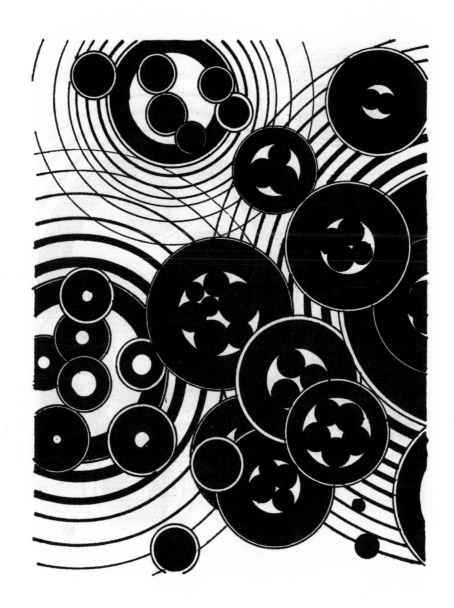

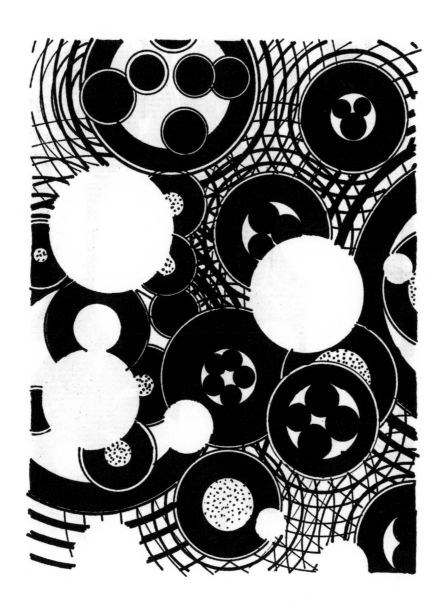

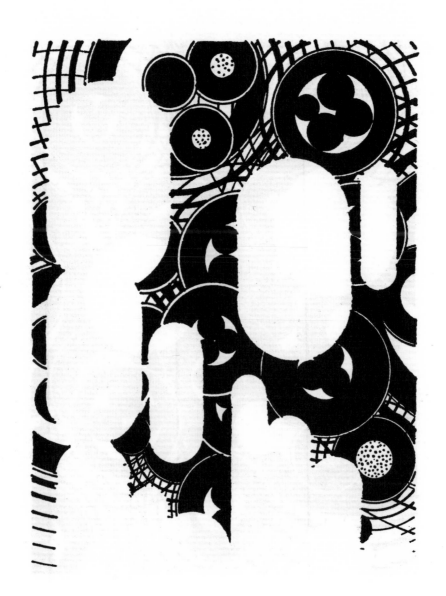

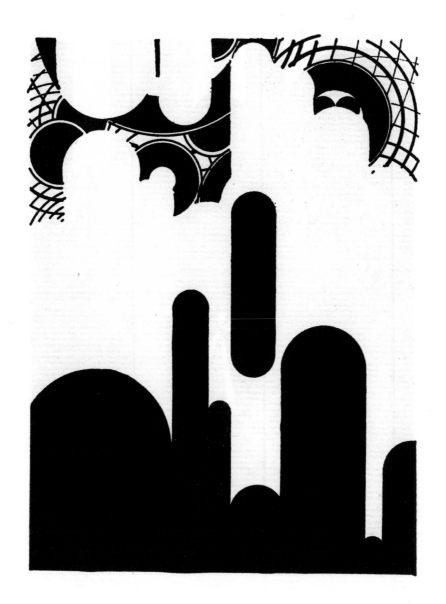

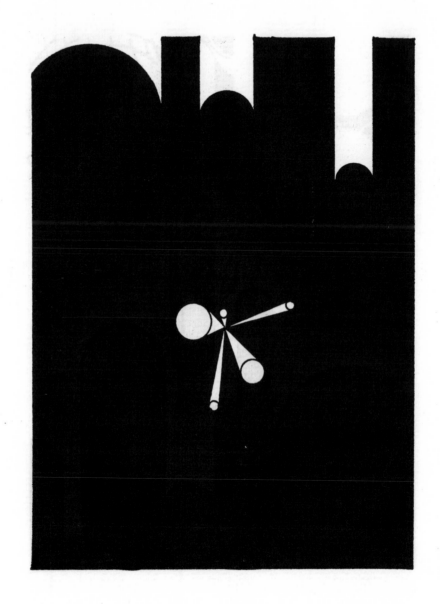

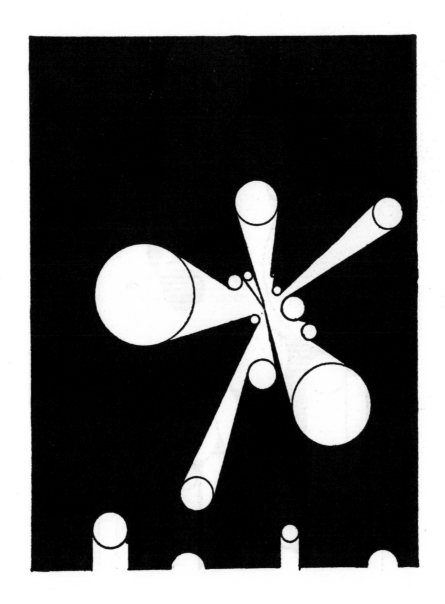

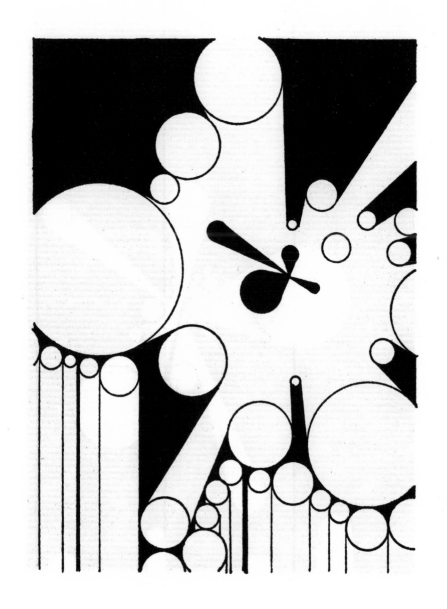

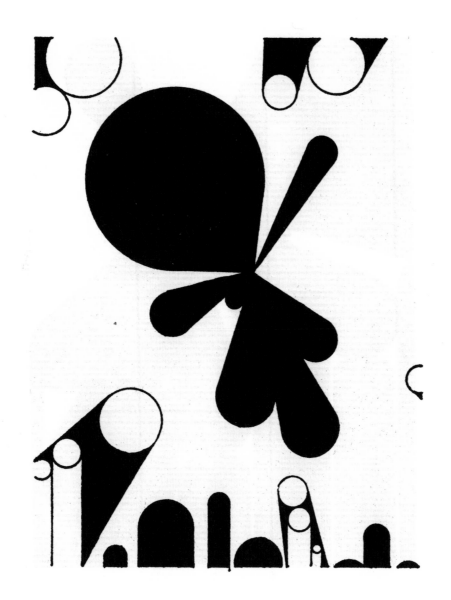

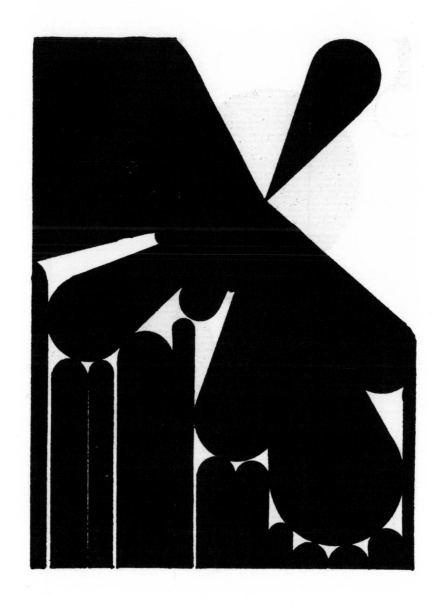

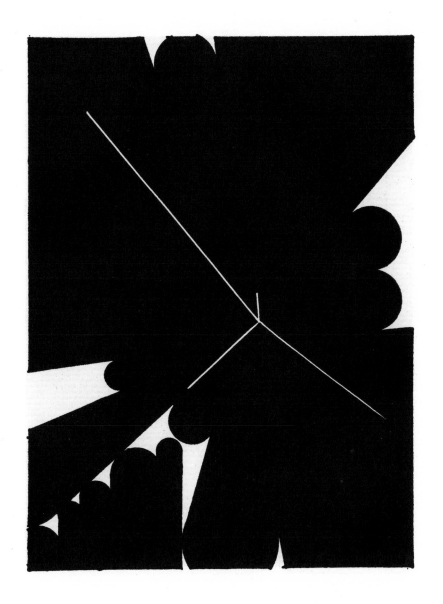

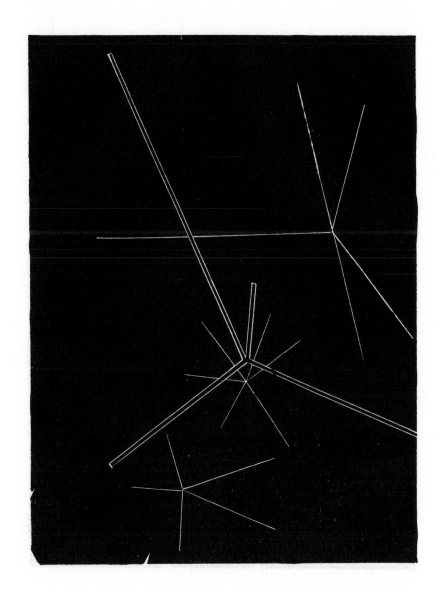

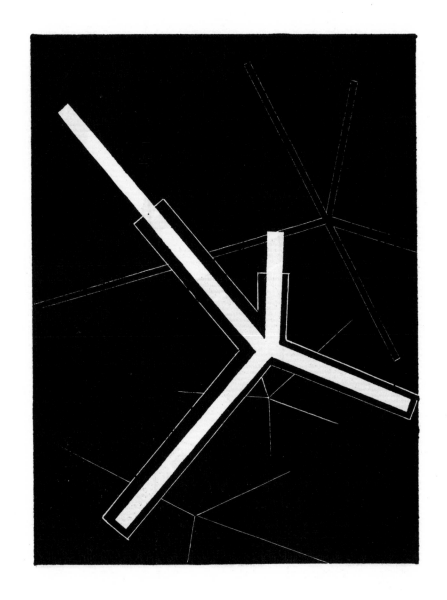

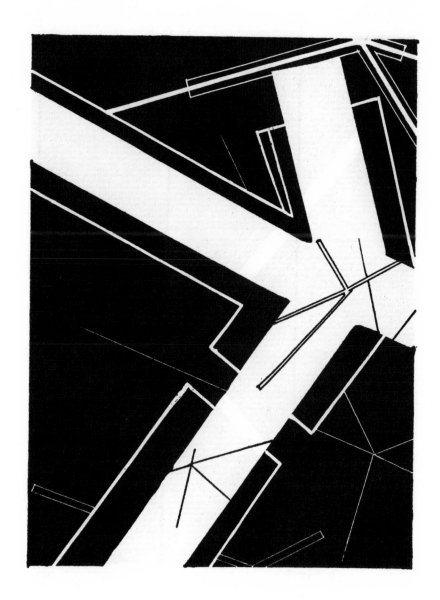

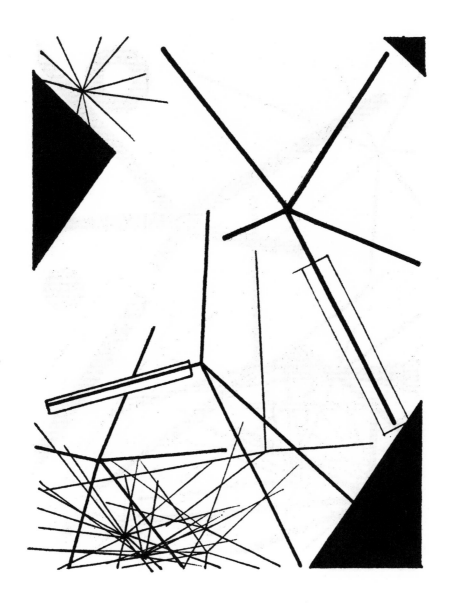

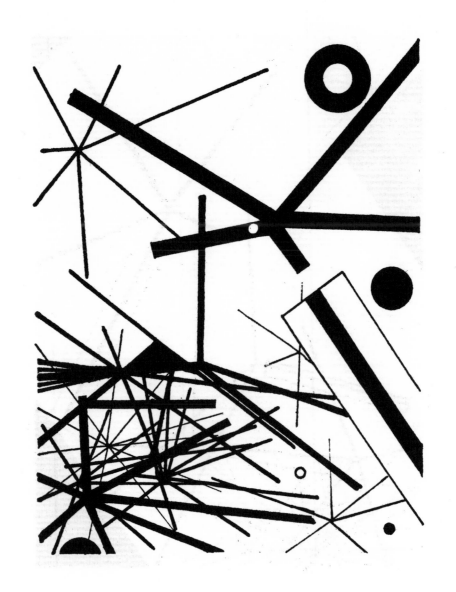

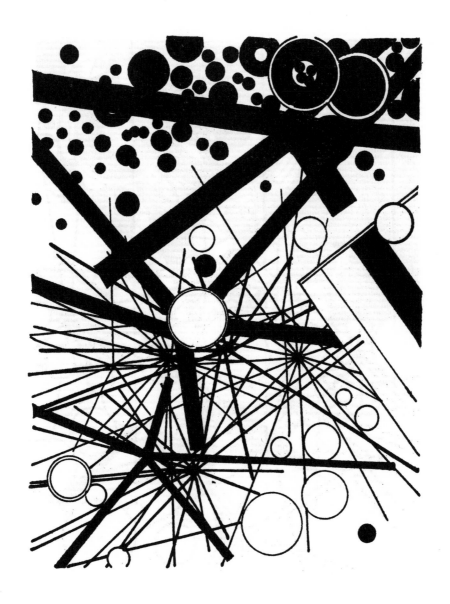

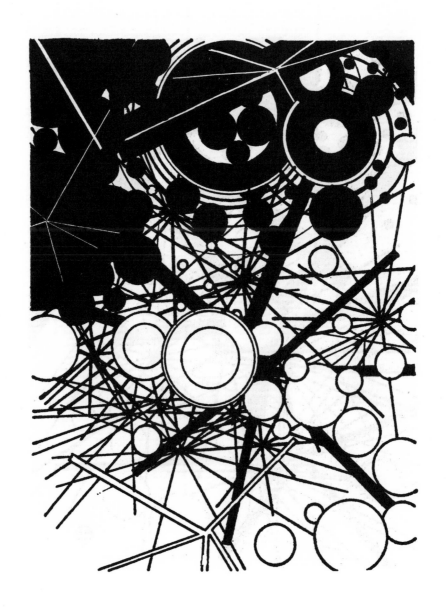

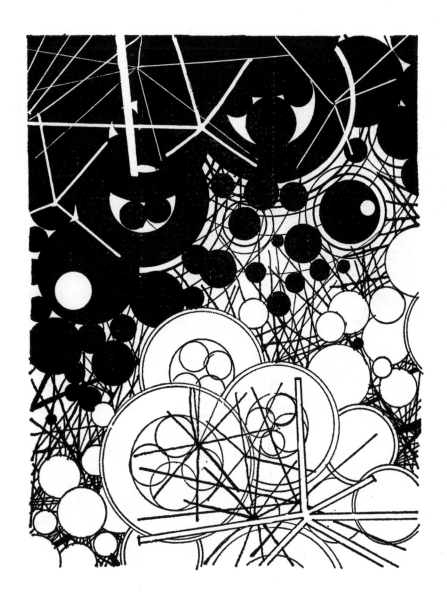

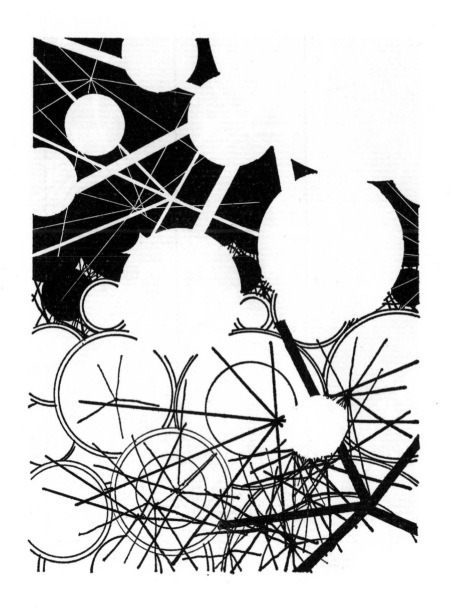

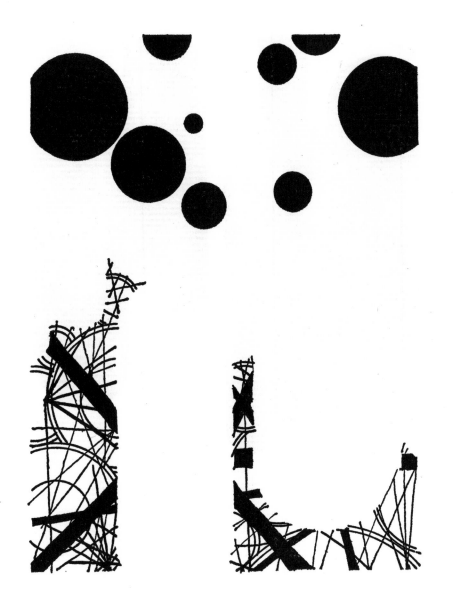

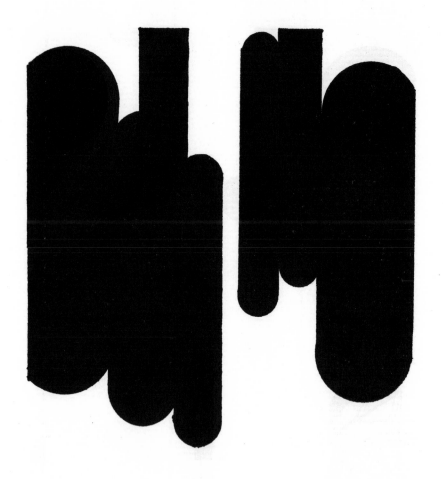

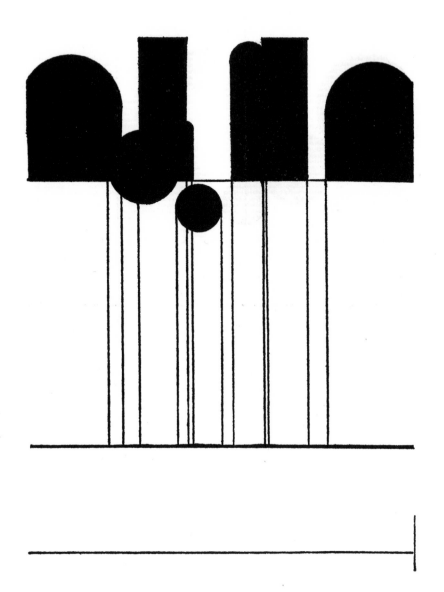

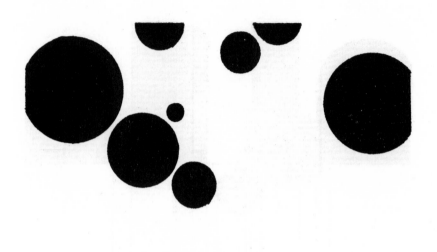

Kurt Kranz
Farbfilm genannt
Leporello
1930–31

32 Phasen in Mischtechnik
die Originale sind auf Leinwand kaschiert
in Leporelloform
Größe der Originale und Tafeln: 17,5 x 14,5 cm
Länge des Leporellos: 352 cm

Kranz arbeitete an diesem Farbfilm-Entwurf im Herbst 1930. Im Bauhaus Dessau gab es keine Malklasse, obwohl dort die Meister der modernen Malerei Deutschlands wie Kandinsky, Klee, Feininger, Albers und Schlemmer lehrten. Zwei bekannte Theorien sind z. B. Klees „pädagogisches Skizzenbuch" oder Kandinskys „Punkt und Linie zur Fläche". Die Seminare dieser Künstler waren außerordentlich interessant, aber unzusammenhängend.

Auch hier eine Teilung . . . in funktionelles Industrieentwerfen, Architektur der Weltverbesserung . . . und in die esoterische Kunst, den überflüssigen Luxus.

Kranz flüchtet in eine Bildreihe. Er benutzt Aquarell, Tempera und farbige Tuschen. Bauplanhafte Formen unterteilen sich wachsend. Rote und gelbe Lichterstäbe dringen sich überschneidend ein. Ein vertikaler Lichtschnitt wischt jalousienartig die grauen Pläne hinweg. Es taucht ein winziges Stabmotiv auf. Zwei Lichtpole bilden sich, die die Stäbe „magnetisch" um sich ordnen. Die wachsenden Lichtformen vereinen sich, während die Stäbe sich zunächst zu Schraffuren, dann zu Geweben verdichten. Die wachsende Lichtform füllt die Szene. Ein zartes, reiches Punktthema variiert in großen und kleinen Zirkelschlägen, in die mit großer Gewalt rote und blaue Spiralzüge einmünden, die sich verengend zusammenfließen zu einer blauen Fläche. Die erneut auftauchenden Kreise, die allmählich an Größe zunehmen, verblassen im Verfall der Bläue und verschwieden im fleckigen Dunkel. Die Balance, die Klee und Kandinsky anstrebten, wird zugunsten dynamischer Formen aufgegeben, die von Phase zu Phase drängen, und ihre Gesichter offenbaren.

Es sind konstruktive, technische, biologische Formanklänge, die Kranz inspirierten. Das Verhältnis zu den Bauhausmeistern war oft gespannt. Die jungen Maler, die in der Reklame unterschlüpften, waren vom Surrealismus beeindruckt und übten sich im realistischen tormpe l'œil. So ist auch hier wieder die Flucht des Kranz in seine Bildreihenwelt zu sehen.

Die hier vorliegenden Faksimile-Reproduktionen kommen dem Leporello sehr nahe. Als Kranz 1930–31 diese Arbeit „Entwurf zu einem Farbfilm" nannte, gab es noch keine Farbfilme. Sie kamen erst 1936 auf den Markt. Das unterstreicht den utopischen Charakter, den Kranz seinen Entwürfen beimaß. An eine Verfilmung dieser Entwürfe war in der damaligen Zeit nicht zu denken. Außen der Druck der Nazis und im Innern des Bauhauses, der intellektuelle Marxismus, ließen eine Katastrophe ahnen. So wurde dieses Leporello 1931 kaum jemandem gezeigt. Im Sommer 1932 schloß das Bauhaus. Kranz ging im Herbst nach Berlin, aber auch hier blieb nur die Flucht in den Alltag der Werbung als Existenz gegen den nationalsozialistischen Terror.

Robert Darroll hat das Leporello 1972 filmisch umgesetzt. Die ersten zu einem Streifen zusammengefaßten Filme schließen eine Episode der Erfindung ab.

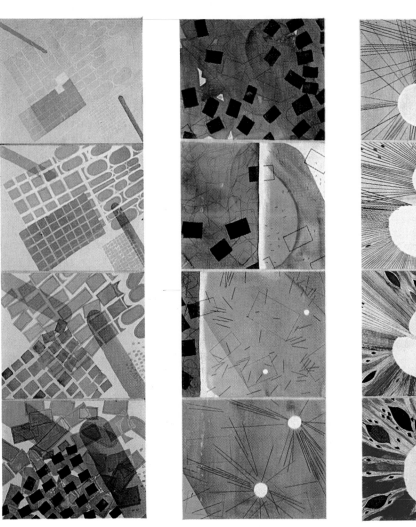
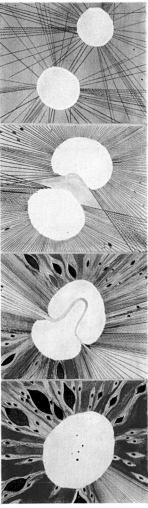
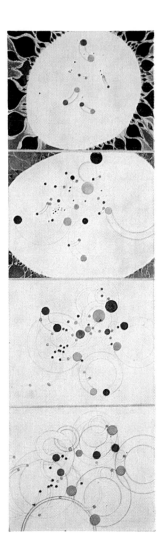

Panel showing complete picture-sequence colour film entitled "Leporello".

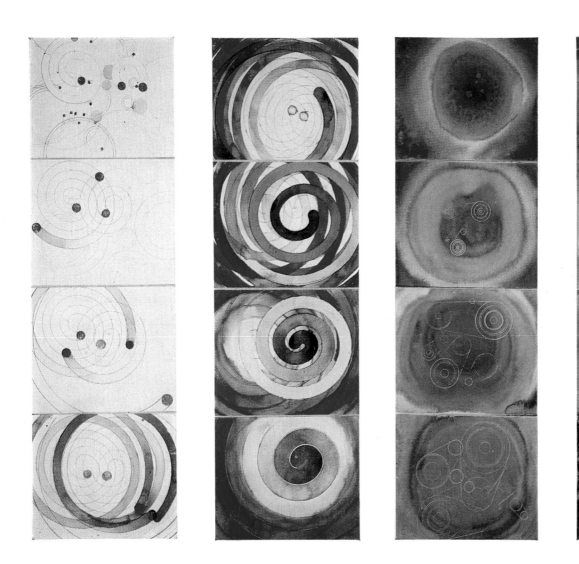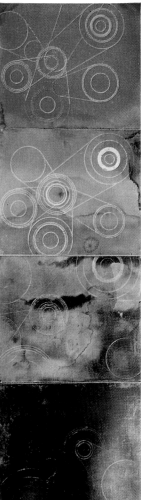

Übersichtstafel der Bildreihe Farbfilm, genannt „Leporello"

Kurt Kranz
Colour Film entitled
Leporello
1930–31

32 phases in mixed media.
The originals are mounted on canvas in
Leporello form.
Size of the originals and plates: 17,5 x 14,5 cm
Length of the Leporello: 352 cm.

Kranz worked on this colour film design in the autumn of 1930. There was no painting class in the Bauhaus at Dessau, although the masters of modern painting in Germany taught there, for example Kandinsky, Klee, Feininger, Albers and Schlemmer. Some of their theories could be studied there from such books as Klee's "Pedagogic sketch book" or Kandinsky's "Point and line to the plane". Their seminars were extraordinarily interesting but bore no relation to one another.

Here also there was a division into... functional industrial design, architecture for social improvement... and into esoteric art, superfluous luxury.

Kranz took refuge in a picture sequence. He uses watercolour, tempera and coloured ink. Forms like building plans keep being subdivided. Red and yellow staves of light penetrate and overlap. A vertical light cut, like a shutter, wipes the grey plans away. A tiny stave motif

appears. Two light poles are formed which arrange the staves "magnetically" around them, the growing light forms combine, while the staves thicken first into cross-hatching and then into textures. The growing light form fills the scene. A delicate, rich point theme varies in large and small circle areas into which red and blue spiral lines force their way; these contract and flow together to form a blue surface. The circles, which appear again and gradually increase in size, fade with the decay of the blue and disappear in the spotty darkness. The balance which Klee and Kandinsky aimed at is rejected in favour of dynamic forms which force their way from phase to phase and unfold the story.

It is constructive, technical and biological form suggestions which inspired Kranz. His relationship with the Bauhaus masters was often a strained one. The young painters, who took refuge in commercial art, were impressed by surrealism and practised realistic trompe l'oeil. Here again was another reason for Kranz's flight into his world of picture sequences.

The facsimile reproductions seen here come very close to the Leporello. When in 1930–31, Kranz called this "work" design for a colour film, there were still no colour films in existence. They did not come onto the market until 1936. This stresses the utopian character with which Kranz judged his films. At that time any possibility of filming the designs was out of the question. The signs of the coming catastrophe were clear to see, externally from the pressure of the Nazis, and internally from the intellectual Marxism of the Bauhaus. So this Leporello of 1931 was hardly shown to anyone. In the summer of 1932 the Bauhaus closed down. In the autumn Kranz went to Berlin, but here also there remained for him no chance against Nazi terror except refuge in commercial art.

Robert Darroll has made the Leporello of 1972 into a film. The first films collected into a single strip conclude an episode in the history of invention.

Leporello 1930-31
32 plates in original size

Leporello 1930-31
32 Tafeln in Originalgröße

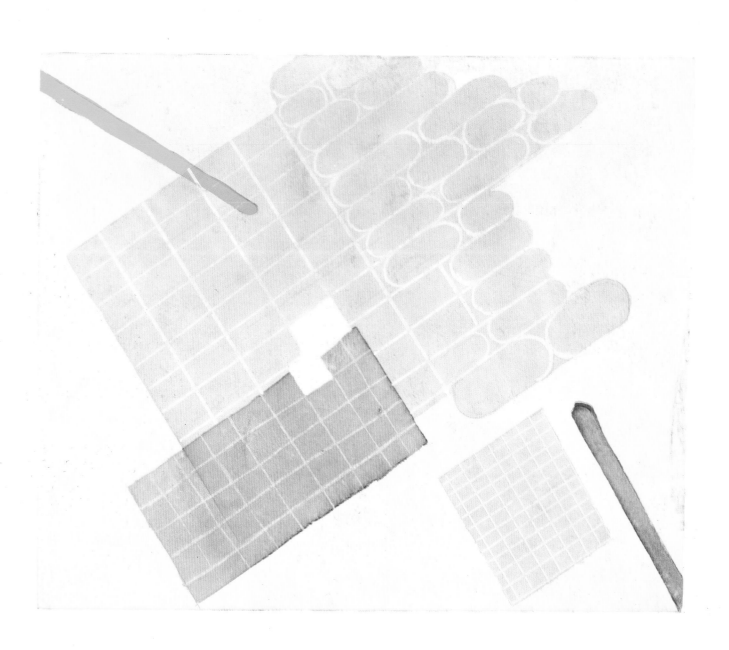

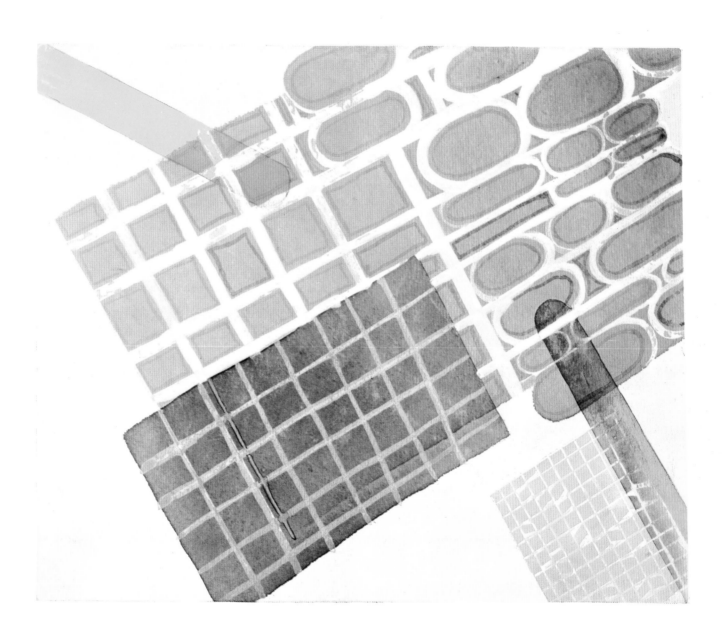

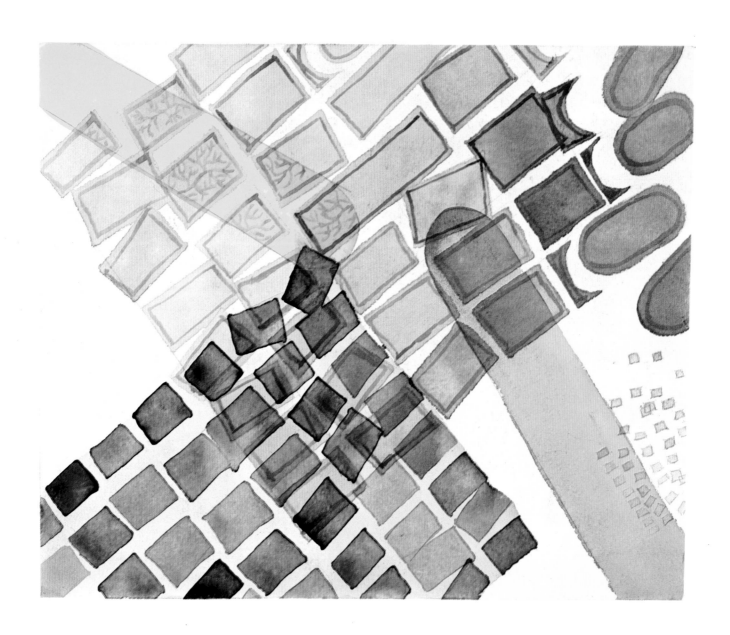

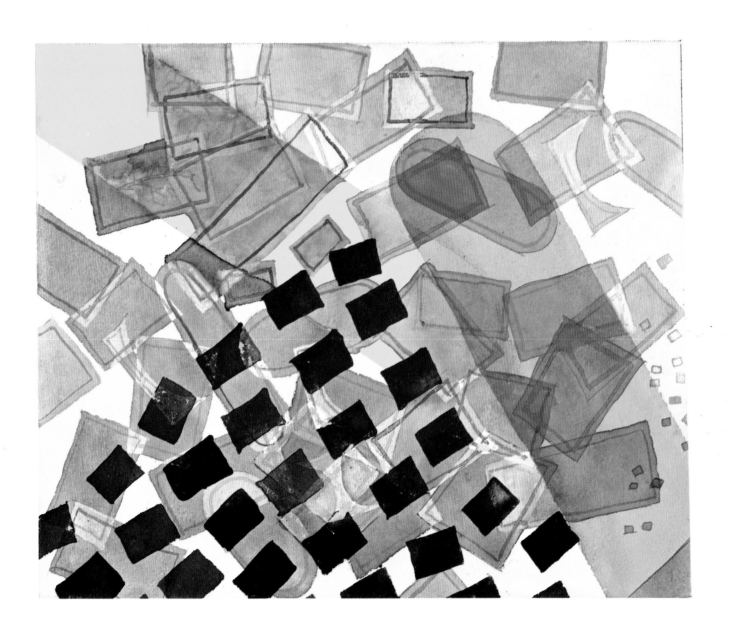

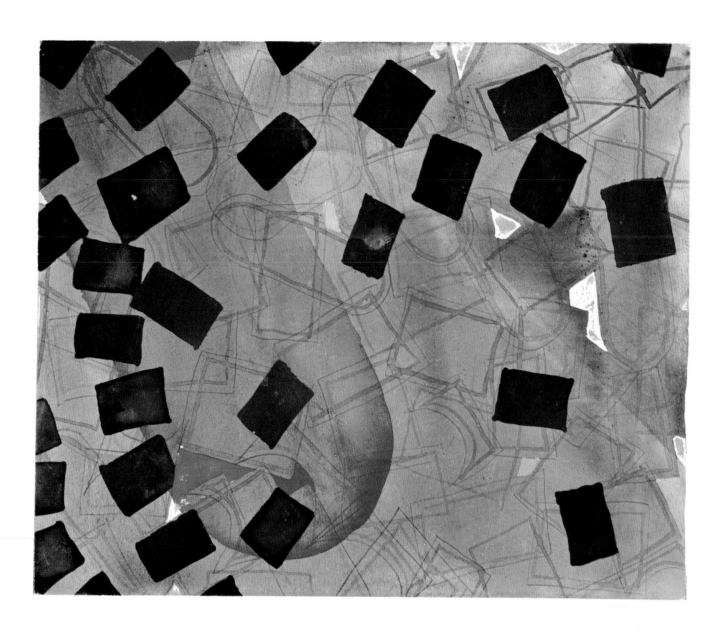

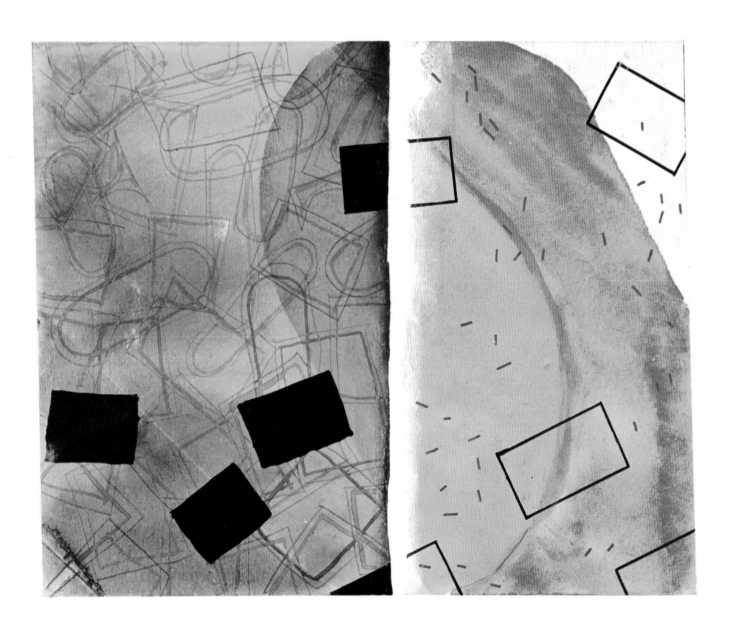

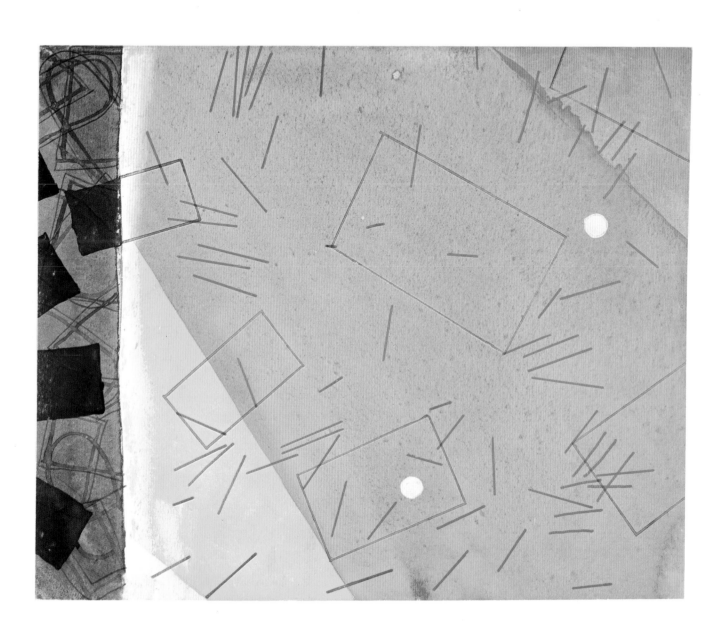

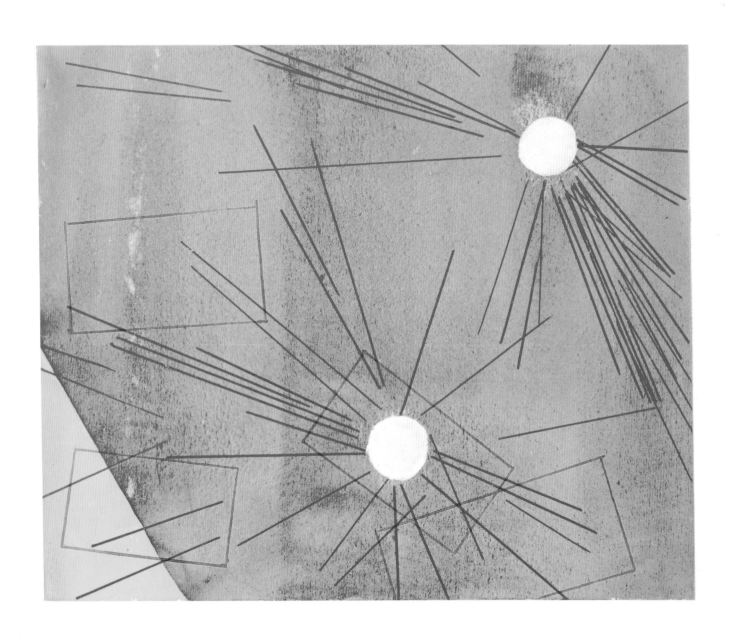

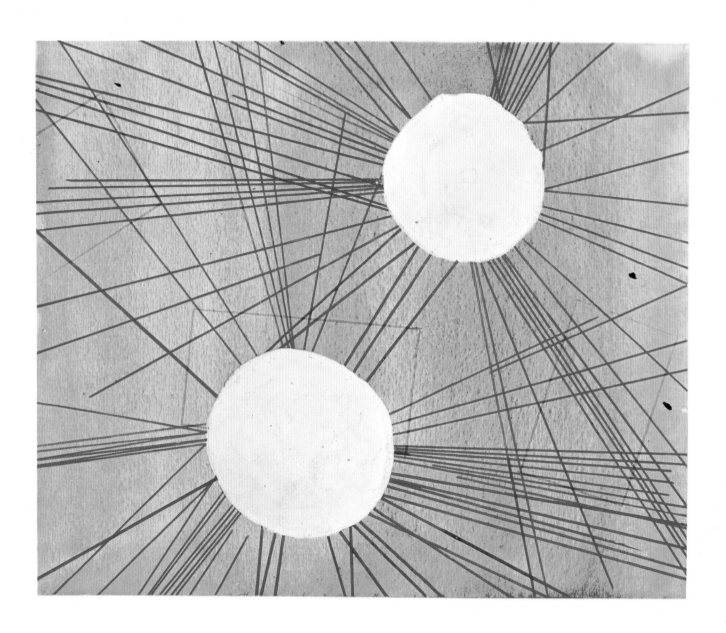

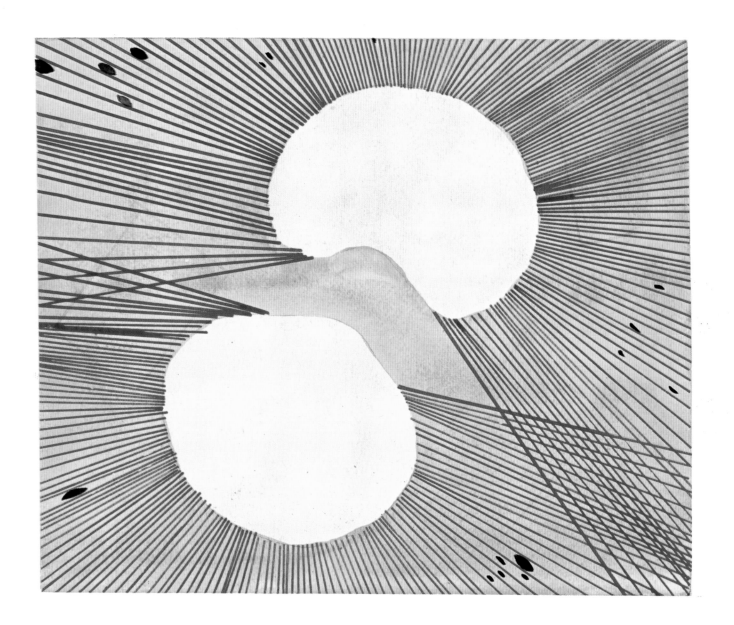

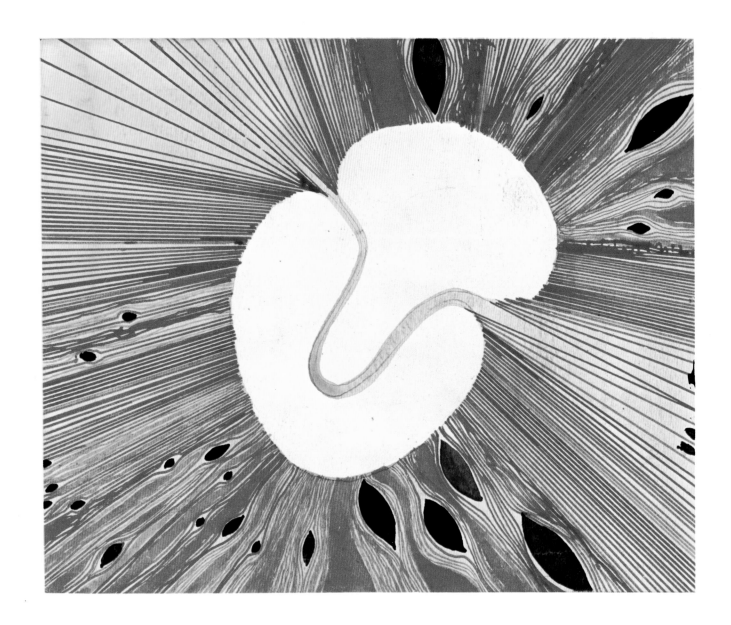

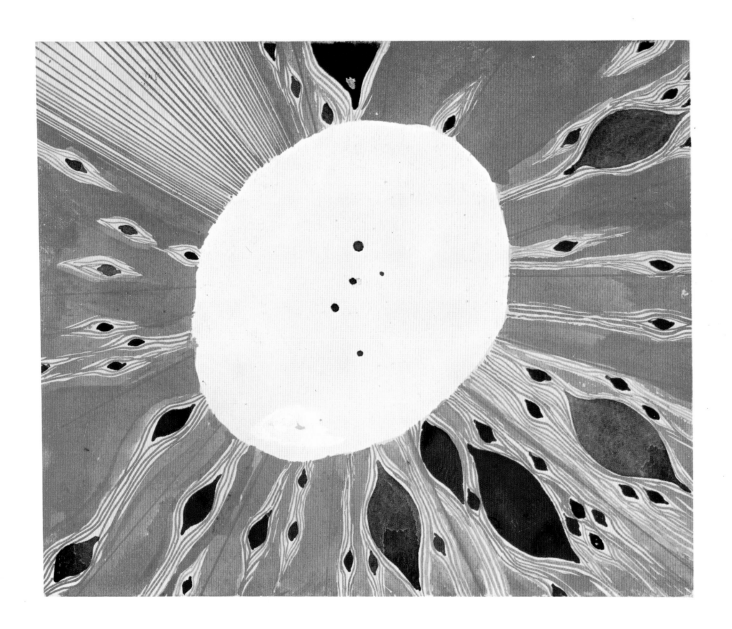

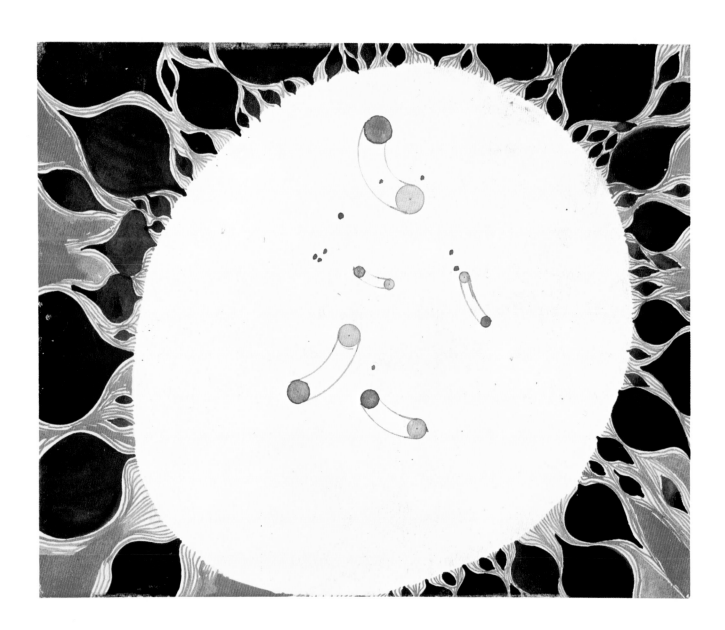

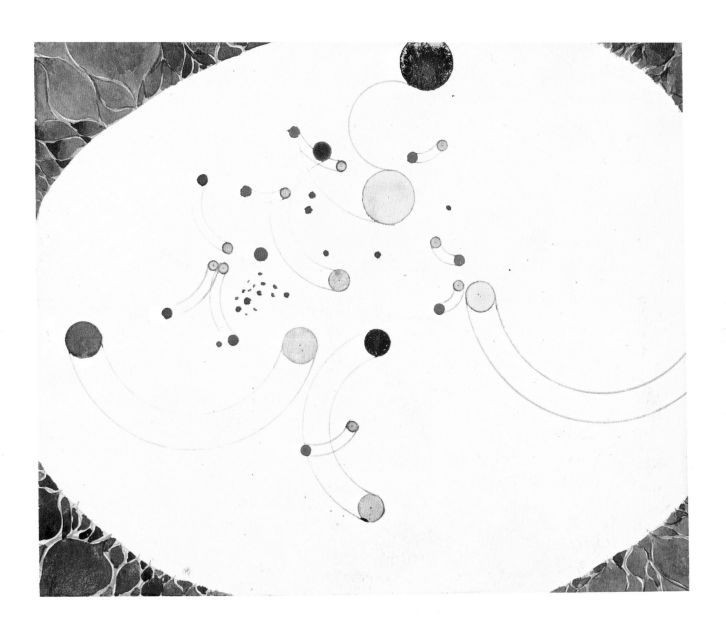

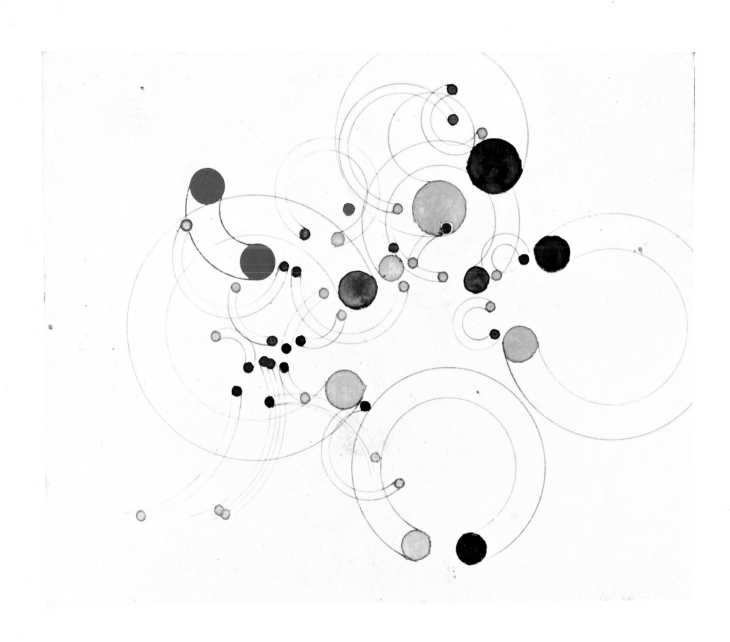

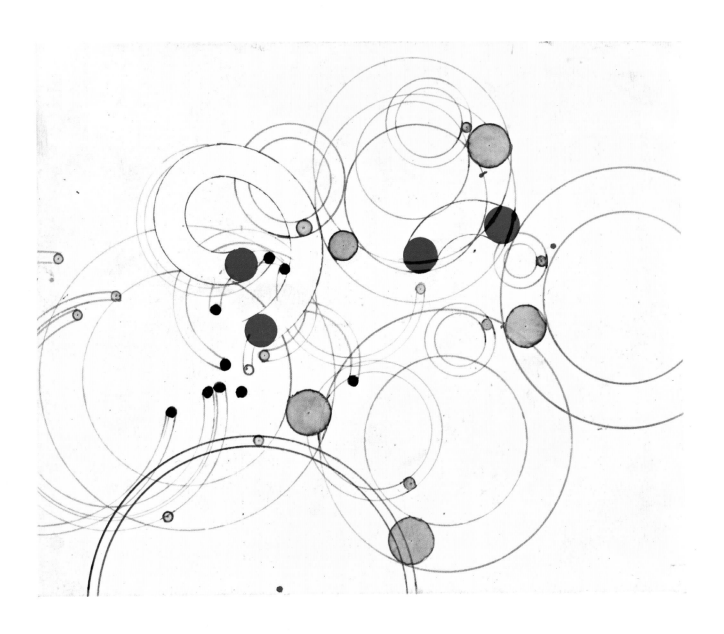

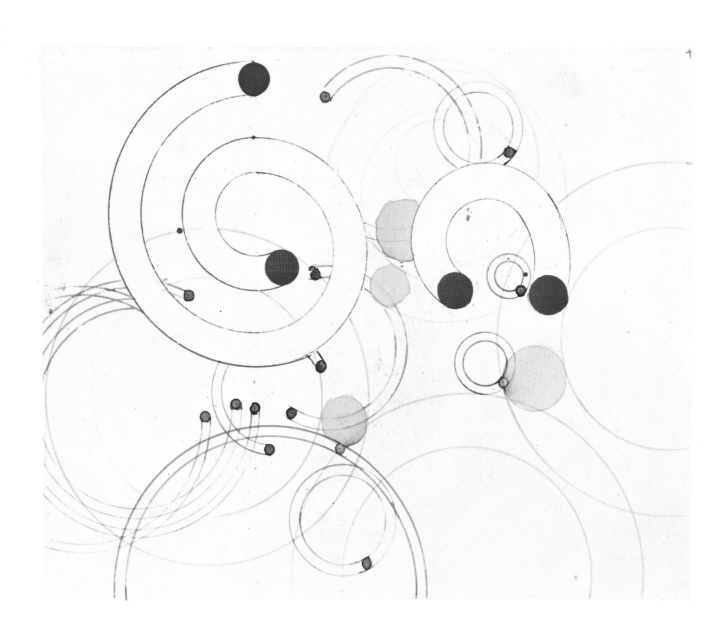

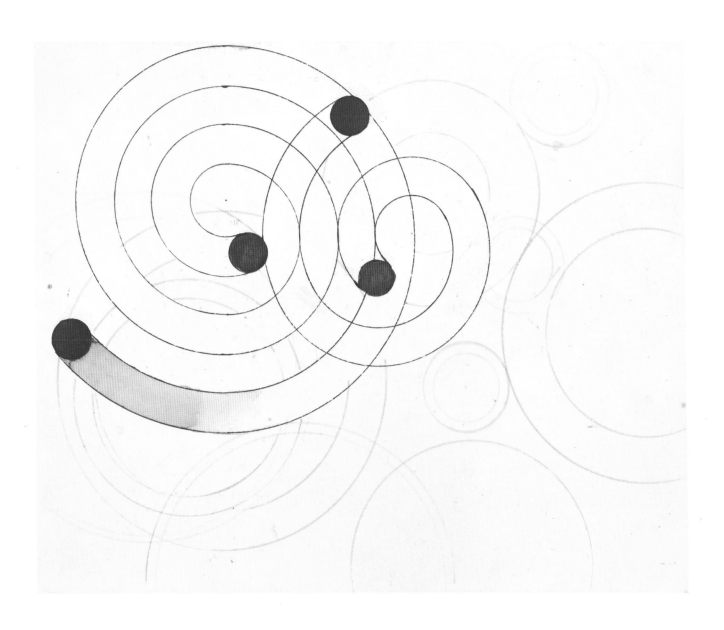

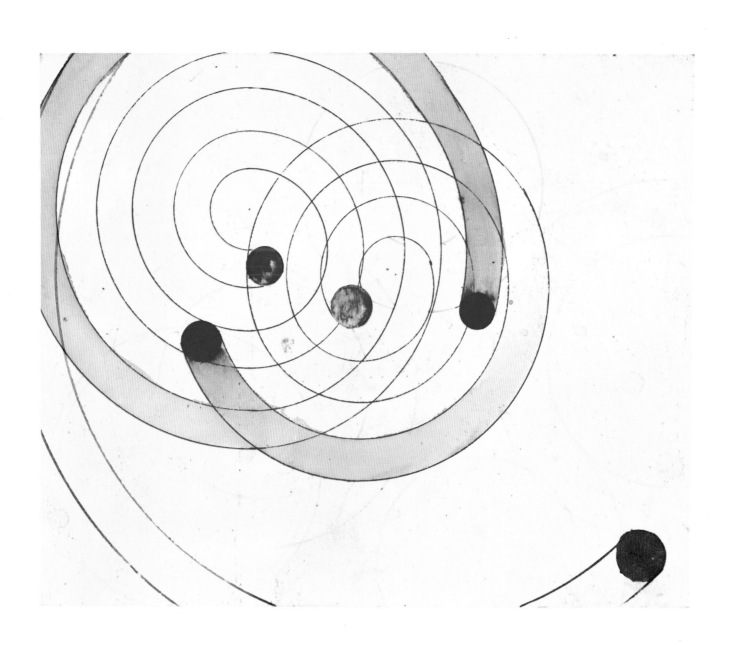

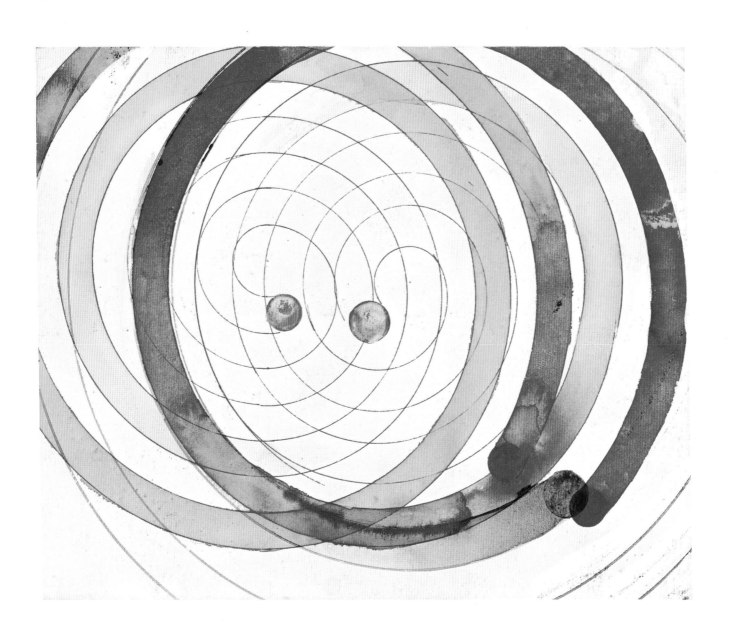

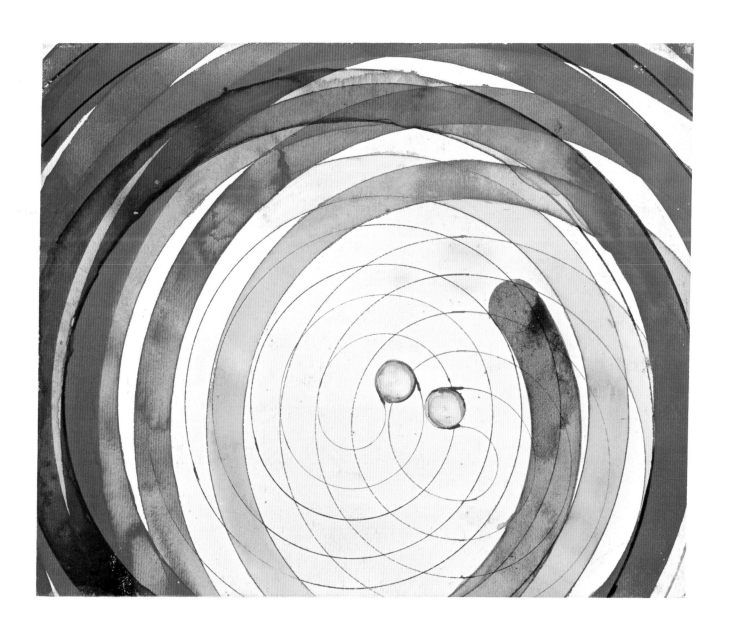

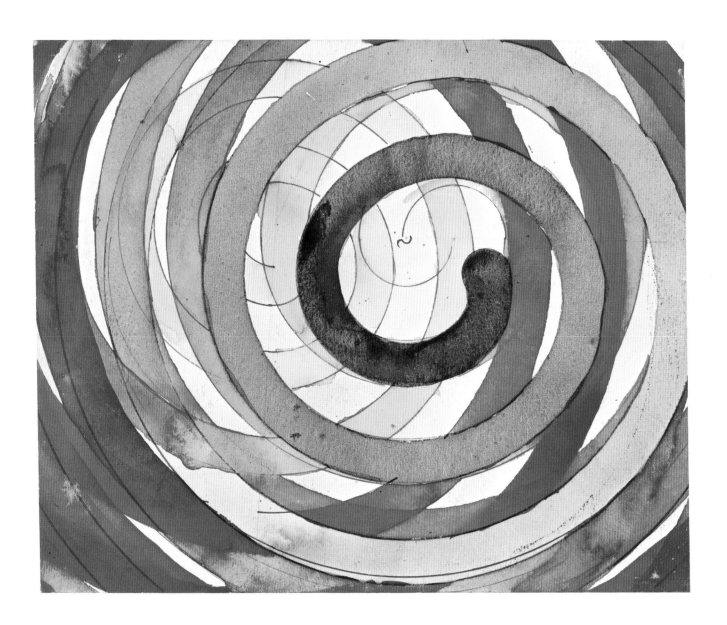

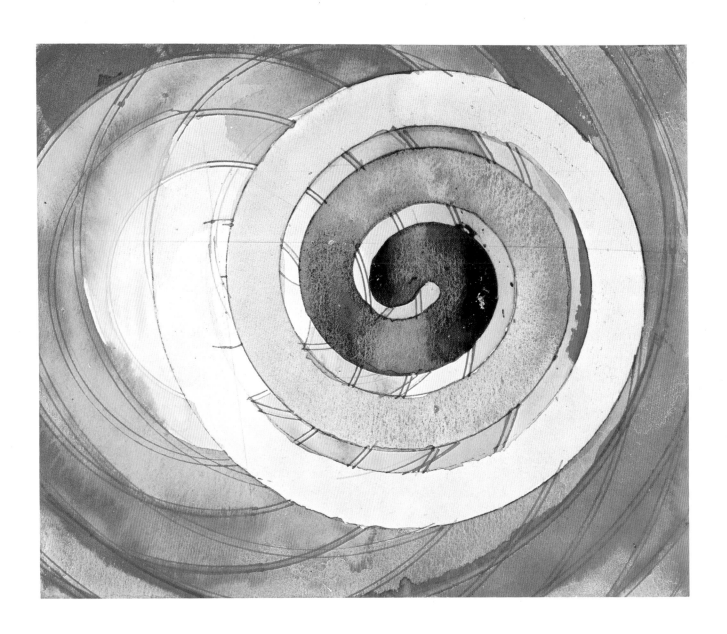

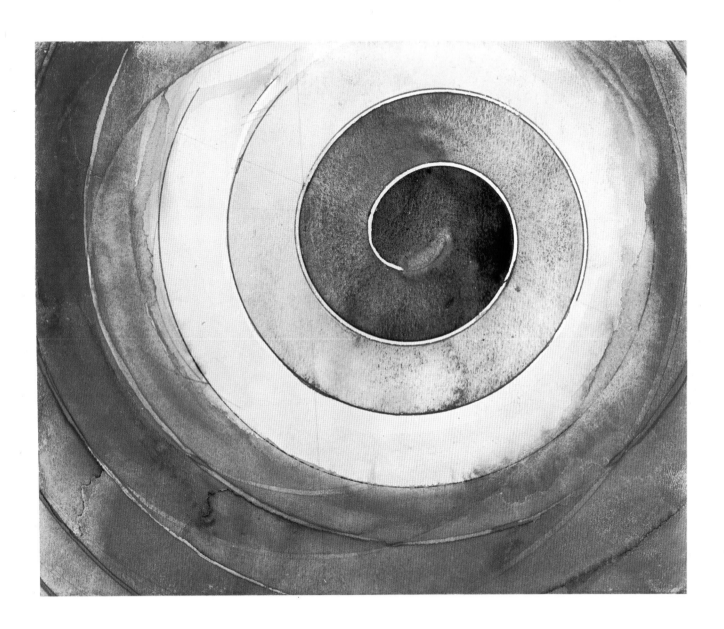

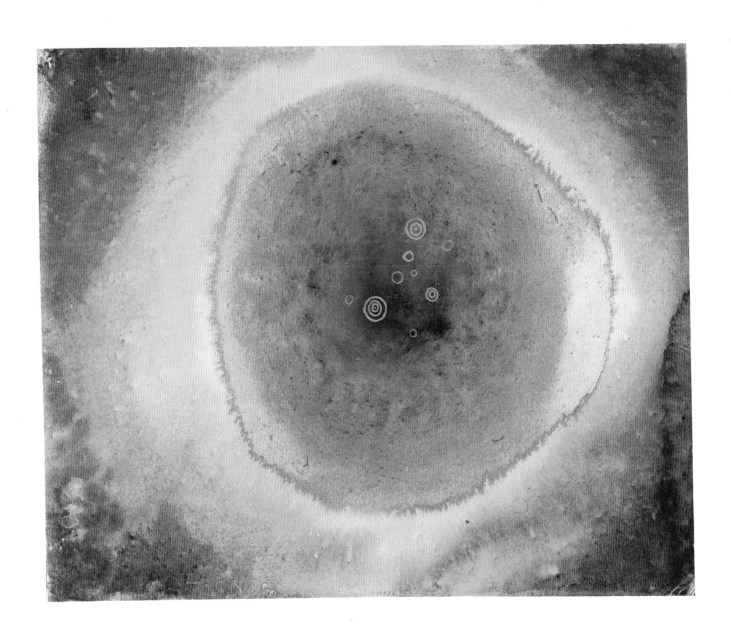

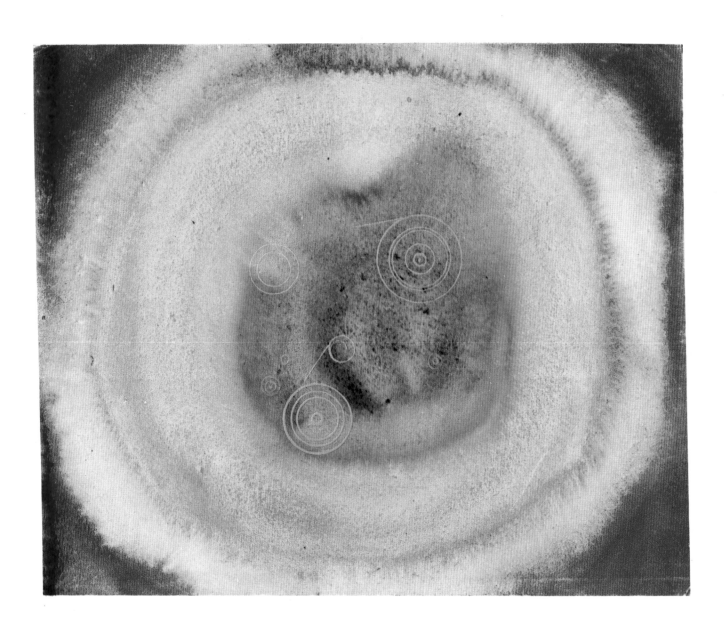

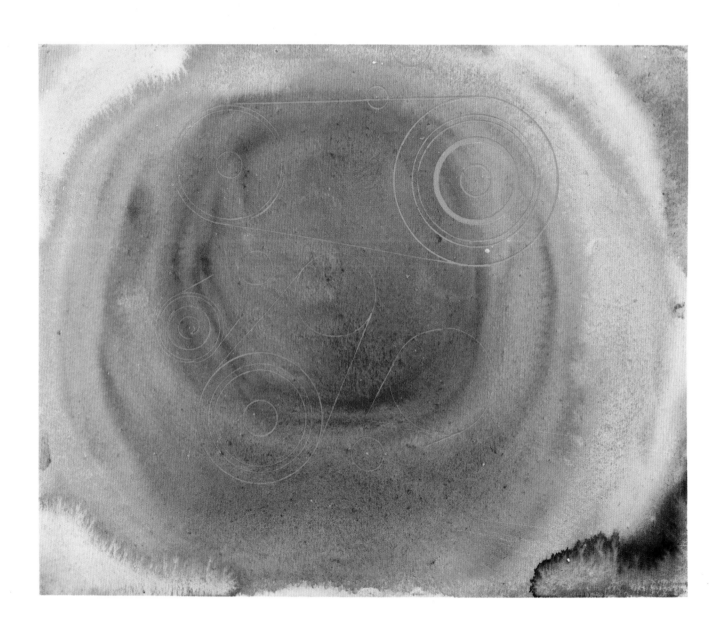

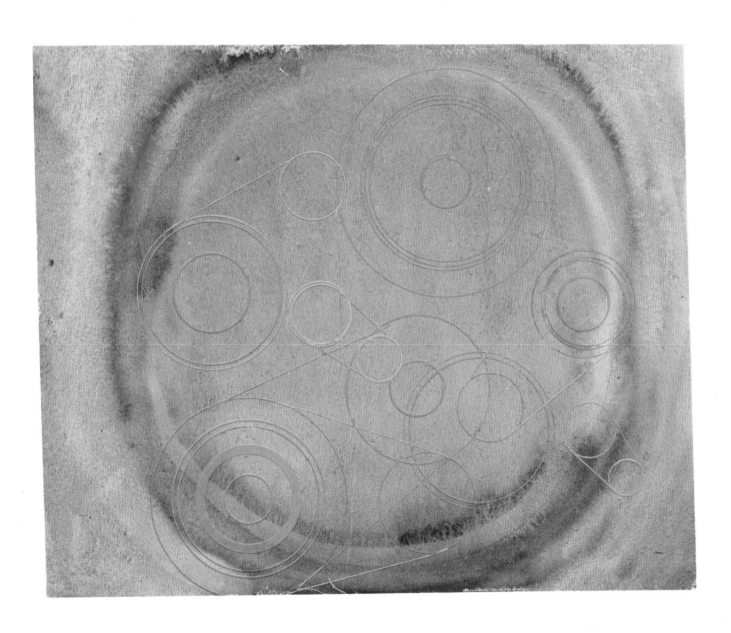

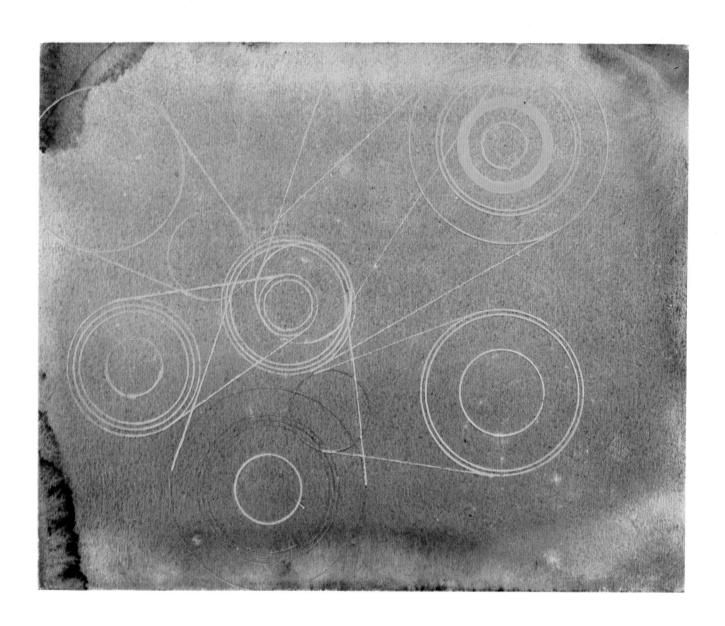

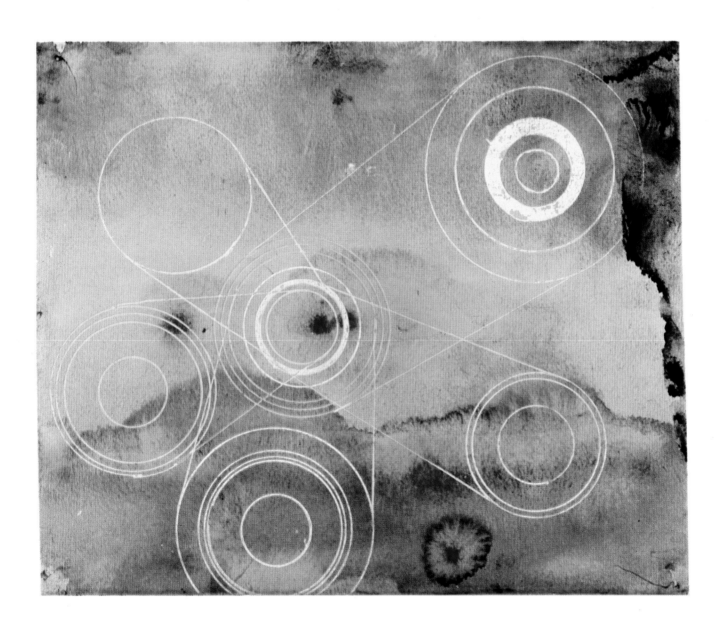

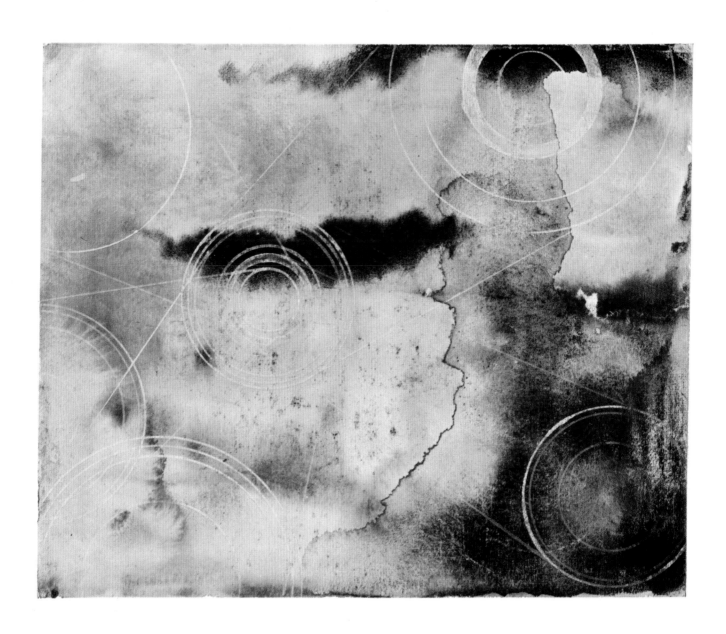

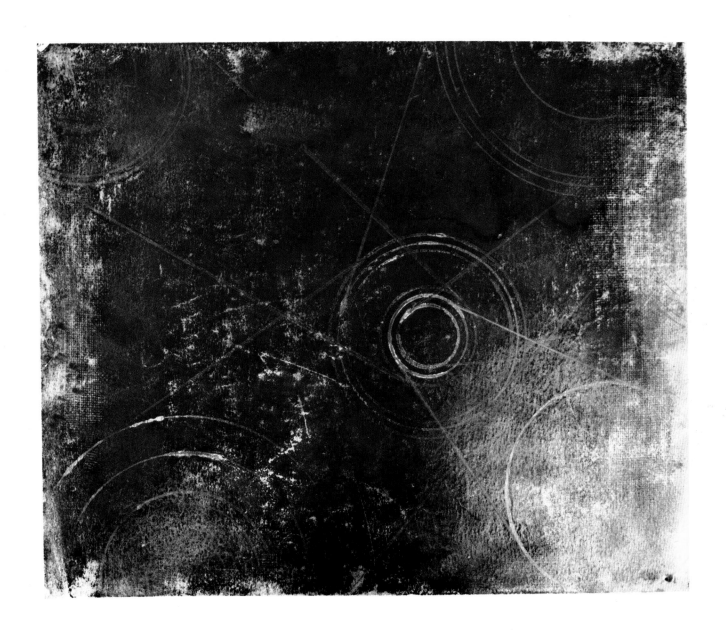

Kurt Kranz
Der heroische Pfeil
1929–30

Original 60 Phasenzeichnungen in Tusche
auf Einzelblättern, Original verlorengegangen.
Nach damaligen Fotoplatten reproduziert
Größe der Originalzeichnungen: 10,5 x 14,5 cm
Gesamtlänge des Leporellos: 330 cm,
beidseitig bedruckt
Größe der Tafeln: 5 x 7,4 cm

1930 befindet sich Kranz im Bauhaus Dessau. Das Oeuvre
und die Theorien der großen Meister wirken wie ein Druck
auf ihn und rufen zwei Reaktionen hervor. Er reagiert ironisch mit Fotomontagen wie z. B. die „Erdzerteilung" oder
„Vereinsamung". Diese Titel wie auch „Versinkende" oder
„Spielt euer Spiel" zeigen das deutlich. Zum anderen kehrt
Kranz zurück zu seinen vertrauten Bildreihen, die jetzt aber
von vorherein als Filmentwürfe angelegt werden. Er wählt
als Thema den im Bauhaus so oft strapazierten Pfeil.
Die Geschichte des Pfeils ist als Tuschzeichnung auf wei-
ßem und schwarzem Papier durchgeführt. Die Größe der
60 nicht gebundenen Originalblätter war 14,5 x 21 cm. Leider
sind nur noch die damals angefertigten Glasnegative er-
halten geblieben.

Die Bildgeschichte mit dem Pfeil als Helden hat ausgesprochen filmischen Charakter, so das Überwinden, Sichdurch-
setzen mit und ohne Trabanten gegen alle Arten von Wider-
ständen. Fast nur lineare Mittel sind angewandt. Hat der
Held ein Feld von Pfeilangeln passiert, wird er von einem
scharfen, unerbittlichen Widersacher halbiert, geschieht
eine Anteilnahme mit der abstrakten Form, wie sie eigentlich nur Personifiziertem, Lebendigem entgegengebracht
wird. Verkleinerung, Vergrößerung, beides im Übermaß
führt zur bleibenden Linie, der „Seele" des Pfeils. Sie
endet in der Kreisform, dem Symbol des Endlosen. Damals
hat Kranz alles Erreichbare an abstrakter Malerei oder
über abstrakte Filme studiert. Im Bauhaus gab es keine
Hilfen. Moholy, der sehr interessiert am Film war, befand
sich in Berlin. Kandinsky, dem Kranz seine Bildreihen
zeigte, wollte das Ganze gedruckt sehen. Als er einen
Mäzen fand, war die wirtschaftliche Krise so weit fortge-
schritten, daß an eine Drucklegung nicht zu denken war.
Damals traten zuerst zwei abstrakte Filme als Blickfang in
den Alltag der Werbung. In Berlin war es Fischinger, der
abstrakte Formen nach Walzer- und Foxtrottklängen sich
bewegen ließ. Kranz war damals nicht damit einverstanden.
Die Vereinfachung, das Praktikable der Technik, sah er
nicht, sondern das ferne Ziel der Animation oder die Be-
seelung der Formen. Er mußte die Realisation der Filme
immer wieder hinausschieben, weil die Herstellungskosten
und Geräte für den damals mittellosen Kranz zu hoch waren. Auch heute wäre die Durchzeichnung des Entwurfes in
einzelne Phasen ein zeitlich kaum zu bewältigendes Problem. Zwischen den einzelnen Bildern der Storyboards
müßten 30–100 Phasen hergestellt werden. Das lineare
Bild des Pfeils ließe es technisch zu. Es würde aber außer-
ordentliche Mittel erfordern, z. B. einen Computer zur Herstellung der Phasen.
Inzwischen ist auch der Film mit Einblendungen der 60
Bilder des „heroischen Pfeils" fertiggeworden und rafft das
Geschehen in einem Ablauf von etwa 6 Minuten.

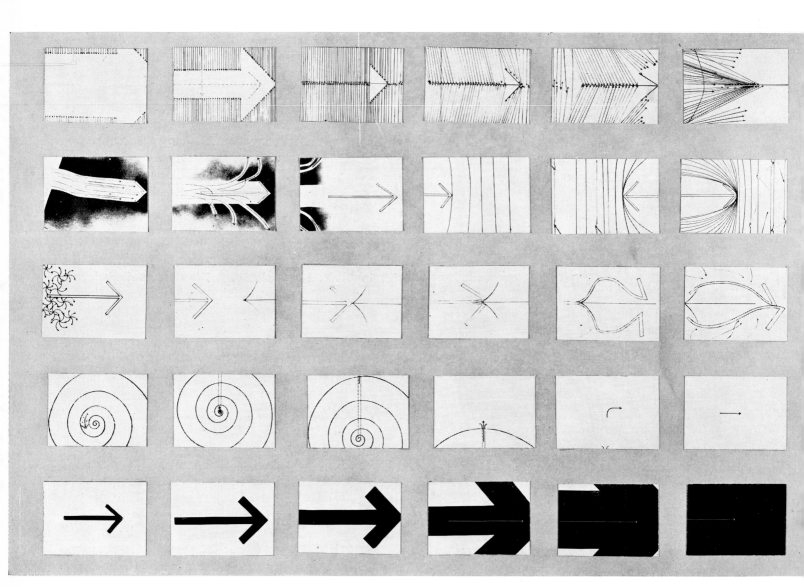

Panel showing complete picture-sequence "the heroic arrow".

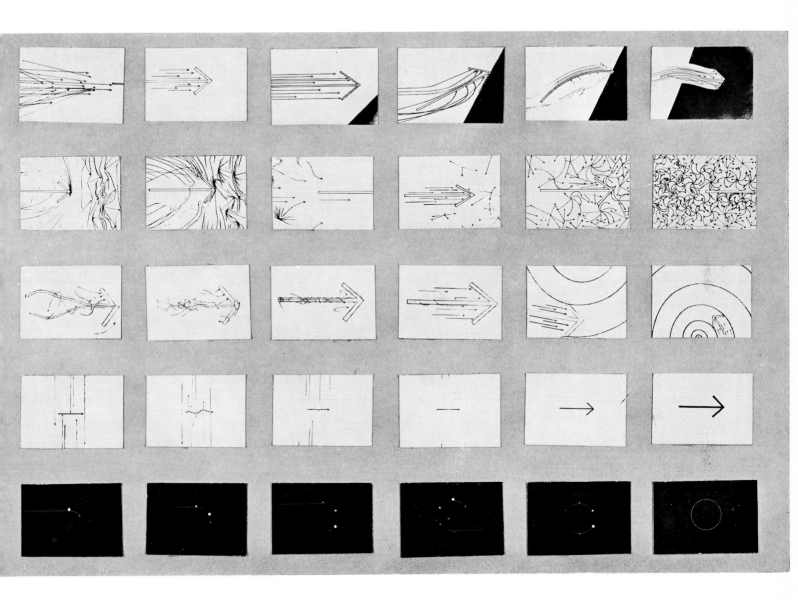

Übersichtstafeln der Bildreihe „Der heroische Pfeil"

171

Kurt Kranz
The Heroic Arrow
1929–30

Original 60 phase pen and ink drawings
on separate sheets; original lost.
Reproduced from photographic plates of that time,
size of original drawings: 10 x 4,5 cm
Total length of the Leporello: 330 cm,
printed on both sides
size of the plates: 5 x 7,4 cm.

In 1930 Kranz is in the Bauhaus at Dessau. The oeuvre and the theories of the great masters exert a sort of pressure on him and evoke two reactions. His first is an ironic reaction with such photomontages as "Dividing up the earth" or "Isolation". These titles or "Play your games" show this quite clearly. Secondly, Kranz returns to his familiar picture sequences, which are now, however, from the very beginning composed as film designs. As a theme he chooses the well worn one in the Bauhaus of the arrow.

The story of the arrow is reproduced in the form of pen and ink drawings on black and white paper. The size of the 60 unbound original sheets was 14,5 x 21 cm. Unfortunately only the glass negatives made at the time have survived intact.

The picture story with the arrow as hero has pronounced film characteristics, for instance the survival over and surmounting of all difficulties against all types of resistance, with or without satellites. Practically only linear media are used. When the hero has passed by a field of arrow barbs, he is cut in half by a sharp and relentless foe, thus arousing a feeling of compassion normally reserved for the personified, the living. Reduction, enlargement, both carried to exaggeration, lead to the remaining line, the "soul" of the arrow. It ends in the circular form, the symbol of infinity. At that time Kranz was studying everything available on the subject of abstract painting and abstract films. There was no one in the Bauhaus itself to help him. Moholy, who was very interested in the film, was in Berlin; Kandinsky, to whom Kranz showed his picture sequence, wanted to see the whole thing printed. When he found a sponsor, the economic crisis had assumed such proportions that printing was quite out of the question.

At that time two abstract films were the first to catch the attention of the advertising world. In Berlin, it was Fischinger who made abstract forms move to the sound of waltz and foxtrot music. Kranz did not approve of this. He was not interested in the simplification or the practicabiltity of the technique, he had his eye on the distant goal of the animation of forms, of endowing them with a soul. He kept having to postpone the production of his films because the costs of production and instruments were too high for a man who at that time was completely penniless. Even today the drawing of the design in its individual phase would be an almost insuperable problem because of the time factor. 30–100 frames would have to be produced between the individual pictures of the storyboard. This would be technically possible for the linear picture of the arrow. But very special media, for instance a computer, would be required for the production of the phases.

In the meantime the film has also been completed with mixes of the 60 pictures of the "heroic arrow" and has been edited down to a running time of about 6 minutes.

Picture-sequence „the heroic arrow", 1930-31,
60 phase pictures

Bildreihe „Der heroische Pfeil", 1930-31,
60 Phasen-Bilder

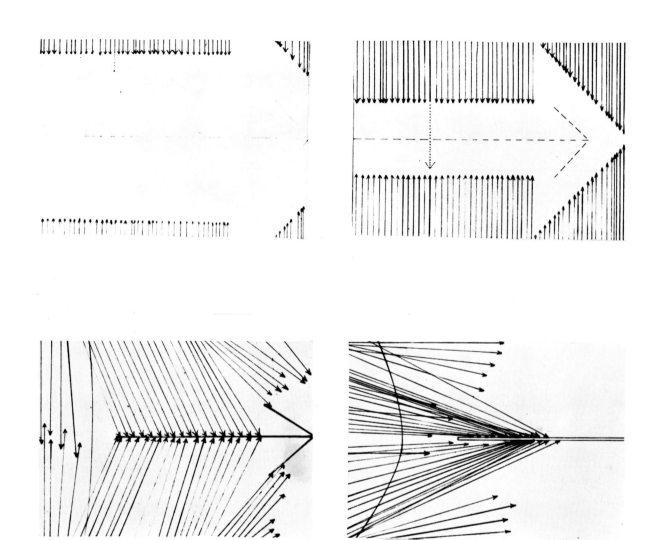

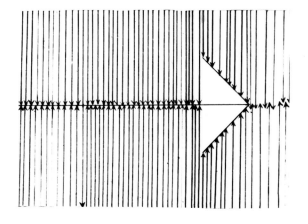 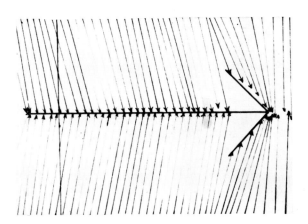

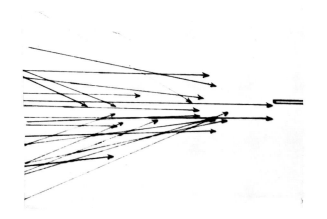 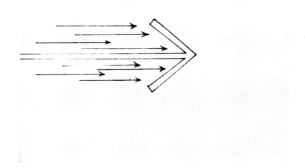

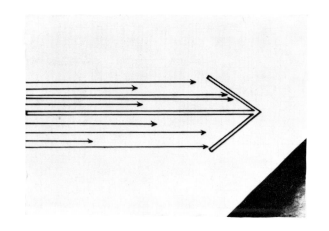
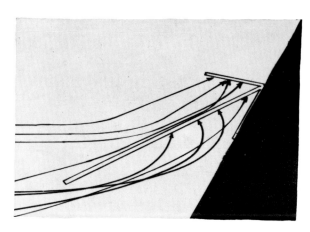
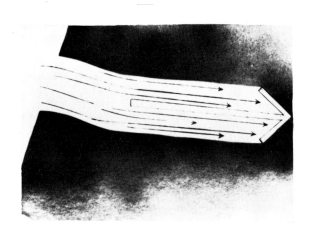
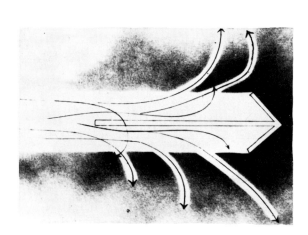

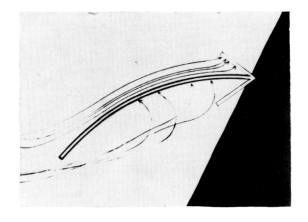

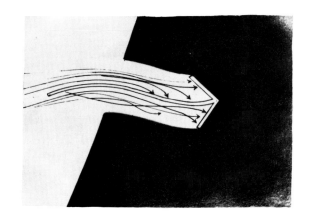

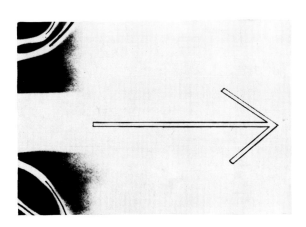

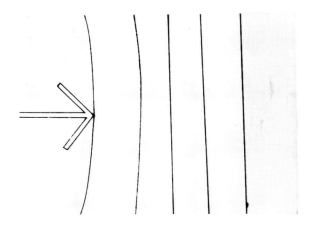

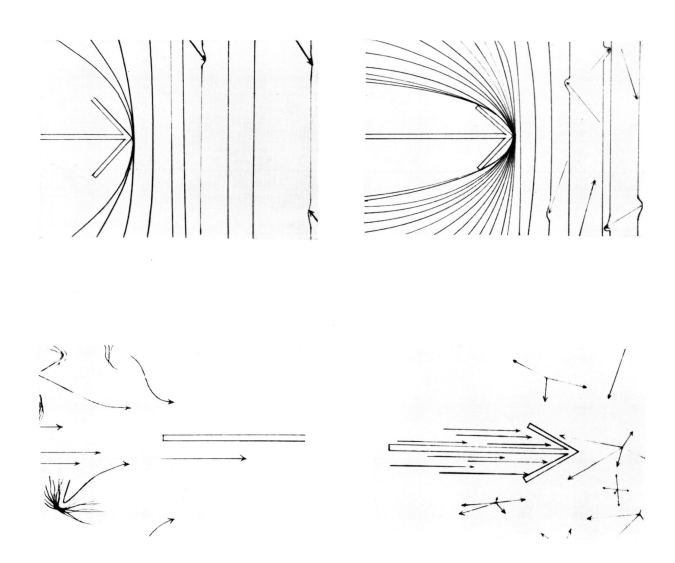

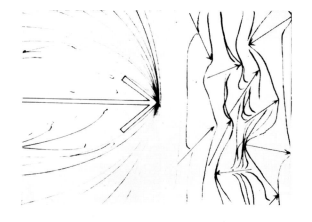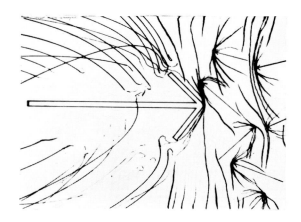

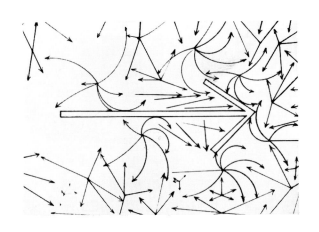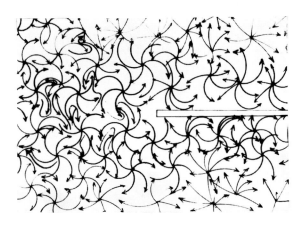

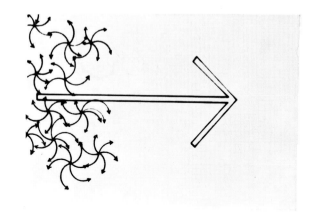

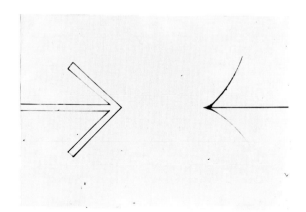

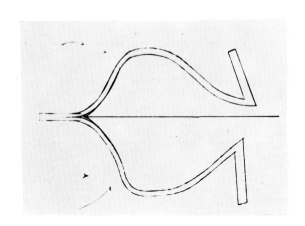

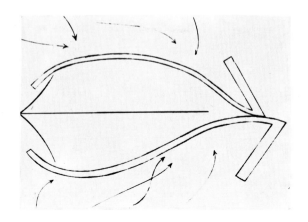

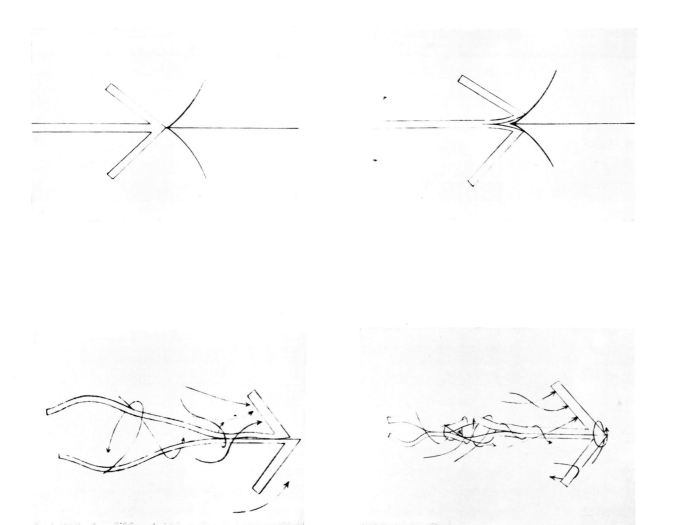

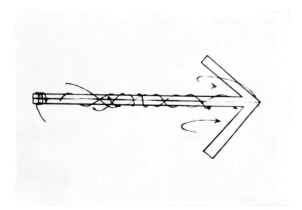 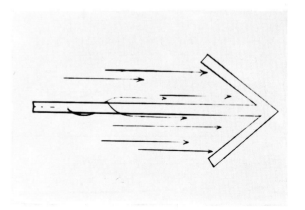

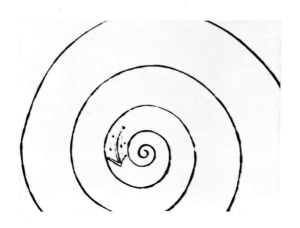 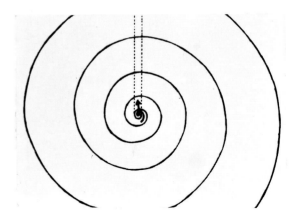

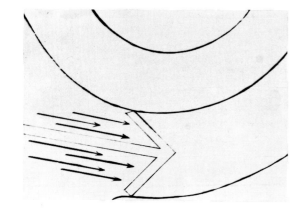

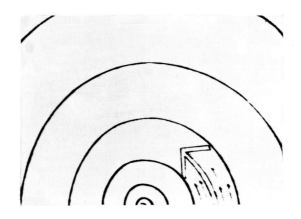

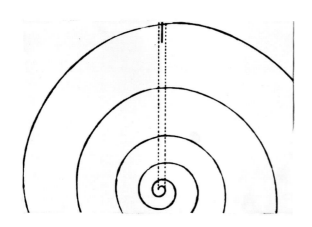

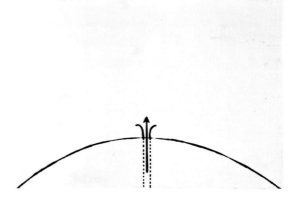

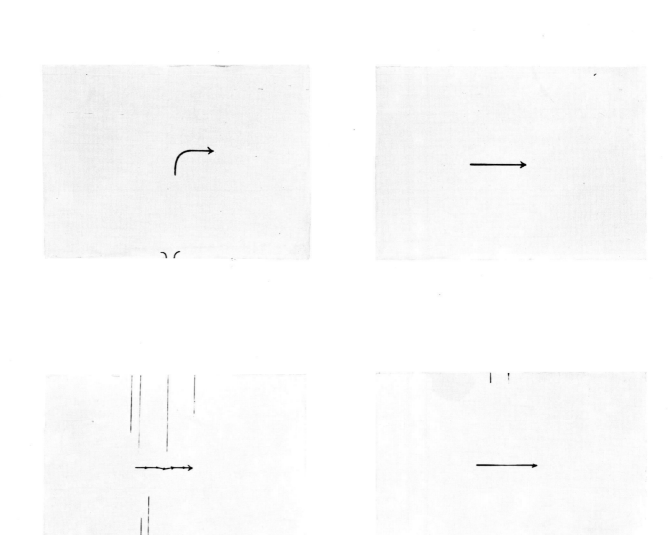

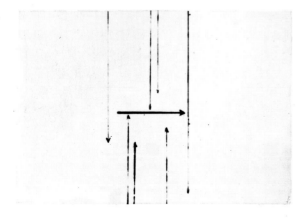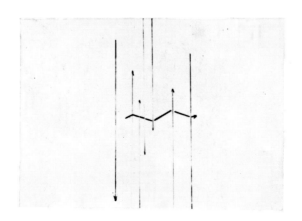

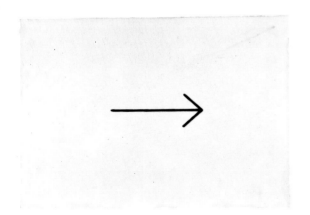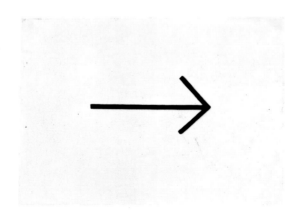

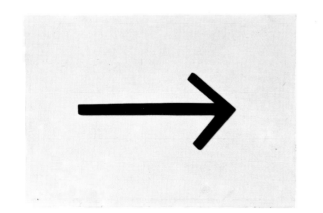 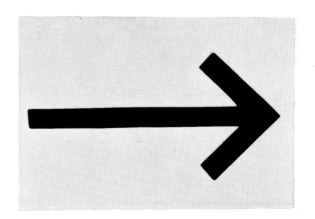

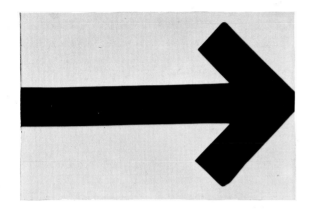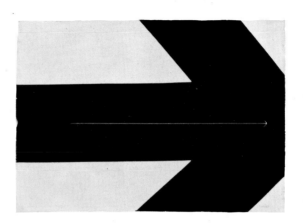

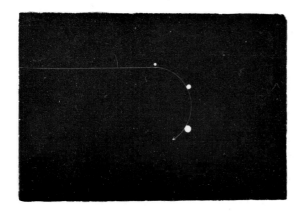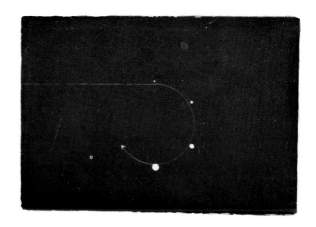

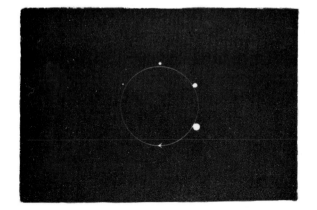

Kurt Kranz
Observations on picture sequences and serial technique in visual art.

Before the background of the scientific concept of nature and technology, today even abstract art has the effect of a reproduction. Scientists arrange data and facts in series so that from an overall survey and from the field of their observations they can detect new combinations or deviations. Concealed in the infinite row of individual data is the actual form of reality. What is hidden in time and in the multitude of phases comes to light, unseen.

Nature herself reproduces on the serial principle. The constant form of reproduction, the uniformity, is interrupted by mutations and – though infinitely slowly – undergoes change. The phyla, the groups of species all developing along individual lines, are subject to variation over very long but nevertheless limited periods of time. It is against this conception of natural processes and modern technology that modern artistic forms are to be viewed.

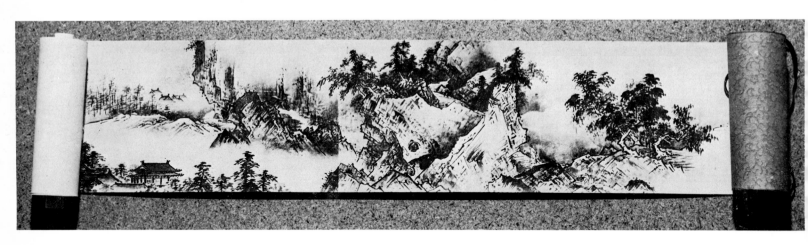

Sesshu: The Four-Season Landscape Scroll, 1486, Tokyo National Museum. This scroll is made up of 17 sheets. In the classic manner of ink drawing, calligraphic groups of trees, rocks and houses glide over the field of view. Bobbing up and then disappearing in the fog, they are varied with emblems of the seasons.

Sesshu: Bildrolle, Vier Jahreszeiten, 1486, Tokyo National-Museum. Diese Bilderrolle ist aus 17 Bogen zusammengesetzt. In klassischer Tuschmalweise gleiten kalligraphische Gruppen von Bäumen, Felsen und Häusern über das Sichtfeld. Auftauchend und im Nebel verschwindend werden sie durch die Embleme der Jahreszeiten variiert.

Kurt Kranz
Betrachtungen über Bildreihen und serielle Verfahren in der visuellen Kunst.

Vor dem Hintergrund des wissenschaftlichen Naturbildes und der Technik wirkt heute selbst die abstrakte Kunst wie eine Abbildung. Die Forscher ordnen Fakten und Daten in Reihen, um aus dem Überblick, aus dem Feld der Beobachtungen neue Zusammenhänge oder Abweichungen ablesen zu können.

Verborgen im endlosen Band der einzelnen Daten ist die eigentliche Form oder die Realität. Das in der Zeit und in der Menge der Phasen Verborgene, Unsichtbare tritt ans Licht.

Natur selbst reproduziert nach seriellen Prinzipien. Die gleichbleibende Reproduktion, die Invarianz, wird durch Mutationen durchbrochen und – wenn auch unendlich langsam – variiert. Die Phyla, die Bündel der einzelnen Entwicklungslinien der Arten, variieren zwar über sehr lange, aber begrenzte Zeiträume. Vor dieser Vorstellung des Naturgeschehens und der modernen Technik sind die künstlerischen Verfahren der Moderne zu sehen.

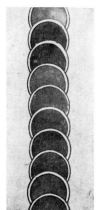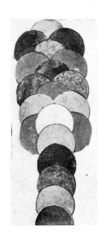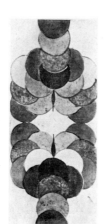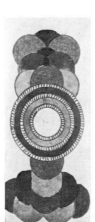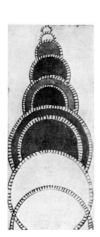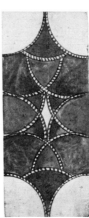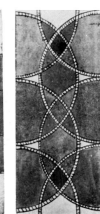

Painting Western India, about 18th century, from a manuscript of the Suddhacittavani, instructional course in correct comprehension.
The sequence shows 3 coexisting forces: creation, preservation, dissolution.

Malerei, Westindien, ca. 18. Jh., aus einem Manuskript der Suddhacittāvani, Lehrgang des rechten Verstehens.
Die Reihe zeigt drei koexistierende Kräfte: Schöpfung – Erhaltung – Auflösung.

The reproduction, the interpretation of this world, ranges from the photo, academic drawing and painting to reconstruction and imitation, from the variation of minor deviation to deformation and to new fantastic discovery.

Perception.
As in Nature, everything, except the perfect sphere, has many aspects; there emerges a permanently changing and flowing picture. In addition occurs the change of form resulting from the background and multiplicity of overlappings. There are many reasons why we make a selection from this flow of aspects, the "panta rhei". In this way the real picture is created in us, a collection of characteristic phases as conception; finally these form the fiction of a type.

The genesis.
Growth brings with it continuous change. Biological growth shows progression, stagnation and regression. Metamorphosis is the richest form of change of shape. The whole of life is subject to the law of ups and downs, of life and death.

Inorganic growth.
Sediments grow in steps and layers, crystals in grids, and erosion destroys. The sequence of earth pictures is in a continual state of change.

The basic pattern.
Each replica is traceable not only to the object in question but also to a basic pattern. Only on the basis of this pattern can free variations be made. Over and above this, imagination can invent new patterns and develop new sequences. It is here that the wide field of transformation belongs with all its different keys.

Human action.
Individual actions grow into processes. If they are strung together in a row, a sequence of events becomes apparent. Actors and mimicry, dance movements and changes of scenery lead to picture sequences, picture series. The cartoon is a naive or skilful serial technique of this type, which appeals to both the illiterate and the intellectual. Picture sequences and diagrams of cosmic happenings have been discovered in many prehistoric finds. Here magic and writing are bound together in the picture, as, for instance, locked in the burial chambers of the Egyptians, picture sequences of gods, battles and scenes of men at work. Other examples are the picture sequences, biblia pauperum, on the walls of christian churches or the illustrated stations of Mount Calvary; in modern times, the murals of Diego Rivera and Orozco in Mexico City.
As in mediaeval times, wood-cut sequences, altars with picture sequences, block-books and broadsheets with picture sequences served to provide the illiterate with information. Picture sequence and diagrams of cosmic happenings have today attracted considerable attention (Tantra art).

Japanese and Chinese picture-rolls possess the purest form of expressing a chronological sequence, a penetration of place and time with action. Rolls by Sesshu, Hokusai and Utamaro deal with various themes. The four seasons with a unified topos, or battle scenes with changing time and place, or intimate human processes in ever changing surroundings are very complex serial techniques. The action is spread over long paper rolls. The composition is open. Ink drawing and its execution is able to make the action fade away or by means of tiny details to revive it again. When looking at the roll-pictures, the field of vision, owing to the winding and unwinding, ranges like a cut-out over the band. The story, the connecting idea becomes during its unwinding a picture sequence. Looking ahead or looking back or looking at the whole are actions of the observer

Die Wiedergabe, die Reproduktion, die Deutung dieser Welt reicht von der Abbildung des Fotos, des akademischen Zeichnens und Malens bis zur Rekonstruktion und Imitation, von der Variation der kleinen Abweichung bis zur Deformation und zur neuen phantastischen Erfindung.

Die Wahrnehmung.

Da in der Natur jedes Ding, außer der idealen Kugel, viele Ansichten hat, entsteht ein ständig verändertes, fließendes Bild. Hinzu kommt die Veränderung der Form durch den Grund und die vielfältigen Überschneidungen. Wir wählen aus vielen Gründen aus dem Fluß der Ansichten, dem πάντα ῥεῖ aus. So entsteht das wirkliche Bild in uns: eine Sammlung von charakteristischen Phasen als Vorstellung; sie bilden schließlich die Fiktion eines Typs.

Die Genese.

Der Wuchs bringt ständige Veränderung. Der biologische Wuchs zeigt Progression, Stillstand und Regression ... die Metamorphose ist die reichste Form der Formverwandlung. Alles Leben unterliegt dem Gesetz von Auf und Ab, von Leben und Tod.

Anorganischer Wuchs.

Sedimente wachsen in Stufen und Schichten, Kristalle in Gittern, und die Erosion baut ab. Ständig verändert sich die Reihe der Erdbilder.

Das Grundmuster.

Jede Nachbildung ist nicht nur auf das Objekt, sondern auch auf ein Grundmuster zurückzuführen. Erst auf Grund dieses Musters wird frei variiert. Darüber hinaus kann die Phantasie neue Muster finden und neue Reihen entwickeln. Das große Feld der Transformation mit ihren verschiedenen Schlüsseln gehört hierher.

Die menschliche Aktion.

Die Einzelaktionen wachsen zu Abläufen. Werden sie aneinandergereiht, so wird das Geschehen ablesbar. Akteure und Mimik, Tanzgestik und Szenenwechsel führen zur Bildfolge, zur Bildreihe. Der Cartoon ist eine solche naive oder raffinierte Reihentechnik, die den Analphabeten wie den Intellektuellen anspricht. Bildergeschichten sind uralt. Bei vielen vorgeschichtlichen Funden sind Reihen von Bildern entdeckt worden. Hier sind im Bilde Magie und Schrift eingebunden, so z. B. in den Grabkammern verschlossene Bildreihen von Göttern, Kampf und Arbeitsszenen der Ägypter usw. Andere Beispiele sind die Bildreihen biblia pauperum an den Wänden der christlichen Kirchen oder die bebilderten Stationen des Calvarienberges; in der Neuzeit die Wandbilder von Diego Rivera und Orozco in Mexiko-City.
Wie im Mittelalter hatten Holzschnittreihen, Altarbilder mit Bildfolgen, Blockbücher und Flugblätter mit Bildreihen die Aufgabe, den Analphabeten zu informieren. Bildreihen und Diagramme kosmischen Geschehens sind heute in den Blickpunkt der Aufmerksamkeit gerückt (Tantra-Kunst).

Japanische und chinesische Bildrollen haben die reinste Ausdrucksform eines Nacheinanders, einer Durchdringung des Orts, der Zeit mit der Handlung. Rollen von Sesshu, Hokusai und Utamaro haben unterschiedliche Themen. Die vier Jahreszeiten mit einem einheitlichen Topos, oder Kampfgeschehen mit wechselnder Zeit und wechselndem Raum, oder intime menschliche Vorgänge in immer anderer Umgebung sind sehr komplexe Reihentechnik. Das Geschehen breitet sich über lange Papierbänder aus. Die Komposition ist offen. Tuschmalerei mit ihren Verläufen hat die Möglichkeit, das Geschehen verklingen und aus winzigen Details neu aufleben zu lassen. Beim Betrachten der Rollenbilder wandert das Blickfeld als Ausschnitt durch das Auf- und Abrollen über das Band. So verwendet auch Takahashi Shohachiro für seine visuelle Poesie „Wasser – Land/Feuer

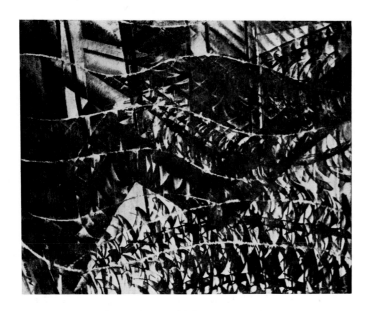

Balla: Swifts: Path of Movement + Dynamic Sequences. 1913, oil on canvas, 100 x 120 cm. The Museum of Modern Art, New York.
The long title of this futuristic painting is a complete acknowledgement of sequence technique. The patterns of the flight phases are interwoven in an undulating and zigzag grid. The sequences are sub-divided by almost vertical lines which function as a measure of time.

Balla: „Schwalben: Bewegungsspuren + dynamische Reihen", 1913, Öl auf Leinwand. Museum of Modern Art, New York.
Der lange Titel dieses futuristischen Gemäldes bekennt sich voll zur Reihentechnik. Die Muster der Flugphasen verweben sich in einem Wellen- und Zickzackraster. Unterteilt werden die Reihen durch vertikale Linien, die wie ein Zeitmaß fungieren.

demanded by the sequence. The actual message to be conveyed lies in the whole. It is very clear that the roll-pictures are the forerunners of the idea of the film. Thus it is quite natural that the abstract film began with abstract roll-pictures. (Richter, Eggeling.)

Phase photos are a serial technique which have a direct effect on art and daily life. First it was the film with its successor, television, then came video technique.

Scientific discoveries and their application:
The phase picture is a cut, a momentary picture, a picture often hidden from the eye — something rigid. Without the sequence of phases, it is not easily understandable. The greater the gaps, the intervals, the more the observer has to use his imagination. This is what the picture story lives on, the cartoon, which since the advent of pop-art, has appeared in a new light. Here in leaps and bounds the phases and scenes, in more or less separate cut-outs, are strung together and connected with word and text fragments. Mostly the contents are of a trivial nature, designed for general consumption.

The phase photo has had a very strong influence on futurism. With overlapping phases and cubist distortions, the futurists suggest the tempo which they seek to glorify. The composition has been dynamized far beyond the edge of the picture, almost similar to a cosmic cut-out. Phases,

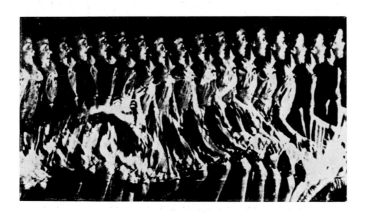

W. Schmittel: Cut-out from a stroboscopic photo. The penetration of the individual running phases produces an undulating sequence.

W. Schmittel: Ausschnitt aus einer stroboskopischen Aufnahme. Die Durchdringung der einzelnen Laufphasen ergibt eine wellenförmige Reihe.

Land" (1970) die traditionelle japanische Bildrolle. Die Erzählung, der verbindende Gedanke wird in seinem Ablauf zur Bildreihe. Das Vor- und Zurückgreifen oder der ganze Überblick sind Aktionen des Betrachters, die die Reihe fordert. Die eigentliche Botschaft liegt im Ganzen. Es ist sehr deutlich, daß die Rollenbilder Vorläufer filmischen Denkens sind. So ist es natürlich, daß der abstrakte Film mit abstrakten Rollenbildern begann (Richter, Eggeling).

Phasen-Fotos sind eine Reihen-Technik, die auf die Kunst und den Alltag unmittelbar einwirken. Zuerst war es der Film mit seinem Nachfolger, dem Fernsehen, dann die Video-Technik.

Die wissenschaftlichen Erkenntnisse und ihre Anwendung: Das Phasenbild ist ein Schnitt, ein Momentbild, ein oft verborgenes Bild für das Auge ... etwas Erstarrtes. Ohne die Reihe der Phasen bleibt es leicht unverständlich. Je größer die Abstände, die zeitlichen Zwischenräume, je mehr muß der Betrachter aus seiner Vorstellungskraft etwas hinzufügen. Davon zehrt die Bilder-Geschichte, der Cartoon, der seit Pop art in einem neuen Licht erscheint. Hier werden in Sprüngen die Phasen und Szenen in mehr oder weniger abgeteilten Bildausschnitten aneinandergereiht und mit Wort- und Textresten verbunden. Sie haben zumeist triviale Inhalte, die für den Konsum für jedermann bestimmt sind.
Das Phasen-Foto hat den Futurismus sehr stark beeinflußt. Die Futuristen suggerieren mit übereinandergelagerten Phasen und kubistischen Verwerfungen das von ihnen verherrlichte Tempo.
Die Komposition wurde dynamisiert weit über den Rand des Bildes hinaus, gleichsam zu einem kosmischen Ausschnitt. Phasen, Progressionen und Variationen über Grundformen und Raster zerstückeln die Form, die sich auf der Fläche verteilt, um Brennpunkte zu bilden.
Mehrere Fluchtpunkte, auch Spiralen und Kreiszentren dynamisieren die Form-Anordnungen.

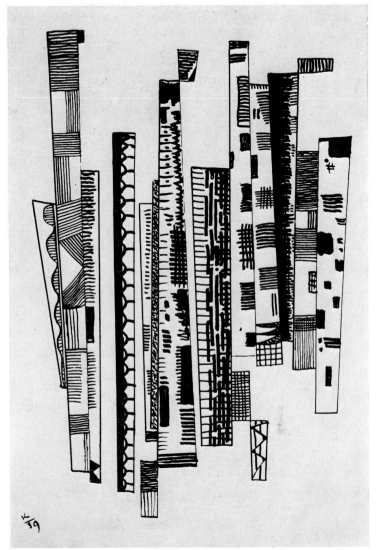

Kandinsky: Drawing no. 10, 1939, ink, 21,5 x 16 cm.
A variation sequence of trapezes and almost rectangular vertical with rich interior drawing.
Kandinsky: Zeichnung Nr. 10, 1939, Tusche, 21,5 x 16 cm.
Eine Variationsreihe von Trapezen und fast rechteckigen, vertikalen Leisten mit reicher Binnenzeichnung.

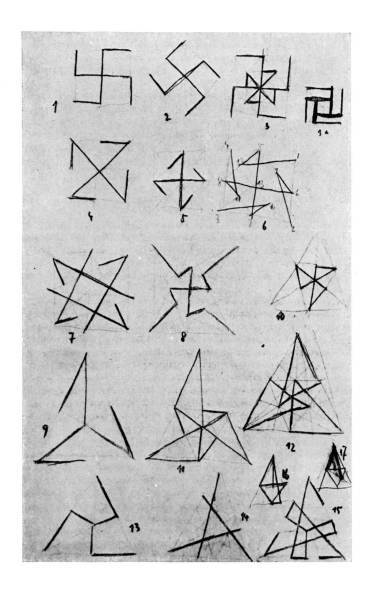

progressions and variations on basic forms and grids mutilate the form, which spreads over the surface to establish focal points. Several vanishing points as well as spirals and centres of circles dynamize the form arrangements.

Abstract art.

Pure colour and form pictures came into being at the same time as futurism. Abstract painting and sculpture use the pure artistic media, colour, form, volume, material as language. Kandinsky's picture-language consists of changing basic forms which, in consonance and dissonance, "resound" into new variations. In his theoretical work "Point and line to the plane", Kandinsky makes a systematic sequence of investigation into the expressive power of the media and their ability to act as an artistic language. Through the oeuvre of the founder of abstract art runs the changing sequence of articulated form.

Kandinsky and Schönberg, the creator of the serial technique of twelve-tone music, had become friends through the "Blauer Reiter" group.

Klee's "The thinking eye" is full of growth and development. Elements in its capacity for combinatorial analysis form logical variation sequences. In his study of nature, he seeks the inner structure, the basic patterns. Clear pictorial media arrange themselves in rhythm and in the grid provided. Repetition, rhythm and variation are elementary technical serial media. The progressing beat is articulated by the rhythm and urged forward by the variation.

Klee: Study sheet, about 1923.
Klee's comment: "1—6 static interpretation of the Swastika" and "7—17 dynamically preferred position of the Swastika".
This study on variation sequences provides an insight into the systematic pictorial conceptions of this painter.

Klee: Studienblatt, ca. 1923.
Anmerkung Klees: „1–6 Statische Deutung des Hakenkreuzes" und „7–17 Dynamisch bevorzugte Position des Hakenkreuzes". Diese Studie über Variationsreihen gibt einen Einblick in das systematische bildnerische Denken dieses Malers.

Abstrakte Kunst.
Reine Farb- und Formbilder entstanden zur gleichen Zeit wie der Futurismus. Die gegenstandslose Malerei und Skulptur verwendet die reinen künstlerischen Mittel: Farbe, Form, Volumen, Material als Sprache. Kandinskys Bilder-Sprache besteht aus langen Reihen von sich wandelnden Grundformen, die in neuen Variationen in Konsonanz und Dissonanz „erklingen". In seinem theoretischen Werk „Punkt und Linie zur Fläche" gibt Kandinsky eine systematische Reihenuntersuchung über die Ausdruckskraft der Mittel und ihre Fähigkeit, als künstlerische Sprache zu wirken. Durch das Oeuvre des Begründers der abstrakten Malerei zieht sich die sich wandelnde Reihe der artikulierten Form. Kandinsky und Schönberg, der Schöpfer der Reihentechnik der Zwölfton-Musik, waren über die Gruppe des „Blauen Reiters" befreundet.

Klees bildnerisches Denken ist voll von Wachsen und Entwicklung. Elemente in ihrer Kombinatorik bilden logische Variations-Reihen. In seinem Naturstudium sucht er die innere Struktur, die Grundmuster. Klare bildnerische Mittel gliedern sich im Rhythmus und im vorgegebenen Raster. Wiederholung, Rhythmus und Variation sind elementare reihentechnische Mittel. Der fortschreitende Takt wird durch den Rhythmus gegliedert ... und durch die Variation vorangetrieben.
Pfeile sind Hilfe und Steigerung dieser Bewegung von Formen, Stufen und Farbreihen und geben der Reihe Richtung. Ähnlich den Mutationen ist der Zufall eine willkommene Quelle der Variation im Werk Klees.

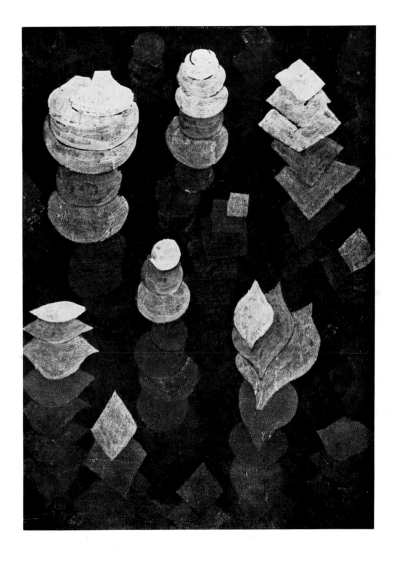

Klee: "Growth of nocturnal plants", 1922
Geometrical form sequences rise in progression and rotation . . .
Colour sequence . . . gives the picture its name and content

Klee: „Wachstum der Nachtpflanzen", 1922
Geometrische Formreihen steigen in Progression und Drehung
Farbreihe . . . gibt dem Bild seinen Namen und Inhalt.

John Whitney: 24 variations on a graphical matrix, abstract film 1940.
The form sequences shown here are black screens which served as material
for an abstract film. By duplication or other mixtures they were varied serially
and provided the frames for the film. They produced mobile compositions,
which were planned like serial music, sequences, which by inversion,
retrograde etc, as in 12 tone music, led through simple or multiple overlapping to further varied film-strips.
Today John Whitney works with electronic systems.

John Whitney: 24 Variationen über eine graphische Matrix, abstrakter
Film 1940.
Die abgebildeten Formreihen sind Schwarzblenden, die als Material
für einen abstrakten Film dienten. Durch Verdoppelung oder
andere Mischungen wurden sie seriell variiert und lieferten die Frames für
den Film. Sie ergaben Bewegungskompositionen, die wie serielle Musik
geplant waren, Sequenzen, die durch Umkehrung, Krebs usw. wie in der
Zwölftontechnik durch einfaches und vielfaches Überlagern zu immer weiter
variierten Filmstreifen führten.
Heute arbeitet John Whitney mit elektronischen Systemen.

Graeff: Film score composition 11/22, 1922, watercolour, 18 x 102 cm.
Werner Graeff obviously started work on the abstract film in Weimar almost
at the same time as Eggeling and Richter. The ideas remained in
storyboard form because at that time the technical equipment required
for abstract film experiments was too expensive.
At the same time Hirschfeld-Mack in Weimar invented reflecting moving
pictures, with which, by the use of simple media, coloured form
sequences could be made as well.

Graeff: film score composition. 11/22, 1922, watercolor, 18 x 102 cm.
Graeff: Film-Partitur 11/22, 1922, Aquarell, 18 x 102 cm.
Werner Graeff hat in Weimar offensichtlich fast gleichzeitig mit Eggeling
und Richter am abstrakten Film gearbeitet. Die Ideen sind beim Storyboard geblieben, weil die aufwändige Technik für abstrakte Film-Experimente
nicht erreichbar war.
Hirschfeld-Mack erfand in Weimar zur gleichen Zeit die reflektorischen
Lichtspiele, die mit einfachen Mitteln auch farbige Formsequencen möglich
machten.

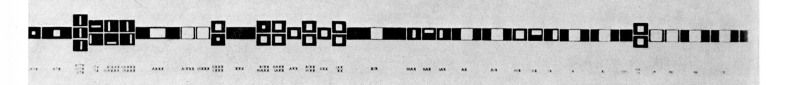

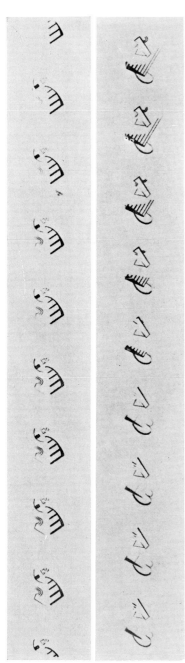

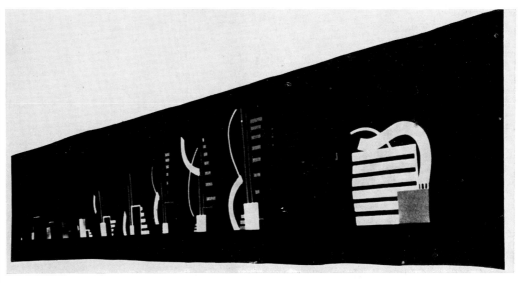

Richter: Rhythm 23, scroll, 69 x 404 cm.
A form sequence similar to the scrolls which Hans Richter developed very
early on in serial technique. These picture-sequences and other experiments
in co-operation with Eggeling led to the beginnung of the abstract film.

Richter: Rhythmus 23, 1923, Bildrolle, 69 x 404 cm.
Eine Formreihe ähnlich den Bildrollen, die Hans Richter schon sehr früh
in serieller Technik entwickelte. Diese Bildreihen und andere
Experimente führten in Zusammenarbeit mit Eggeling zum Beginn des
abstrakten Films.

Eggeling: Diagonal symphony, Animations Film, 1923
This film is made up of abstract form-sequences only. The individual
form-sequences, comparable with the musical phases in a symphony, were
photographed.
Eggeling's Diagonal Symphony as well as Richter's "Rhythm 21" are of
classical importance. The modern animation films very seldom achieve the
effectiveness and power of the initial films.

Eggeling: Diagonalsymphonie, Animations-Film, 1923.
Dieser Film besteht nur aus abstrakten Formreihen.
Die einzelnen Formreihen sind, vergleichbar den musikalischen Abläufen
in einer Symphonie, fotografiert worden.
Eggelings „Diagonalsymphie" sowie Richters „Rhythmus 21" haben
klassische Bedeutung. Die heutigen abstrakten Animations-Filme erreichen
sehr selten die Konsequenz und Kraft der Anfänge.

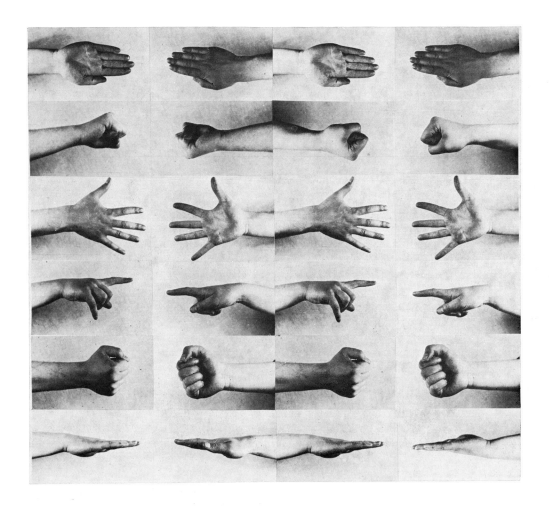

Kranz: Photo sequences form 1930/31, Bauhaus, Dessau, Peterhans
photography course.
Hand gesture sequences—an astonishingly early anticipation of the
picture-sequence of body gestures, which today have very much come to the
fore through concept art. The same applies to the wide field of video
practice.

Kranz: Fotoreihen von 1930/31, Bauhaus Dessau, Foto-Kurs Peterhans,
Handgesten-Reihen – eine erstaunlich frühe Vorwegnahme der Bildreihe von
Körpergesten, die heute durch die Concept-Kunst sehr ins Blickfeld
gerückt sind. Das gleiche gilt für das große Feld der Video-Praxis.

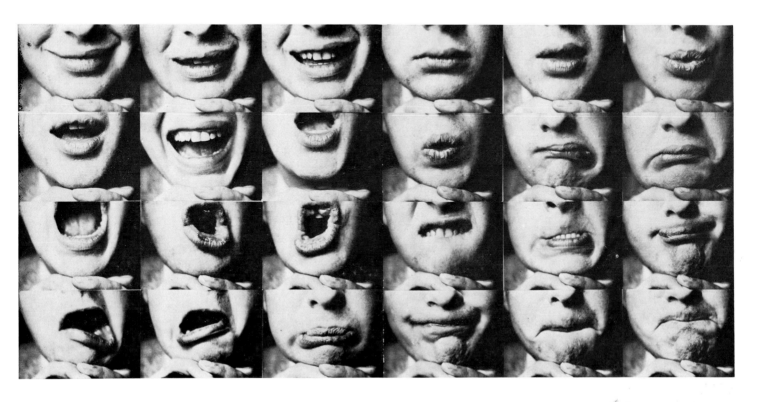

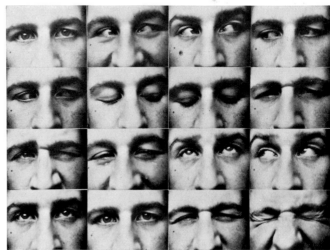

Kranz: Mimicry-sequences of eyes and mouths taken by a fixed camera show a sequence of mime variations. Body language, which is one of the primordial means of communication, is given renewed artistic significance through the mass media (video).

Kranz: Mimik-Reihen von Mündern und Augen zeigen bei stehender Kamera eine Reihe von mimischen Variationen. Durch die Massenmedien (Video) gewinnt die Körpersprache, die zu den Uranfängen der Kommunikation gehört, erneute künstlerische Bedeutung.

Arrows aid and accelerate this movement of forms, steps and rows of colours give direction to the sequence. Like the mutations, chance is a welcome source of variation in Klee's work.

Albers is strictly against chance and demands precise articulation and systematic invention. The yardstick is the proportion of effort expended and efficacy. The work of this master is a persistent progression in picture sequences. Extreme limitation in the choice of motifs leads to closely confined sequences with great inner richness. Serial technique and sequence here begin to overlap.

The stereotyped repetitions, comparable with basso ostinato, are the lowest forms of the sequence. Combinatorial analysis unites different forms into a new grouping. All the possibilities of combinations and the resultant arrangements of forms can only be worked out mathematically. The succession is conceivable as continuing in geometrical progression or in free variations. The book you have in front of you provides examples in ample measure.

In the language of modern art appreciation, serial technique is understood as prefabricated, recurring parts, which are sometimes differently coloured or treated with other media. Very often one uses serigraphy, stamps or photos (Warhole). Other serial forms are repetitions of certain patterns and arrangements, which are then orchestrated in colour (Vasarely). Serial technique is represented in sculpture on a lavish scale, particularly there where movement is involved, motor or wind propulsion, mobile plastic, which continually changes in form or which draws mechanically or which destroys itself, is a wide field for transformation (Calder, Tinguely, Rickey).

Sculpture, which can be taken to pieces, offers a variety of aspects. Its parts, mounted individually, can be observed one after the other and be integrated into a whole (Imposteguy, Berocal).

Sequences can also be produced by technical optical transformation, for instance by coloured moving pictures projected onto screens or thrown into the room (Schoeffer, Piene). Other kinetic objects use chemical opposites and climatic real time systems to produce permanent transformations (Haake). Plastic parts, which can be observed from various angles, provide new pictures (Agam).

Parts of pictures, which with the help of magnets can be freely changed by the public on the surface, provide endless serial variations (Fahlstrom).

Another possibility of variation is to divide the picture into parts and fit it together again in any number of different variations. Another kinetic form permits one to compose anew a part of the picture's surface which is movable. Here it concerns a picture sequence with a given repertoire, in which the observer can make his own choice (Yo Ichikawa, Kranz). This catalogue of kinetic art shows a number of processes, all of which satisfy the pressure of our age for variation. Here is formed an aesthetic of movement, of temporary paces, of steps; the aesthetic of the totality of the sequence. But in the early moderns as well, variation played an important role. A particularly clear example of sequence and transformation is the sequence of tree studies by Mondrian. Out of a naturalistic study he develop a graduated rhythmic, geometric division or surface. This sequence is a classic example of constructivist nature study.

The suite "Les Femmes d'Alger", which Picasso painted after the picture by Delacroix, is a self-contained variation sequence. His own elements of style and transformation, experience and inspiration, combined with the luck of a painter's fist, show also here the urge of our age for variation.

Similar to parameters in science, in visual art grid fields are often the constructive base in which variation sequences are inserted; thus symbol fields are created.

Computer technique, when correctly programmed, can express an apparently unlimited succession of variations. Without the help of human imagination, relying only

Albers wendet sich streng gegen den Zufall und fordert die präzise Artikulation und die systematische Erfindung. Das Maß ist Proportion von Aufwand und Wirkung. Die Arbeit dieses Meisters ist ein beharrliches Fortschreiten in Bildfolgen.

Äußerste Begrenzung in der Motivwahl führt zu engumgrenzten Reihen mit großem innerem Reichtum. Serielle Technik und Reihe beginnen sich hier zu überschneiden.

Die stereotypen Wiederholungen, dem ostinaten Baß vergleichbar, sind die untersten Formen der Reihe. Kombinatorik verbindet verschiedene Formen zu neuer Gruppierung. Die Möglichkeiten der Kombinationen und die so zusammengesetzten Formen unterliegen der Mathematik. Die Sukzession, die Folge, ist fortschreitend in Progressionen oder bis zur freien Variation denkbar. Das vorliegende Buch zeigt in reichem Maße Beispiele.

Im Sprachgebrauch der modernen Kunstbetrachtung versteht man unter dem Seriellen vorfabrizierte, wiederkehrende Teile, die manchmal verschieden coloriert oder ähnlich behandelt sind. Sehr oft verwendet man Serigraphie, Stempel oder Foto (Warhole).

Wiederholungen gewisser Muster und Gliederungen, die dann farbig orchestriert werden, sind andere serielle Formen (Vasarely).

Serielle Technik ist in der Skulptur sehr reich vertreten, besonders da, wo Bewegung hinzukommt, motor- oder windangetriebene, mobile Plastik, die ihre Form ständig ändert oder die maschinenhaft zeichnet oder sich selbst zerstört, ist voller Verwandlung (Calder, Tinguely, Rickey).

Die unterteilbare Plastik bietet eine Reihe von Ansichten. Ihre einzeln montierten Teile können nacheinander betrachtet und zu einem Ganzen zusammengefügt werden (Imposteguy, Berocal).

Durch technisch-optische Verwandlungen entstehen ebenfalls Reihen, so z. B. durch farbige Lichtspiele, die auf Schirme projiziert oder in den Raum geworfen werden (Schoeffer, Piene).

Andere kinetische Objekte verwenden chemische Gegensätze und klimatische Realzeit-Systeme zur Herstellung ständiger Verwandlungen (Haake).

Plastische Teile, die aus verschiedenen Winkeln betrachtet werden, ergeben neue Bilder (Agam).

Bildteile, die mit Hilfe von Magneten auf der Bildfläche vom Publikum frei verändert werden können, stellen endlose Variationsreihen dar (Fahlström).

Eine weitere Variationsmöglichkeit ist, das Bild zu unterteilen und es beliebig wieder zusammensetzen zu lassen.

Eine andere kinetische Form erlaubt einen Teil der Bildfläche, die beweglich ist, neu zu komponieren. Hier handelt es sich um eine Bildreihe mit gegebenem Repertoire, in dem der Betrachter seine eigene Wahl treffen kann (Yo Ichikawa, Kranz).

Dieser Katalog der kinetischen Kunst zeigt vielerlei Verfahren, die alle dem Verwandlungsdruck unserer Zeit entsprechen. Hier bildet sich eine Ästhetik der Bewegung, der vorläufigen Schritte, der Stufen: die Ästhetik der Gesamtheit der Reihe. Aber auch in der frühen Moderne spielt die Variation eine große Rolle. Ein besonders deutliches Beispiel für Reihe und Transformation ist die Serie der Baumstudien von Mondrian. Er entwickelte aus der naturalistischen Studie eine stufenweise, rhythmische, geometrische Flächenaufteilung. Diese Reihe ist ein klassisches Beispiel für konstruktivistisches Naturstudium.

Die Suite „Les Femme d'Algèr", die Picasso nach dem Bild von Delacroix malte, ist eine geschlossene Variations-Reihe.

Eigene Stilelemente und Transformationen, Erfahrung und Einfall, verbunden mit dem Glück einer Malfaust, zeigen auch hier den Variationsdruck unserer Zeit.

Ähnlich den Parametern in der Wissenschaft, sind häufig in der visuellen Kunst Rasterfelder der konstruktive Grund, in dem Variations-Reihen eingetragen werden. So entstehen Zeichenfelder.

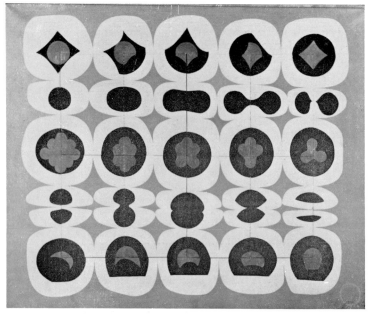 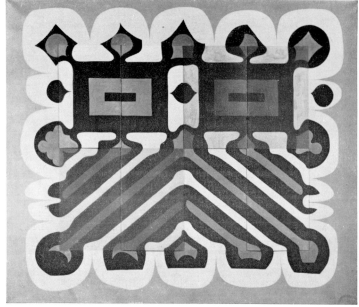

Kranz: Other combinations. 1968, 74 x 110 cm, acrylic on canvas
with movable metal parts and magnets sewn on. Two constellations of
34 variations.
5 horizontal form sequences in variations. New variations are added
from the layers below by means of hinged parts. The observer selects his
constellations from the repertoire.

Kranz: Andere Verbindungen. 1968, 74 x 110 cm, Acrylic auf Leinwand
mit aufgenähten, beweglichen Metallteilen und Magneten. Zwei Konstellationen von 34 Variationen.
Fünf horizontale Formreihen variieren. Durch aufklappbare Teile
kommen aus den darunterliegenden Schichten neue Variationen hinzu.
Der Betrachter wählt aus dem Repertoire seine Konstellationen.

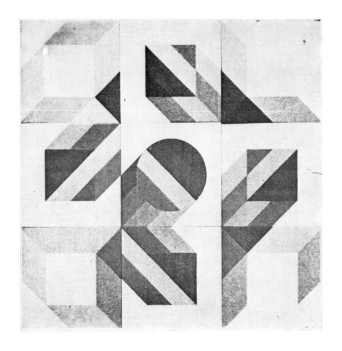 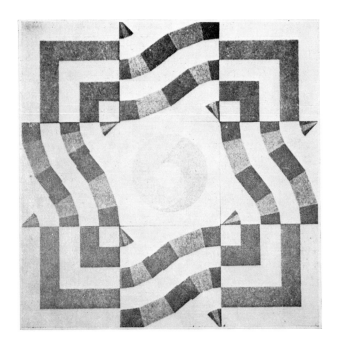

Yo Ichikawa: "Livre d'heures", acrylic on plywood, 75 x 75 cm, 1972.
By rearranging and rotating the panels, an almost infinite number of
variations can be produced by the transformable with its theme sequence
on 9 panels; to be exact 9! x 4⁹) —1 = 7.597.829.999 possibilities.
Yo Ichikawa: "I do not give different titles to the transformables.
. . . the activity of rearranging the panels by a viewer seems somewhat like
that of reading a book."

Yo Ichikawa: Stundenbuch, Acrylic auf Sperrholz, 75 x 75 cm, 1972.
Das transformable Bild mit seinen seriellen Themen auf neun Feldern
erlaubt durch die Drehung und Auswechslung der Tafeln eine fast unendliche
Variation. Genauer: 9! x 49) –1 also 7 597 829 999 Möglichkeiten.
Ichikawa: „Ich gebe meinen Transformables keine verschiedenen Titel,
ich nenne jedes einfach ‚Stundenbuch' . . . die Aktion des Betrachters,
der die Tafel neu umordnet, erscheint mir wie das Leben eines Buches."

Yo Ichikawa: "Livre d'heures", acrylic on plywood, 75 x 75 cm, 1972.
Yo Ichikawa remarks: "I try to be faithful to an imagined world, existing
only in my mind, by utilizing combinations of forms that are not
found in nature. I do not wish to give these forms a religious character.
Yet I do wish that they be eternal." (Leonardo VII-1, p. 10.)

Yo Ichikawa bemerkt:
„Ich versuche meiner Vorstellungswelt treu zu bleiben, die nur
in meinem Geiste existiert und benutze Formen, die nicht aus der Natur
gefunden sind. Ich möchte nicht, daß diese Formen einen religiösen
Charakter * bekommen, aber ich wünsche mir, daß sie Dauer haben."
(Leonardo VII. – 1. p. 10.)

on the programmes, the computer produces permutational art. The permutation is a field of possibility which is limited by rules, for instance sequence technique, combinatorial analysis and the like. This technique is used in particular by John Whitney for his abstract films. After he had together with his brother produced abstract films by the use of stencils in progressions, he synchronized them with synthetic music. In his latest works, each "frame" is designed by the computer. The abstract film began, as mentioned above, with picture rolls in the sense of scrolls. The Zurich Dadaists, Viking Eggeling and Hans Richter, were the pioneers. In 1923 Eggeling developed the first abstract film, "the diagonal symphony". Today it still has its value as pure form sequence in film technique. With modern computer, video and film technique, a rich field lies open in the future for form sequences.

Computer technique in experimental poetry and in musical art is serial technique subject to the laws of chance like dice throwing. The field of permutational art extends from the Markow chain of sound intervals and sounds to the variation texts with their word-chains.

Significant is the new music notation which makes use of visual media in picture sequences in order to give full expression to complicated "clusters" or the like (Haubenstock, Ramati).

Technique, a never finished structure, which, under the ceaseless pressure of ever expanding scientific discoveries, is itself at the spearhead of development subject to continual change, arouses the emotions for necessary change or stirs the curiosity of futurologists.

In addition there is the attrition of visual signs and acoustic forms, which acts as a permanent urge towards new discoveries. This wear and tear puts new demands on the artists. Innovation, the new, in sequence pictures develops into the movable. Within the sequence, in contrast to the absolutely identical series produced by a machine, the changing of the sequence is the new factor which enters. This gradual unveiling of the new is an important part of the message. The method of serial technique is opposed to chance or coincidence. In contrast to mutation in Nature, it proceeds in steps and stages, in constructive units to simplification and to processes which have as their final aim – order.

Serial technique is abstraction and constructivism, without being tied to any "ism". It is a technique not tied to art and it is reflected in human thought. When one looks at the oeuvre of the artists and groups of artists of the last decades, it includes whole bunches of work sequences, pictures sequences.

The picture sequence, when observed over a longer period of time, is one of the keys to recognizing that there is artistic evolution as well in the world.

Die Computer-Technik kann mit den entsprechend vorgegebenen Programmen in scheinbar unbegrenzter Sukzession Varianten ausdrücken. Ohne die Hilfe der menschlichen Phantasie, nur auf die Programme gestellt, produziert der Computer permutationelle Kunst. Die Permutation ist ein Möglichkeitsfeld, das durch Regeln, z. B. durch Reihentechnik, Kombinatorik und ähnliches, eingeengt wird. Diese Technik wird ganz besonders von John Whitney für seine abstrakten Filme angewandt. Nachdem er mit seinem Bruder abstrakte Filme unter Verwendung von Schablonen in Progressionen hergestellt hatte, synchronisierte er sie mit synthetischer Musik. In den letzten Arbeiten ist jeder „Frame" mit dem Computer gezeichnet. Begonnen hatte der abstrakte Film, wie oben erwähnt, mit abstrakten Rollenbildern im Sinne der Makemonos. Die Züricher Dada-Mitglieder Viking Eggeling und Hans Richter waren die Pioniere. 1923 entwickelte Eggeling den ersten abstrakten Film, „Die Diagonal-Sinfonie". Sie hat heute noch ihren Wert als reine Formsequenz in der Filmtechnik. Mit der heutigen Computer-, Video- und Filmtechnik wird ein zukünftiges reiches Feld der Formsequencen sich öffnen.

Computer-Technik in der experimentellen Poesie und Tonkunst ist Reihentechnik mit dem Würfelwurf des Zufalls. Von der Markow-Kette der Tonintervalle und den Tönen bis zu Variations-Texten mit ihren Wortketten breitet sich das Feld der permutationellen Kunst aus.

Bezeichnend ist die neue Musik-Notation, die sich visueller Mittel in Bildreihen bedient, um komplizierte „Clusters" oder dergleichen zum Ausdruck zu bringen (Haubenstock, Ramati).

Die Technik, ein ewig unfertiges Gebilde, das unter der stetig sich erweiternden Flut der Forschungsergebnisse sich an der Front der Entwicklungen ständig verändert, erweckt das Gefühl des notwendigen Wandels oder die Neugier der Futurologie. Hinzu kommt der Verschleiß visueller Zeichen und akustischer Formen, der zu immer neuen Erfindungen drängt.

Diese Abnutzung fordert an den Formenden die Erneuerung. Die Innovation, das Neue wird in der Reihe zum Bewegenden. Innerhalb der Reihe, im Gegensatz zur völlig gleichen Serie der Maschinenproduktion, ist das Verändernde der Reihe das Neuhinzutretende. Das schrittweise sich entschleiernde Neue ist ein wichtiger Teil der Botschaft. Die Methode der Reihentechnik stellt sich gegen den Zufall. Im Gegensatz zur Mutation in der Natur geht sie in Schritten und Stufen, in konstruktiven Einheiten zur Vereinfachung und zu Verfahren über, die als letztes Ziel die Ordnung haben.

Reihentechnik ist Abstraktion und Konstruktivismus, ohne an einen Ismus gebunden zu sein. Sie ist eine nicht an die Kunst gebundene Technik, die sich im menschlichen Denken widerspiegelt. Beobachtet man die Oeuvre der Künstler und Künstlergruppen der letzten Jahrzehnte, so bilden sie ganze Bündel von Werkreihen, Bildreihen.

Die Reihe, die sich über einen längeren Zeitraum beobachten läßt, ist einer der Schlüssel, auch die künstlerische Evolution in der Welt zu erkennen.

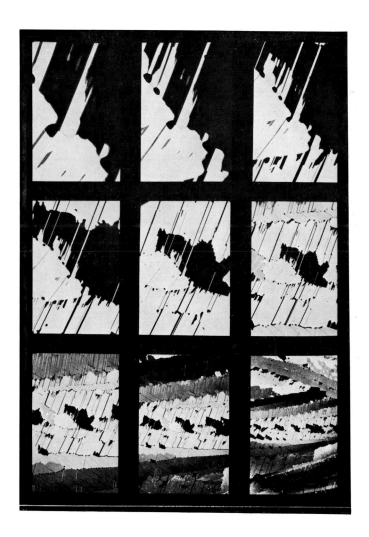

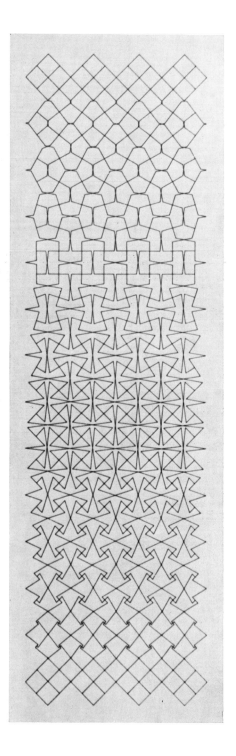

Kage: Morpholin System, Sequence B, 1972
During the chemical transformation process of a crystalline preparation, selected steps are photograped and formed into a sequence.

Kage: „System Morpholin", Serie B, 1972;
Während des chemischen Verwandlungsprozesses eines
Kristallpräparates sind ausgewählte Stufen fotografiert und zu einer Reihe
geformt worden.

Glasmeier: Catametric structure, 1966,
Hochschule für Gestaltung, Ulm,
Germany.
The computer transforms a diamond
lattice. The sequence is constantly
deformed into concave octagons through
rotation. These transformations can
also be regarded as variations which
return to the original lattice configuration.

Glasmeier: Katametrische Struktur,
Computergraphik, 1966,
Hochschule für Gestaltung, Ulm.
Der Computer transformiert ein
quadratisches Gitter. Über konkave
Achtecke wird die Folge durch Drehung
fortlaufend deformiert. Man kann
diese Änderungen auch als Varianten
auffassen, die schließlich zum
Ausgangsgitter zurückkehren.

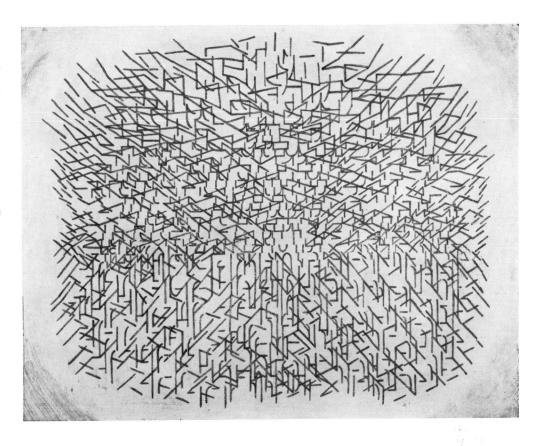

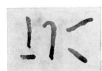

Kranz: Landscape, 1959, 77 x 100 cm, tempera on canvas.
The original complex consists of 4 straight lines of different lenghts
and of one straight line with a quarter arc. This basic form-sequence,
the theme, which is here described as original complex, is
continually being transformed by nets and broken grids. Everywhere
can be seen signlike shapes, polygonous letters and numbers. Symmetrical,
vertical and horizontal reflections produce a centred space. Since
1955 Kranz has been using this method for drawing fields. Herewith he
discovered a technique comparable with computer-graphics, which
was developed at a later date.

Kranz: Landschaft, 1959, 77 x 100 cm, Tempera auf Leinwand.
Der Ausgangskomplex besteht aus vier Geraden verschiedener Länge und
aus einer Geraden mit einem Kreisbogen-Viertel.
Diese Grund-Formreihe, das Thema, das hier als Ausgangskomplex
bezeichnet ist, wird durch Netze und gebrochene Raster ständig transformiert. Es entstehen neue Formreihen. Überall sind zahlreiche Gebilde,
polygone Buchstaben und Zahlen zu erkennen. Symmetrische, vertikale und
horizontale Spiegelung stellen einen zentrierten Raum her.
Diese Methode hat Kranz seit 1955 für Zeichenfelder angewandt. Er fand
damit eine Technik, die mit der später entwickelten Computer-Graphik
vergleichbar ist.

Kurt Kranz: Vita

1910   geboren in Emmerich am Rhein.
1925–30   handwerkliche Lehre als Lithograph.
1930   Eintritt ins Bauhaus; Albers und Joost Schmidt;
Peterhans; Kurse bei Klee und Kandinsky.
1932   Im fünften Semester mit dem Bauhaus nach Berlin
unter Mies van der Rohe. Danach bei dem
Bauhausmeister Herbert Bayer, Lehre und später
Zusammenarbeit; gebrauchsgraphische Arbeiten,
Titelblätter für ›Neue Linie‹.
1938   Selbständig im eigenen Atelier.
Im zweiten Weltkrieg in Norwegen und Finnland.
1946   Rückkehr nach Berlin.
1950   Berufung als Dozent an die Landeskunstschule
Hamburg für Grundlehre.
1955   Ernennung zum Professor an der Staatlichen
Hochschule für bildende Künste Hamburg.
1957   Gastdozent an der Tulane University, New Orleans,
USA.
1958   Rückkehr nach Hamburg.
1960   Leitung der Klasse für freie und angewandte Graphik
an der Hochschule für bildende Künste.
1965   Gastdozent an der University of California,
Santa Barbara.
1966   Artist in residence an der Academy of Honolulu.
Vorlesungen an der Nihon-Universität in Tokio, Japan.
1967–68   Gastdozent an der Havard University, Cambridge.
1972   Emeritus der Hochschule für bildende Künste
Hamburg, lebt jetzt in der Nähe Hamburgs und in
Südfrankreich.

Kurt Kranz: Curriculum vitae

1910   born in Emmerich on Rhine.
1925–30   Litography apprenticeship.
1930   Entered Bauhaus; teachers: Albers, Joost Schmidt,
Peterhans; attended courses given by Klee and
Kandinsky.
1932   In his fifth semester at Bauhaus went to Berlin
to study under Mies van der Rohe and afterwards
under Herbert Bayer. Later cooperated with
the latter; commercial art work, title pages for
"Neue Linie".
1938   Freelance work in his own studio
Spent world war II in Norway and Finland.
1946   Returned to Berlin.
1950   Appointed lecturer at Hamburg School for
Basic Art.
1955   Appointed Professor at Hamburg Academy
of Fine Arts.
1957   Guest lecturer at Tulane University, New Orleans,
USA.
1958   Return to Hamburg.
1960   Director of the class for free and applied graphics
at Hamburg Academy of Fine Arts.
1965   Guest lecturer at the University of California,
Santa Barbara.
1966   Artist in residence at the Academy of Honolulu.
Lectures at Nihon University in Tokyo, Japan.
1967–68   Guest lecturer at Harvard University,
Cambridge Mass.
1972   Professor Emeritus of Hamburg Academy of Fine
Arts. Now lives near Hamburg and in the South
of France.

Ausstellungen: Exhibitions: 1971   Mickelson Gallery, Washington, D. C., USA
                                                                    Goethe House New York, NYC, USA

                                                            1972   Academy of the Arts, Easton, Maryland, USA
                                                                    Musee d'Art Contemporain, Montreal, Canada
1931   Buch- & Kunsthandlung Otto Fischer, Bielefeld   Pollock Gallery Ltd, Toronto, Canada
                                                                    Carpenter Center, Cambridge, Mass., USA,
1933   Staatsbibliothek Berlin   Beteiligung an der Ausstellung ›Transformationen‹.
                                                                    Galerie at, Wiesbaden
1949   Buch- & Kunsthandlung Otto Fischer, Bielefeld   Galerie Ariadne, Wien
                                                                    Agnes Etherington Art Centre, Kingston,
1950   Beteiligung an der Ausstellung der Berliner   Ontario, Canada
        Bauhäusler in Berlin-Neukölln, Amt für Kunst   McMaster University Art Gallery, Hamilton,
                                                                    Ontario, Canada
1957   University Tulane, Art Gallery, New Orleans, USA   Corcoran Gallery of Art, Washington, D. C., USA

1962   Galerie Anna Roepcke, Wiesbaden
                                                            1974   New Orleans Museum of Art, New Orleans, USA
1965   Museum of Art, Santa Barbara   High Museum of Art, Atlanta, Georgia, USA
        Feigen-Palma Gallery, Los Angeles, USA   Pollock Gallery Ltd., Toronto, Ontario, Canada
                                                                    Virginia Polytechnic Institute of Art,
1966   Academy of Honolulu, Art Gallery Design Corner,   Blacksburg, Va., USA
        Matzuja, Tokio, Japan   Little Rock Art Center, Little Rock, Arkansas, USA
                                                                    Dane G. Hansen Memorial Museum, Longan,
1967   Ward-Nasse Gallery, Boston, USA   Kansas, USA
        Charlotte Thomsen Gallery, Cambridge, Mass., USA   Hayden Gallery, MIT, Cambridge, Mass., USA
                                                                    New York Cultural Center, NYC, USA
1969   Overbeck-Gesellschaft, Lübeck
        Kunsthalle Bielefeld
        Kunstverein Oldenburg
                                                            1975   Museum of South Texas, Corpus Christi, Texas, USA
1970   Rheinisches Landesmuseum Bonn,   Carnegie Institute Museum of Art, Pittsburgh,
        Beteiligung ›50 Jahre Bauhaus‹ mit Photomontagen   Penns., USA
        und pädagogischer Methodik.   Arts Club of Chicago, Chicago, Illinois, USA
        Kunsthaus Hamburg   Beteiligung an der Gruppen-Ausstellung:
        Kasseler Kunstverein   ›Artists Make Toys‹, The Crocktower, NYC, USA

Animation Films
In 1972 films were made from the picture sequences here published. These photographs are based on the original designs. The individual pictures have been linked together by the technique of superimposing and focussing one still upon another. Phases have not been produced. Robert Darroll was responsible for the actual filming. Atlantik-Film Hamburg made the copies. The artist owns all the film rights.
The form sequences 1–4 were combined to make one film.

Title No. 1:
20 pictures from the life of a composition
Length: 150 m, Duration: approx 8 minutes, Colour

Title No. 2:
Black : White
Length: 408 m, Duration: 12 minutes, Black/White

Title No. 3:
The heroic arrow
Length: 170 m, Duration: 9 minutes, Black/White

Title No. 4:
Colour film called Leporello
Length: 172 m, Duration: 9 minutes, Colour

Title No. 5:
12 variations on a theme
Length: 560 m, Duration: 22 minutes, Black/White.
The original is a sketch pad from the end of the war 1944/45.

Title No. 6:
Variations on a geometrical theme
Length: 618 m, Duration: 20 minutes, Black/White.
The originals (15 x 21 cm) are in various media.
Excellent productions of these appeared in book form in 1956 in Prestelverlag Munich.

Animations-Filme
Nach den hier veröffentlichten Bildreihen sind 1972 Filme entstanden. Die Original-Entwürfe liegen diesen Aufnahmen zugrunde. Die einzelnen Bilder wurden untereinander durch Einblendungen verbunden. Phasen sind nicht hergestellt worden. Die filmtechnische Ausführung hat Robert Darroll betreut. Die Kopien stellte der Atlantik-Film Hamburg her. Alle Film-Rechte sind beim Künstler.
Die Formreihen 1–4 wurden zu einem Film zusammengesetzt.

Titel Nr. 1:
20 Bilder aus dem Leben einer Komposition
Länge: 150 Meter, Dauer: ca. 8 Minuten, Farbfilm

Titel Nr. 2:
Schwarz : Weiß
Länge: 408 Meter, Dauer: 12 Minuten, Schwarzweißfilm

Titel Nr. 3:
Der heroische Pfeil
Länge: 170 Meter, Dauer: 9 Minuten, Schwarzweißfilm

Titel Nr. 4:
Farbfilm, genannt Leporello
Länge: 172 Meter, Dauer: 9 Minuten, Farbfilm

Titel Nr. 5:
12 Variationen über ein Thema
Länge: 560 Meter, Dauer: 22 Minuten, Schwarzweißfilm.
Das Original ist ein Skizzenbuch, das am Ende des Krieges 1944–45 entstanden ist.

Titel Nr. 6:
Variationen über ein geometrisches Thema
Länge: 618 Meter, Dauer: 20 Minuten, Schwarzweißfilm.
Die Originale (je 15 x 21 cm) haben unterschiedliche Materialien. Sie sind 1956 in sehr guten Reproduktionen im Prestel-Verlag, München, als Buch erschienen.

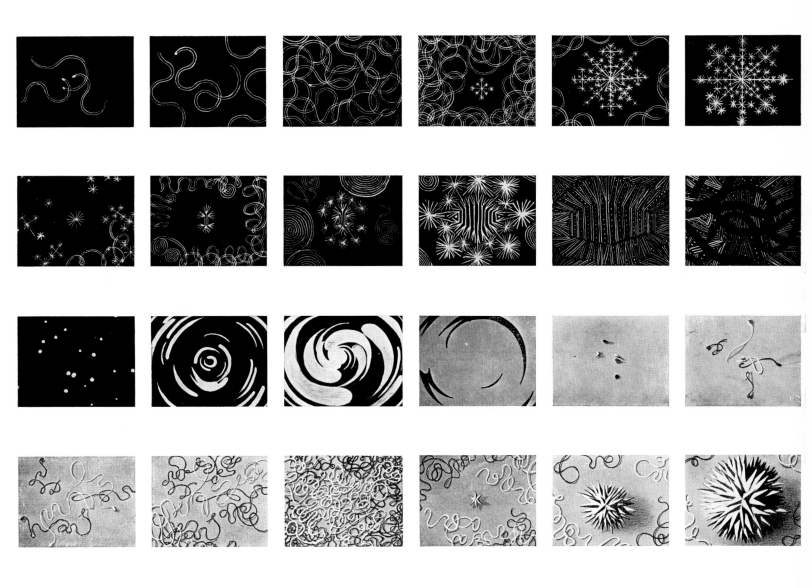

Content of the picture sequence: 12 variations on a theme, 1944   Ausschnitt aus der Bildreihe „12 Variationen über ein Thema", 1944

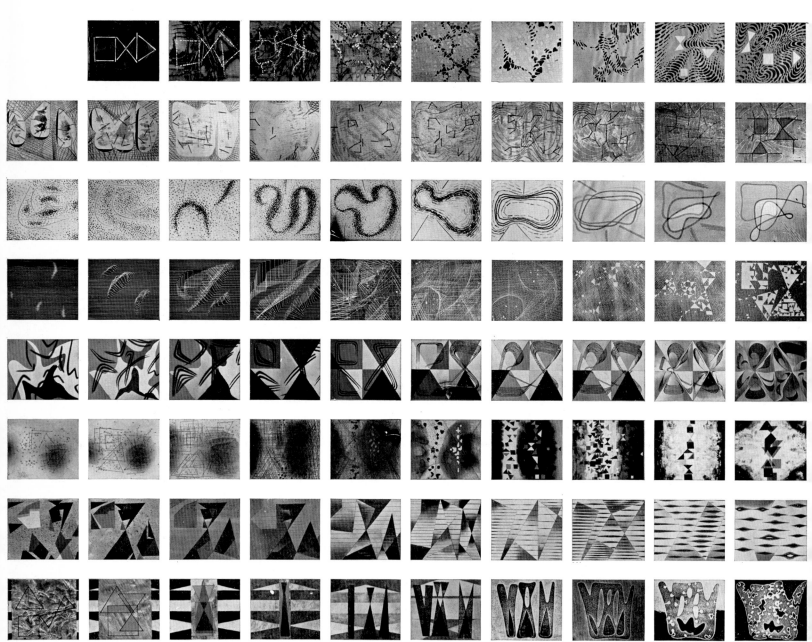

Master panel of the picture sequence "Variations on a geometrical theme", 1953

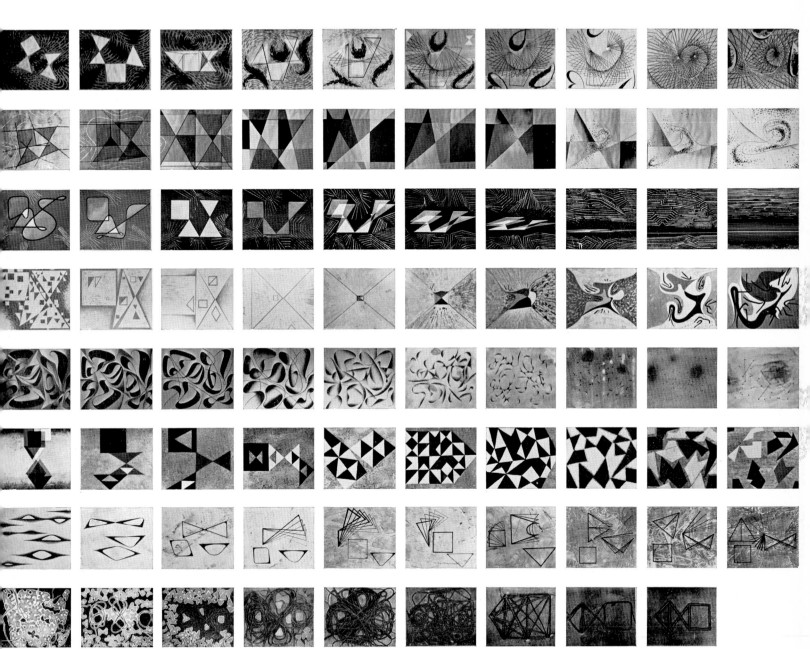

Übersichtstafel der Bildreihe „Variation über ein geometrisches Thema", 1953

Bibliographie: Bibliography:

Christian Frenzel, Kritik zur 1. Ausstellung 1931,
Westfälische Zeitung, Bielefeld

1970, ›Kurt Kranz zum 60. Geburtstag‹, Hamburger
Abendblatt

Eberhard Hölscher: ›Kurt Kranz, Hamburg‹,
Gebrauchsgraphik, München 1954/4

›Variationen über ein geometrisches Thema. Aus einem
Buch von Kurt Kranz‹, Gebrauchsgraphik, München 1957/3

›Rapportlose Tapeten von Kurt Kranz‹, Gebrauchsgraphik,
München 1961/4

A. Wannemacher: ›Materialkompositionen als Grundlage
der modernen Formgebung‹, Heidelberg 1950/7

Max Bense:
›Für Kurt Kranz‹, Katalog zur Ausstellung des Museums für
Kunst und Gewerbe Hamburg, Verlag Hans Christians 1960

›Zum Werk von Kurt Kranz‹, Katalog zur Ausstellung
der Overbeck-Gesellschaft Lübeck, 1969

›Kurt Kranz, Bildreihen und Bilder mit beweglichen Teilen‹,
Hamburg 1970, Kiepenheuer & Witsch, Köln, Berlin 1970

›Sign-Images by Kurt Kranz‹, Katalog Kurt Kranz bauhaus
and today, Washington 1973, Smithsonian Institution

Wulf Herzogenrath: 50 Jahre Bauhaus, Katalog,
Seite 196, 270, 342

Iwao Yamawaki: KOGA 1933/12, ›Kurt Kranz im Bauhaus
Dessau‹, Seite 381–387, Tokyo

Bauhaus Weimar–Dessau–Berlin
Iwao Yamawaki, Selbstbiographie, Tokyo 1973,
Kapitel über Kurt Kranz

Joachim Thiele: ›Verfahren der statistischen Ästhetik‹,
Verlags-Vertriebs-Gesellschaft mbH. Hamburg-Altona, 1966
›Zur Beschreibung von Graphiken‹, Seite 51–62

Stephen B. Reichard: ›Beyond Bauhaus and Today‹,
Kurt Kranz, Katalog Smithsonian Institution, Washington
1973

George Rickey: ›Tulane, 1957–1958‹,
Katalog Smithsonian Institution, Washington 1973

Alfred Moir: ›Santa Barbara, 1965–1966‹,
Katalog Smithsonian Institution, Washington 1973

Eduard F. Sekler: ›Harvard, 1967–1968‹,
Katalog Smithsonian Institution, Washington 1973

Joachim Thiele: ›Konstellations- und Faltgraphik‹,
Katalog Kranz, Christians Verlag, Hamburg 1969

Bazon Brock: ›Kurt Kranz . . . Meister der Phase‹,
Katalog Kranz, Christians Verlag, Hamburg 1969

Dietrich Helms: ›Über Kurt Kranz, Bildreihen und Bilder mit
beweglichen Teilen‹, Christians Verlag, Hamburg 1970

Dietrich Helms: ›Allmanach Kurt Kranz‹, Christians Verlag,
Hamburg 1970

Dietrich Helms: Katalog ›Kurt Kranz Aquarelle‹,
Galerie Denis René, Hans Mayer, Düsseldorf 1973

Benjamin Forgey: ›Kurt Kranz by Michelson‹,
Washington 1971

Kristian Sotriffer: ›Form und Phantasie‹,
Die Presse, Wien 1972

Gilles Toupin: Kurt Kranz, ›L'Eveilleur‹,
La Presse, Montreal 1972

Michael White: Kurt Kranz, ›Bringing the Bauhaus to Montreal‹, The Gazette, Montreal 1972

John David Farmer: ›Kurt Kranz' Retrospektive‹, Vie des Arts, Toronto 1972

Kay Kritzwizer: Kurt Kranz, ›Warmth and Feeling Despite the Bauhaus‹, Toronto 1973

Theodor Allen Heinrich: ›An Authentic Bauhaus Man‹, Artscanada, Toronto 1972

Art Gallery Magazin: ›Kurt Kranz, Bauhaus and Today‹, Washington 1973

Benjamin Forgey: ›Kranz is Bauhaus Updated‹, The Washington Star News, Washington, D. C. 1973

Paul Richard: ›Behind Exquisite Toys, A Talent‹, The Washington Post, Washington, D. C. 1973

Albert Collier: ›Kurt Kranz Will Be Guest at Noma‹, Restrospective, The Timms Picayune, New Orleans 1974

Helen C. Smith: ›I love color, Kranz Comments on New Exhibit‹, The Atlanta Constitution, Atlanta 1974

Kurt Kranz Showing at High Museum, Journal Constitution, Atlanta 1974

Clyde Burnett: ›Kurt Kranz Exhibit one of Better One Man Shows‹, The Atlanta Journal, 1974

Robert Taylor: ›Sharing the Triumph of Kurt Kranz‹, The Boston Sunday Globe, 1974

Sarah Faunce: ›Kurt Kranz at the New York Cultural Center‹, Art in Amerika, New York 1974

Ken Baker: ›Kurt Kranz at NYCC‹, Studio International, London 1974

Lurry Rosing: ›Kurt Kranz, Bauhaus and Today‹, Artnews, New York 1975

Veröffentlichungen des Künstlers:

Publications of the Artist:

Harlekin und Bandolina, Berlin 1948, Selbstdruck

Variationen über ein geometrisches Thema, Prestel Verlag München 1956

Mit eigenen Augen sehen, Verlag F. Bruckmann KG München 1956

Sehen, verstehen, lieben. Die Schritte in die Kunst, Verlag Mensch und Arbeit, München 1963

Amerikanische Ausgabe: Art The Revealing Experience, Shorewood Verlag N. Y. 1964

Holländische Ausgabe: kunst-zien, begrijpen, waarderen, Verlag G. J. A. Ruys, Amsterdam 1964

Italienische Ausgabe: Capire l'arte moderna, Edizione di Comunità Milano 1964

Finnische Ausgabe: nähdä ymmärtää kiintyä, Kustannusosakeyhtiö Aalto Helsinki, 1964

Schwedische Ausgabe: se förstå och uppleva konst, Allhems Förlag, Malmö 1964

Index of illustrations

201 Paul Klee: „Wachstum"

201 Paul Klee: Wachstum der Nachtpflanzen, 1922

202 John Whitney: 24 variations on a graphical matrix,
abstract film 1940
Werner Graeff: Film score composition 11/22, 1922,
watercolour, 18 x 102 cm

202 John Whitney: 24 Variationen über eine graphische
Matrix, abstrakter Film 1940

202 Werner Graeff: Film-Partitur 11/22, 1922, Aquarell,
18 x 102 cm

203 Hans Richter: Rhythm 23, 1923, oil on canvas,
69 x 404 cm
Viking Eggeling: Diagonal symphony,
animations film, 1923

203 Hans Richter: Rhythmus 23, 1923, Bildrolle,
69 x 404 cm

203 Viking Eggeling: Diagonalsymphonie, Animations-Film

204 K. K.: Photo-sequences from 1930/31,
Bauhaus Dessau

204 K. K.: Fotoreihen von 1930/31, Bauhaus Dessau

205 K. K.: 2 mimicry-sequences of eyes and mouths,
1930/31, Bauhaus Dessau

205 K. K.: 2 Mimikreihen von Mündern und Augen,
1930/31, Bauhaus Dessau

208 K. K.: Other combinations, 1968, 74 x 110 cm,
acrylic on canvas

208 K. K.: Andere Verbindungen, 1968, 74 x 110 cm,
Acryl auf Leinwand

209 Yo Ichikawa: 2 transformables, titles: "Livre
d'heures", acrylic on plywood, 75 x 75 cm, 1972

209 Yo Ichikawa: 2 transformable Bilder, Titel:
Stundenbuch, Acryl auf Sperrholz, 75 x 75 cm, 1972

212 Manfred P. Kage: System morpholin, serie B, 1972
Rolf Glasmeier: Catametric structure, 1966,
Hochschule für Gestaltung Ulm, Germany

212 Manfred P. Kage: System Morpholin, Serie B, 1972

212 Rolf Glasmeier: Katametrische Struktur,
Computer-Graphik, 1966, Hochschule für Gestaltung,
Ulm

213 K. K.: Landscape, 1959, 77 x 100 cm,
tempera on canvas

213 K. K.: Landschaft, 1959, 77 x 100 cm,
Tempera auf Leinwand

217 K. K.: Cut-out from the film "12 variations
about a theme"

217 K. K.: Ausschnitt aus dem Film „12 Variationen
über ein Thema"

218 Panel showing complete picture-sequence
"Variations about a geometrical theme"

218 Übersichtstafel: „Variationen über ein
geometrisches Thema"

Aus: Paul Klee, „Das bildnerische Denken,
Benno Schwabe, Basel

Stichwörterverzeichnis

Index

Register

Die halbfetten Ziffern beziehen sich auf die englischen Texte.

The numbers in semi-bold type refer to the English textes.

Ortsregister